CRITICAL PERSPECTIVES ON EDUCATIONAL LEADERSHIP

Deakin Studies in Education Series

General Editors: Professor Rob Walker and Professor Stephen
Kemmis, Deakin University, Victoria, Australia

Deakin Studies in Education Series: 3

CRITICAL PERSPECTIVES ON EDUCATIONAL LEADERSHIP

Edited by
John Smyth

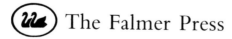 The Falmer Press

(A member of the Taylor & Francis Group)
London, New York and Philadelphia

UK The Falmer Press, Falmer House, Barcombe, Lewes, East Sussex, BN8 5DL

USA The Falmer Press, Taylor & Francis Inc., 242 Cherry Street, Philadelphia, PA 19106-1906

First published 1989   Reprinted 1994

British Library Cataloguing in Publication Data
Critical perspectives on educational leadership.—(Deakin studies in education series).
   1. Education administration. Leadership.   I. Smyth, W. John (William John), 1944–
379.1′5.
ISBN 1-85000-524-9
ISBN 1-85000-525-7 (pbk.)

Library of Congress Cataloging-in-Publication Data
Critical perspectives on educational leadership / edited by John Smyth.
      p.   cm.—(Deakin studies in education series)
   Bibliography: p.
   Includes index.
   Contents: Leadership, power, and symbols in educational administration / Peter Watkins—Towards a critical practice of leadership / William Foster—New leadership and the possibility of educational reform / Lawrence Angus—Educational leadership, a feminist critique and reconstruction / Jill Blackmore—Leadership and the rationalisation of society / Richard Bates—Educational leadership as reflective action / John Codd—A pedagogical and educative view of leadership / John Smyth—In defence of organizational democracy / Fazal Rizvi.
   ISBN 1-85000-524-9 — ISBN 1-85000-525-7 (pbk.)
   1. School management and organization. 2. Leadership.
I. Smyth, W. John. II. Series.
LB2805.C70   1989
371.2—dc 19   88-27230

Typeset in 12/13 Garamond by
The FD Group Ltd, Fleet, Hampshire

Jacket design by Caroline Archer

Printed in Great Britain by Burgess Science Press, Basingstoke on paper which has a specified pH value on final paper manufacture of not less than 7·5 and is therefore 'acid free'.

Contents

General Editors' Introduction

The Deakin Studies in Education Series aims to present a broad critical perspective across a range of interrelated fields in education. The intention is to develop what might be called a 'critical educational science': critical work in the philosophy of education, curriculum, educational and public administration, language education, and educational action research and clinical supervision. The series strives to present the writings of a rising generation of scholars and researchers in education.

A number of researchers based at Deakin University have been closely associated with the development of the critical perspective across these fields. For such reasons, people in the field have sometimes spoken of a 'Deakin perspective'. We do share some common views from which we hope to contribute to contemporary debates about the future development of educational enquiry; at the same time, our disagreements seem as fruitful for us as our agreements.

The Deakin Studies in Education Series provides an opportunity for extending this debate about the nature and future development of education and educational enquiry. It will include the writings of a variety of educational researchers around the world who, like ourselves, are interested in exploring the power and limitations of the critical perspective in the analysis of educational theory, policy and practice.

The central themes of the series will not be dictated by the alleged boundaries between 'foundational' disciplines in education, nor by an unexamined division of the tasks of education and educational research between 'practitioners' and 'theorists', or between 'practitioners' and 'policy-makers'. On the contrary, one of the tasks of the series is to demonstrate, through careful research and scholarship across a range of fields of practical, political and theoretical endeavour, just how outmoded, unproductive, and ultimately destructive these divisions are both for education and for educational research. Put positively, the central themes and questions to be addressed in the series include:

> the unity of educational theory and practice — expressed, for example, in the work of educational practitioners who research their practice as a basis for improving it, and in the notion of collaborative, participatory educational research, for example, in educational action research;
>
> the historical formation, social construction and continual reconstruction of education and educational institutions and reforms through processes of contestation and institutionalization — expressed, for example, in the work of critical researchers into the curriculum and educational reform; and
>
> the possibilities of education for emancipation and active and productive participation in a democratic society — expressed, for example, in the development of critical pedagogy and the development of communitarian perspectives in the organization of education.

These are enduring themes, touching upon some of the central questions confronting our contemporary culture and, some would say, upon the central pathologies of contemporary society. They are all too easily neglected or obscured in the narrow and fragmented views of education and educational research characteristic of our times. Yet education is one of the key resources in what Raymond Williams once described as our societies' 'journey of hope' — the journey towards a better, more just, more rational and more rewarding society. Education has always aimed to nurture, represent, vivify and extend the values and modes of life which promise to make the best in our culture better. Finding out how this can be done, interpreting our progress, and appraising and reappraising the quality of our efforts at educational improvement are the tasks of critical educational research. They are the tasks of this series.

Stephen Kemmis and Rob Walker

Preface

John Smyth

If we were to try to find a more alluring, seductive (even magnetic) word in the educational language to fire the collective imaginations of educational policy analysts, we would be hard pressed to go beyond the notion of 'leadership'. In its reified form, the term 'leadership' has all the qualities that have instant appeal to those who are looking for a way of remedying what is deemed to be wrong with schools in Western democracies. I can best illustrate the aura attaching to leadership with an example from Tolstoy's *War and Peace*:

> Napoleon was standing a little in front of his marshalls, on a little grey Arab horse, wearing the same blue overcoat he had worn throughout the Italian campaign. He was looking intently and silently at the hills, which stood up out of the sea of mist, and the Russian troops moving across them in the distance, and he listened to the sounds of firing in the valley. His face — still thin in those days — did not stir a single muscle; his gleaming eyes were fixed intently on one spot . . .

> When the sun had completely emerged from the fog and was glittering with dazzling brilliance over the fields and the mist (as though he had been waiting for that to begin the battle), he took his glove off his handsome white hand, made a signal with it to his marshalls, and gave orders for the battle to begin. (cited in McCall, 1976, p.139)

As McCall (1976) puts it, borrowing from the military in this way conjures up precisely the strong and resourceful image of 'courage, stamina, power, [and] charisma' (p.139), that many commentators believe is encapsulated in the term 'leadership'. Couple this with the malaise that has allegedly descended upon schools — as evidenced in the

1

seemingly endless calls for a return to the basics, demands for an increase in academic standards and an extension of testing — and the recent frenzy over educational leadership becomes all the more understandable. Conventional wisdom has it that if we can get school principals to take heed of the research on 'school effectiveness', and act as the visionary custodians they are supposed to be, then schools will emerge from the crisis of competence, educational standards will rise, school discipline problems will dissipate, and schools will once again become the means of effecting social, economic and military recovery.

The problem with such arguments and analyses is that they confuse two things: the loss of public confidence in the efficacy of schools and schooling, and a much more fundamental crisis of confidence in the role of the state in Western democracies generally (Weiler, 1982). In the public mind at least, these two have come to be mischievously linked in a way that suggests that the growing mistrust and accompanying decline of public confidence in the state is somehow 'caused' by the inability of education, and schools in particular, to improve the quality of individual and collective life. As Apple (1983) argues, what we have is an 'exporting' downwards of the crisis. As the state comes increasingly under attack because of a lack of public confidence in its ability to respond to wider structural economic and social dislocations within Western capitalism generally, schooling and education are focused upon as being simultaneously the cause and the means of remedying the situation. That is to say: '. . . rather than attention being directed towards the unequal results and benefits produced by the way our economy is currently organized and controlled, schools and teachers will be focussed upon as major causes of social dislocation, unemployment, falling standards of work, declining productivity, and so on' (p.4). According to Weiler (1982), what emerge are strategic responses that masquerade as educational reform, that are designed to arrest wider public disillusionment with the state, by focusing on ways of improving the 'quality of education'. It is in this context that we hear much about the need to have strong and forthright leadership that will stem the decline in levels of educational attainment, restore classroom discipline and return rigour to curriculum and subject offerings.

It is possible, of course, to construe the strategic response to this situation quite differently. Habermas (1980), for example, presents the argument that when we talk about 'crisis' in these terms, we get it wrong. He argues that there is a tendency towards a crisis of 'legitimation', rather than a crisis of 'competence'. There is a crisis in capitalist societies that is of a cyclical economic kind, which gives rise to a hierarchy of other crises that displace one another; the tendency towards *economic* crisis is displaced into a *rationality* crisis, which in turn is displaced into a *legitimacy* crisis, which is further displaced into a *motivation* crisis. Habermas sees the tendency towards a 'crisis of rationality' taking expression in the form of so-called 'scientific approaches' to solving perceived social and economic problems. Invariably these involve a series of constructed and artificial separations — of facts from values, of means from educational ends, of administration from pedagogy — and the substitution of technical/rational administrative solutions to what amount to complex social questions of equity, access and distribution of society's resources. According to Habermas, there is a deepening 'crisis of legitimacy' as these centrally driven technologized solutions (particularly in respect of education) undergo a displacement as they are translated, justified, packaged, and perpetrated onto the community by recourse to the rhetoric of their supposed cost efficiency and cost effectiveness. Of course, they are nothing of the kind; there is rarely any evidence in support of such extravagant claims for enhanced centralism, and the evidence that does exist is spurious, to say the least. In taking on economistic language and methods to analyze and resolve our social problems, we are required not only to write off the accumulated wisdom and cultural traditions that have enabled us to resolve social problems in the past, but more importantly we destroy the cultural habitus that has held educational communities together. Habermas regards the tendencies of both these crises to displace one another as producing a 'crisis of motivation', as feelings of increasing alienation and powerlessness develop: we feel that control lies 'out there with them' and 'not with us in here, in this institution'. Not only does this produce a loss of meaning, identity and purpose, but more importantly it is accompanied by the imposition of forms of language and discourse that further reinforce and bolster the orientation toward measurement, technocracy and managerialism. While there has been some philosophical discussion in the literature about the precise interrelationship between the last two of these crisis tendencies, and whether they exist simultaneously, analyses of this kind are far more sophisticated and informative than explanations generally offered about what is occurring in education and schooling.

The contributors to this volume start from the presumption that the thinking implicit in technicist solutions involving schools is wrong-headed, superficial and fundamentally flawed. Not only are the premises incorrect, but the perceived solutions, through a recovery led by a restoration of leadership in schools, are equally wide of the mark. The truth, so far as the latter is concerned, probably lies somewhat closer to the situation described by Warren Bennis (1959) some thirty years ago, when he said:

> Of all the hazy and confounding areas in social psychology,
> leadership theory undoubtedly contends for top nomination.
> And, ironically, probably more has been written and less known
> about leadership than about any other topic in the behavioural
> sciences. Always, it seems, the concept of leadership eludes us or
> turns up in another form to taunt us again with its slipperiness
> and complexity. So we have invented an endless proliferation of
> terms to deal with it . . . and still the concept is not sufficiently
> defined. As we survey the path leadership theory has taken we
> spot the wreckage of 'trait theory', the 'great man' theory, and
> the 'situationist critique', leadership styles, functional lead-
> ership, and finally leaderless leadership; to say nothing of
> bureaucratic leadership, charismatic leadership, democratic-
> autocratic-laissez-faire leadership, group-centred leadership,
> reality-centred leadership, leadership by objective, and so on.
> The dialectic and reversals of emphases in this area very nearly
> rival the tortuous twists and turns of child rearing practices. . . .
> (p.259)

The views put forward by the authors in this volume run counter to both
the salvationist and the hegemonic views of leadership implicit in the
pragmatic solutions currently proposed as the way out of the educational
quagmire we are supposedly in. While we certainly have a need for
people who hold a vision of the way schools might be in the future, the
various writers in this book argue that such thinking and acting does not
necessarily lie with those who have been hierarchically anointed, or with
those deemed to possess some special or inalienable qualities or traits. If
there is a common thread to the papers presented here, it is that whatever
leadership acts are, they probably have more to do with processes of
communicating understanding, developing a sense of community and
reconstituting the power relationships which get in the way of educative
processes in schools.

   As a number of the contributors point out, it is not altogether
surprising that the study of and research on educational leadership are
moribund. There are several reasons for this, not the least of which have
to do with the persistent inability of scholars and practitioners to
embrace more robust possibilities. The writers in this book challenge in a
very direct manner the dominant behaviourist and functionalist views
that have come to entrap those who live, work and conduct research on
the area of educational leadership. By drawing in various ways upon the
tenets of critical social theory, the various chapters focus on the largely

ignored political, cultural and social context of schools as the starting point from which to unravel the forms of knowledge, power relationships and social control that *must* be central to any discussion of leadership in schools. The linking argument is that if schools are to be the critical and inquiring communities necessary for a democratic way of life, then the leadership within them will have to be more educative and pedagogical in various ways, rather than bureaucratic and authoritarian. By shifting the focus away from sterile discussions about traits, personalities and styles of educational leadership, and focusing instead on the structures and processes within schools as organizations that frustrate, distort and ultimately stifle educative relationships the writers provide a much needed way of reconceptualizing both thought and action in so-called acts of educational leadership. Construed in this way, the agenda becomes one of empowering school participants by helping *them* to unmask the unquestioned and oppressive managerialist modes that have come to constrain them.

The opening chapter by Peter Watkins, entitled 'Leadership, Power and Symbols in Educational Administration', discusses the origins of hierarchical and functionalist interpretations of leadership and shows how the trait, situationalist and contingency models as explanations of leadership theory are flawed even on their own terms. According to Watkins, when these approaches introduce the notion of power, it is always in a static, uni-directional form. What these accounts of leadership theory fail to acknowledge is that an alternative view of power, which is itself central to any discussion of leadership, must be more inclusive of issues of class, agency, gender, dialectics, symbols and metaphors. Only if we conceive of leadership as embracing these aspects will we be able to break out of a 'line management' view of what leadership means. In this way, Watkins sets the stage for the chapters to follow.

The chapter by Bill Foster, entitled 'Toward a Critical Practice of Leadership', notes that, as a descriptor, leadership covers a great deal of ground; as a consequence it is one of the most misunderstood concepts in our educational language. There is a sense in which leadership *is* understood in the conventional language of schooling as being a real phenomenon, one that does make a difference in schools. He argues that before the term can be utilized sensibly it is necessary to tease out two particular contemporary meanings (the political-historical and the bureaucratic-managerial). It may then be possible to acknowledge the way in which the concept of leadership itself has been swallowed up by the needs of managerial theory. He argues that leadership needs to be seen as transcending management, to involve the critical, the transformative, the educative and the ethical.

Recent attempts to rescue the notion of leadership, via the 'educational reform movement', have been dogged by a failure to understand a number of crucial issues. In his chapter, entitled '"New" Leadership and the Possibility of Educational Reform', Lawrence Angus points to the inadequacy of renewed calls for leadership emerging out of school effectiveness research in the USA. According to Angus, a persistent failure to acknowledge the business management origins of the concept of leadership, a lack of understanding of the notion of 'culture' as it applies to schools, along with an absence of any realistic moral dimension to its conceptualization, have left discussions of leadership in schools in a threadbare state. What we have, he claims, is discussion which is eloquent about matters bureaucratic, but alarmingly silent about the ideological context within which both schooling and leadership occur.

In 'Educational Leadership: A Feminist Critique and Reconstruction', Jill Blackmore argues for a marking out of a territory that has long been neglected, but which holds considerable significance for the redefinition of leadership as a field of study. The central argument of her chapter is that as long as discussions of leadership remain wedded to liberal theories that rely upon abstract notions of individualism and bureaucratic rationality (supported by positivistic theories of knowledge), then the scene will continue to be dominated by masculinist perspectives of leadership. Blackmore contests the patriarchical view of leadership that emphasizes individualism, hierarchical relationships, bureaucratic rationality and abstract moral principles. In its place she advocates a feminist reconstruction of leadership that includes leadership outside formal roles; that envisages power as multi-dimensional and multi-directional; that empowers others to have power; that is concerned with communitarian and collective activities and values.

Richard Bates, in 'Leadership and the Rationalization of Society', argues that leadership as a field of study has for a long time been informed by two fundamental misconceptions: firstly, that the process of abstraction and reification in and of itself constitutes an appropriate path toward powerful theory; secondly, that the language of technique is an appropriate substitute for the discourse of ethics. Taking the 'agency and structure' notions of Giddens, and the 'knowledge and power of social life' of Foucault, Bates mounts the argument that herein may lie the means for addressing the issues of subjectivity and objectivity that feature so prominently in Greenfield's endeavours to reconstruct the notion of leadership. What Bates does is incorporate into the notion of leadership the dialectic of agency and structure, along with the interpenetration of the production and execution of power. We might also, he says, approach leadership in the way Habermas encourages us to think of 'the law' as a process of mediation between interests and values. Such alternative notions need further elaboration, it is true, but at least they open up the possibility of moving leadership beyond being defined as 'technique' or charisma.

The claim that leadership is a form of philosophy in action is the central issue raised by John Codd in his chapter, 'Educational Leadership as Reflective Action'. He makes the distinction, alluded to by other contributors, between the managerial and educational aspects of leadership. He uses this as the basis for developing the argument about the need for critical reflection and collective deliberation to constitute the moral domain of those who profess to be educational leaders. Only when leadership in schools is based upon such moral principles as justice, freedom and respect for persons can learning in schools move beyond a narrow utilitarian concern for skill-related learning. When leadership is regarded as a form of moral action, decisions are made that amount to a considered and informed cognitive and cultural appraisal.

John Smyth's central claim in 'A "Pedagogical" and "Educative" View of Leadership' is that constructs like leadership (as conventionally defined) are not easily transported into schools. Indeed, the notion of one group (leaders), who exercise hegemony and domination over another (followers), is an anti-educational one. Drawing upon Brian Fay's (1987) notion of the 'educative', this chapter sees leadership as constituting a process of school participants incorporating one another in a sense-making process that involves 'deliberative exchanges', thus uncovering the contradictions and dilemmas that have come to constrain and dominate their school lives. This notion of leadership is essentially an 'enabling' one that has to do with school people gaining an understanding of the way they participate in creating self-destructive and self-perpetuating social, cultural and political conditions that make their working lives less than fulfilling. A number of possibilities are presented: working towards reclaiming the pedagogical and the critical in schools; linking the pedagogical with the political in schools; engaging in reflection in action; and developing a more situated pedagogy that acknowledges the importance of dialogical relations in education. Against the background of the current lexicon in leadership discussions, these may appear as rather curious phenomena, but when considered against the background of *what schools are supposed to be about,* they make a good deal more sense than current management imperatives.

It is appropriate that the final chapter in this volume should examine the issue of organizational democracy, which has been an implicit (and sometimes explicit) presumption in all the other chapters of the book. In his 'Defence of Organizational Democracy', Fazal Rizvi reasserts the importance of this as the basis for a reformulated view of educational leadership. He does this by rehearsing the arguments against organizational democracy, especially Michels' arguments of inefficiency and apathy, and concludes with some case study examples from Yugoslavia and Israel that suggest that these arguments have little substance.

The somewhat ambitious dual agenda of this book is therefore one of providing a critique of existing practices in educational leadership, while at the same time engaging in a transformation of the notion itself. The sequencing of the papers reflects a deliberate structure in the argumentation: more of a deconstructionist emphasis (although not exclusively) in the Watkins, Foster, Angus and Blackmore chapters, followed by a more reconstructionist agenda in the Bates, Codd, Smyth and Rizvi papers, as the presenters concentrate increasingly upon what alternative and more 'inclusive' viewpoints might look like (particularly ones that acknowledge the pedagogical and gendered nature of schools).

While the agenda of reformulating a new and much more critical perspective on educational leadership has only just begun, it is clear that above all else there must be a concerted attempt to move thinking about leadership outside itself. I believe this volume does that.

References

Apple, M. (1983) 'Controlling the work of teachers,' *Delta 32,* pp.3-15.
Bennis, W. (1959) 'Leadership theory and administrative behaviour,' *Administrative Science Quarterly,* 4, pp.259-301.
Habermas, J. (1980) *Legitimation Crisis,* London, Heinemann.
McCall, M. (1976) 'Leadership research: Choosing goods and devils on the run,' *Journal of Occupational Psychology,* 49, pp.139-53.
Weiler, H. (1982) 'Education, public confidence and the legitimacy of the modern state: Is there a 'crisis' somewhere?' *Journal of Curriculum Studies,* 15, 2, pp.125-42.

Chapter 1

Leadership, Power and Symbols in Educational Administration

Peter Watkins

The traditional approach to administration and its off-spring educational administration lies within the functionalist paradigm. Indeed, as Burrell and Morgan (1979) have amply illustrated, the bulk of the theoretical debate and research on organizations is accounted for within this paradigm. A major concern of those within the functionalist school is to explore the extent that the designated leaders of organizations determine the outcomes of the organization and the behaviour of its lower ranks (March and Simon, 1958). But this perception of administration presents a static one-directional view of leadership in which the superordinate or leader leads an anonymous, unquestioning mass of subordinates or followers. Administrative research and theory is looked on to serve and give support to those in positions of administrative power, thereby conserving and reproducing the status quo. Moreover, the resultant theory and research 'invokes the unarticulated assumption that managers are both more important and more variable than workers, and that their behaviour is thereby more worthy of study and intervention' (Goldman, 1978, p.24). Such an approach to the study of administration reflects the belief that 'the functionalist researcher/consultant and manager are joined in a similar search: a search for predictability and control' (Smircich, 1983, p.223). One of the foremost theorists of the functionalist paradigm, Merton, has conceded that with regard to the sponsorship of research:

> Of the limited body of social research in industry, the greater part has been orientated towards the needs of management. The problems selected as the focus of the inquiry . . . have been largely thus defined by management, sponsorship has been typically by management, the limits and character of ex-perimental changes in the work situation have been passed upon

by management, and periodic reports have been made primarily to management. No matter how good or seemingly self-evident the reason, it should be noted that this is the typical perspective of social research in industry, and that it limits the effective prosecution of the research. (Merton, 1968, p.625)

Giddens' criticism of functionalism goes further, claiming that its influence has been largely pernicious (1984, p.xxxi). By ascribing rationality to social systems, not to human beings, the functionalist approach does not give an adequate explanation of anything (Giddens, 1984, p.294).

However, recently a number of scholars in administration have presented a view of organizations which stresses the activities of all members and the emancipatory potential of administration (e.g., Forester, 1982a, 1982b; Deetz and Kersten, 1983; Denhardt, 1981; Benson, 1977; Knights and Wilmott, 1982). While the work of these authors has had a considerable impact, it is probably premature in educational administration to argue, as Giddens does with regard to functionalism, that 'the battlefield is largely empty, even if from time to time isolated bolts continue to be launched' (1977, p.96). Nevertheless, because the traditional approach toward leadership and power has exerted such a powerful influence, firstly a critique of that approach in those two areas will be offered; secondly an alternative approach, viewed from two dimensions, will be suggested; and lastly the implications of these approaches will be discussed.

Traditional Views of Leadership and Power

This chapter explores alternatives in leadership to the traditional, functionalist view. The search for alternatives stems from my personal experience over many years in schools that leadership does not necessarily emanate from the senior administrative posts of a school, and from the dissatisfaction of students of educational administration whom I have taught that the traditional views of leadership bear no resemblance to what actually goes on in schools. In many situations the senior administrators, while frequently being members of various school committees, often find that their qualifications, interests or predilections preclude them from being the driving force in the ever-changing organizational life of a school. Traditional stances in leadership take for granted the one-directional flow from the leader to the led, from the principal to the school community, without realizing the reality in which a junior member of staff may be the leader and the principal the follower. More starkly, in the recently reconstituted school councils in Victoria, which entail significant student representation, a student may feasibly arise as a leader in a certain area while principal, teachers and parents become followers.

Thus it would seem to be a futile exercise blandly to label a principal of a school as a leader when anyone in the school community might arise in certain situations at certain times to become what might be termed a leader. The problem seems to be that too often what is in reality a power relationship is obscured by the label of leadership. The result is that the literature on leadership adopts a fairly descriptive, simplistic and naive view of the concept. As McCall and Lombardo put it:

> the accumulated data, even when pulled together, are still contradictory, ambiguous, and narrow. Improvement of our understanding of leadership apparently does not lie in pursuing existing trends or in attempting to integrate existing research. Conceptually and methodologically, leadership research has bogged down. (1978, p.151)

Greenfield (in Macpherson, 1984) has labelled the traditional approaches to leadership as being characterized by superficiality. Manz and Sims (1984) in expressing similar disappointment point to problems of declining productivity, absenteeism and increasing contestation in the workplace as indications that 'traditional approaches to leadership and work design are no longer adequate' (p.410). Sergiovanni (1987) in a change of perspective has acknowledged that the traditional or transactional, as he calls it, view of leadership has run its course and 'can deliver no more than it has with respect to insights and understandings of leadership and management' (1987, p.6). The following discussion of traditional approaches to leadership illustrates why they have fallen into disrepute.

Leadership: A Critique of the Traditional Views

In this section it will be argued that the trait approach, the Ohio situationalist approach and Fiedler's contingency model approach to leadership are static, ahistorical and ideologically based (Watkins, 1986). Moreover, it will be illustrated that the functionalist leadership perspective operates in an authoritative way to sanitize the unequal power relations within an organization. The result is that the class relations inherent within a superordinate and subordinate social hierarchy of the school (see Wright, 1979; Watkins, 1983; and Salaman, 1981) are legitimized and mystified through the 'motherhood' concept of leadership.

The Trait Approach

In the major conceptual and empirical approaches to research into leadership, the initial emphasis was on distinguishing certain 'leadership traits' in the individual's personality or physical make-up. Advocates of the trait approach have spent a considerable time attempting to correlate leadership behaviour and such physical and personality traits as age, height, weight, appearance, fluency of speech, intelligence, introversion/extroversion. Stogdill (1970, original 1948) investigated 124 papers in an attempt to determine the validity of the trait studies of leaders. He found that the correlations, while positive, were low, and that contradictory findings were common. The evidence suggested that 'leadership is a relation that exists between persons in a social situation, and that persons who are leaders in one situation may not necessarily be leaders in other situations' (Stogdill, 1970, p.126). If leadership is situationally based, then traits are of little consequence.

The findings of Stogdill indicated that leadership is not a matter of passive status or of the mere possession of some combination of traits. Also Janda (1960) has pointed out that the five basic factors listed by Stogdill (capacity, achievement, responsibility, participation, status) were characteristics of the leader. It was still unclear whether leadership referred to:

> the behaviour of this individual in interaction with other group members;
> the behaviour of this individual as a group member — perhaps with differentiated role functions to perform;
> the behaviour of other group members in interaction with the member designated as leader;
> the social relationships which existed between the leader and other group members;
> all of the above;
> none of the above.

Thus, while Stogdill helped to cast light on what might be the comparative fruitfulness of the trait approach, he did not clarify what is actually entailed in leadership. No unifying conceptual development was suggested. However, his basic conclusion that the 'qualities, characteristics and skills required in a leader are determined to a large extent by the demands of the situation in which he is to function as a leader' (Stogdill, 1970, p.123) led to establishment of the Ohio situationalist school as the next main development in leadership studies.

But despite the devastating critiques of the trait approach it has persisted in various forms. Very often rather than certain traits being attributed by people to some idealized hero, organizational founders reconstructed history to foster the notion of a 'great man'. Myths were created by public relations men and those ideologically committed to a particular construction of social reality. Teulings (1980) in a perceptive study of the Philips company and the family which controls it comments that:

> The great man approach tends to attribute company successes to the purposeful behaviour of a clairvoyant captain of industry, and failures to the unpredictable, uncontrollable turbulances of the environment, or to the fate of time.

> Once in use this myth becomes a functional prerequisite for the viability of the company as a private enterprise. The myth provides a symbolic continuity, sustains the role of family ownership and prevents the downfall of the great leader, even when he does not distinguish himself at all by acts of wisdom or foresight. (Teulings, 1980, p.153a)

Thus the trait approach still finds favour because it often presents those idealized characteristics with which people would like to typify their imagined symbolic heroes. In addition the approach has been nurtured by business magnates to justify their own position through myths and legends that endorse their prowess (see Angus, this volume). However, because the trait approach was obviously simplistic and could not withstand close scrutiny, the more complex situational approach was developed as part of the human relations strategy of management (see Perrow, 1986a).

The Situational Approach

The situational approach views leadership in terms of function performed rather than in terms of particular leadership traits. This emphasis on the function of leaders dominated the literature on leadership during the 1950s. Halpin (1955) states that this was a natural result of the surveys of Gibb in 1954 and Stogdill in 1948, which indicated that leadership was a 'complex social phenomenon that cannot be treated meaningfully when conceived as an isolated trait or entity viewed apart from related group and institutional factors' (1955, pp.18-19).

The main work on the situational approach came from members of the Personnel Research Board at Ohio State University, especially Hemphill, Stogdill and Shartle. The Ohio school sought to define leadership behaviour in terms of certain situational variables such as the nature and distance of group goal, motivation of the group, etc. As these factors vary with the situation, leadership would also vary. Describing leader behaviour was an amalgam of the perceptions of the leader's subordinates and the way in which the leader himself perceived his own attitude toward his role. The notions of 'consideration' and 'initiating structure' were isolated as basic dimensions of leadership behaviour in formal organizations.

These two dimensions of leader behaviour were used in the Halpin and Winer (Halpin, 1955) adaptation of Hemphill and Coons' original Leader Behaviour Description Questionnaire (LBDQ). Halpin used the questionnaire to attempt to measure leadership ideology and leadership style in both the US Air Force and public education.

Halpin's studies of educational administrators and aircraft commanders promoted a view of effective leadership which is characterized by high initiation of structure *and* high consideration (1969, p.313). However, Greenwood and McNamara's research (in Wrightsman and Deaux, 1981) indicates that the relationships between consideration and initiating structure are generally low. Thus a supervisor who keeps his employees task orientated would not be particularly considerate. This would also indicate that there is independence in regard to success in achieving the two dimensions of leadership.

Graen *et al.* (1972), in reviewing research on the dimensions of consideration and structure, claimed that 'research on the two dimensions of leadership style proposed and operationalized by the Ohio State researchers has not advanced much beyond the initial descriptive stage' (p.216). Indeed, Greenfield describes the LBDQ-based research as unusually restrictive and static. As he puts it, 'At best, the LBDQ gives us a single Brownie camera shot of a complex and obscure process. We know that much went on before we took the photograph; we know that much will go on after it; and we know that our fuzzy LBDQ snapshot represents only a tiny part of what was going on at the time it was taken' (1979, p.178). Similarly Janda (1960) and Yukl (1971) point out that most research has been conducted as if leadership were a unique phenomenon, although most of the conceptions of leadership can be explained in more basic variables. This simplistic, static view of leadership has led researchers to exclude intermediate and situational variables such as power and class relationships. But the consideration of these may be necessary in order to understand how leaders' actions can affect the productivity or well-being of their subordinates.

Intensive contemporary reviews of the literature by Sayles (1966), Lowin (1968), Korman (1966) and Campbell *et al.* (1970) indicated that the relation of leader behaviour to subordinate productivity and satisfaction with the leader was still unclear.

Korman (1966) found that there was very little evidence that leadership behavioural and/or attitudinal variation, as defined by scores on the Leadership Behaviour and Leadership Opinion Questionnaire, were predictive of later effectiveness and/or satisfaction criteria. From his investigation it appears that the majority of validity studies provide *no* evidence, even in cases of positive relationships, that variation on the above scales predicts different kinds of worker behaviour. His other main criticism was of the research designs of the studies investigating the situational approach. While they emphasize that the effects of 'consideration' and 'initiating structure' have become almost bywords in American industrial psychology, it seems apparent that very little is known about how these variables may predict work group performance or about conditions which affect such predictions. Korman concluded then, and it might be suggested still, 'we cannot even say whether they have any predictive significance at all' (1966, p. 360).

But while the situationalist approach to leadership was seen to be virtually worthless on its own terms, of controlling and extracting more work from subordinates, it has also been criticized for working by stealth in seeking to manipulate the employees of organizations (see Leavitt, 1964; Perrow, 1986a; and Tinker and Lowe, 1982). By ignoring inequalities of organizational power, it implied an acceptance of the power status quo. Industrial psychologists sought to present a conception of leadership which might meet the socio-emotional needs of workers, 'thus ending various kinds of irrational hostility in the factory and the "need" for workers to unite in opposition to management (i.e., via unionisation)' (Bramel and Friend, 1981, p. 868). Such manipulative ploys by both industrial psychologists and industrial sociologists were recognized by workers as the management strategies that they clearly were. Indeed, the United Auto Workers described some industrial sociologists as 'cow sociologists seeking to milk the workers and make them more contented' (Tinker and Lowe, 1982, p. 335).

Thus the main thrust of the research was concerned with extracting greater productivity while legitimating the power status quo and the class relations of organizations. However, the same deficiencies are still evident in the most recent influential work on leadership which has been done by Fiedler.

Fiedler's Contingency Model of Leadership

Fiedler has attempted to synthesize the relatively unsuccessful attempts of the 'trait school' and the situationalists of Ohio. In his seminal work detailing this synthesis Fiedler defines the leader 'as the individual in the group given the task of directing and co-ordinating task-relevant group activities or who in the absence of a designated leader, carries the primary responsibility for performing these functions in the group' (Fiedler, 1967, p.8). Twenty years later in his more recent writings he argues more succinctly that 'leadership . . . refers to that part of organizational management that deals with the direction of subordinates' (1987, p.3). Effectiveness is evaluated in terms of group performance on the group's primary assigned task. Morale and member satisfaction are seen as by-products rather than as measures of task-group performance. However, Fiedler recognizes that this relationship may change in the case of the military or schools in which the building of morale or the increase of member satisfaction is the primary goal of the leader and is his explicit task. Fiedler's model of leadership is termed a Contingency Model of Leadership because the model assumes that the leader's contribution to group performance depends on both his leadership style in terms of either task orientation or person orientation, and the favourableness of the situation for the leader.

As Shiflett and Nealey (1972) point out, the contingency model hypothesizes that the leader's style, as indicated by the leader's esteem for his Least Preferred Co-Worker (the LPC score), interacts with the group-task situation to determine group productivity. There are thus two main components: the group-task situation and the leader's style (the LPC score); these are correlated together to form the contingency model (for a more detailed description and analysis see Watkins, 1986).

The need for constant revision has indicated the many problems of the LPC, which has caused many writers to have misgivings on the Contingency Model (see Graen *et al.,* 1970, 1971, 1972; Yukl, 1970; McMahon, 1972; O'Brien, 1969; Sample and Wilson, 1965; Fishbein *et al.,* 1969a, 1969b). Fishbein *et al.* consider that a consistent general halo may not occur when leaders evaluate their least preferred co-worker. 'That is, when high LPC Ss are asked to rate their least preferred co-worker on Fiedler's Esteem Scale, they are a markedly different type of person than are low LPC individuals' (Fishbein *et al.,* 1969b, p.184). In this way the leader's attitudes about the task-relevant attributes of a co-worker may be independent of his attitudes about the co-worker's social attributes. Moreover, a number of studies, which found no correlation, have been made into the behavioural correlates of LPC scores. Yukl (1970) concludes that the absence of a clear conceptual interpretation for LPC scores is paralleled by a lack of empirical data concerning the relation of LPC scores to leader behaviour. Graham (1973) concludes that in spite of nearly twenty years of research on the psychological meaning of LPC, the main predictor variable in the contingency model remains a mystery (p.60).

Mitchell *et al.* (1970-71) also point out that a number of studies have not supported the interpretation of the LPC score as relating to 'task-versus-relationship' orientation. Steiner (1959) found that low LPC subjects were socially more expansive on three social distance measures and less extrapunitive than high LPC persons. Mitchell *et al.* (1970-71) found that low LPC subjects were more concerned about the interpersonal relation in a task setting than were the high LPC subjects. Moreover, high LPC subjects were more aware of position power and task structure than were low LPC subjects in judging leadership situations. These findings led Mitchell to call for a re-examination of the conceptualization of the LPC.

Fiedler himself saw the LPC as being very similar to the Ohio model of consideration and initiating structure. He considers any divergences as 'relatively minor' (Fiedler, 1970). However, a study by Weissenberg and Gruenfeld (1966) found little correlation between the two. Graen *et al.* (1971) also found a low correlation. Fishbein *et al.* (1969a, 1969b) after a review of the literature concluded that it is still not clear just what the LPC is measuring. McMahon (1972) also found that there is a lack of agreement on what the LPC is measuring. Indeed, he argued that the contingency theory seems to be lacking in substance and explanatory power, which should be one of the primary goals of any theory. Fishbein *et al.* (1969b) have illustrated that Fiedler keeps changing ground on his LPC score. In 1958 he viewed the LPC score as a measure of a leadership effectiveness trait. In 1961 he saw low LPC persons as being more controlling and task orientated, and high LPC as being compliant and interpersonally orientated. In 1969 he emphasized a motivational rather than a behavioural basis to the LPC. In 1969 he introduced the variable of stress. In 1972 (Fiedler, 1972a, 1972b) he tried to combine some of these disparate variables into a new model of LPC.

Some general criticisms of the contingency model. Ashour (1973) also has criticized the theoretical adequacy of the contingency model. He argues that from an analysis of the cumulative results Fiedler's claims are not fully supported by the empirical evidence. Ashour points out that:

> Not *only does a theory have to offer valid and nontrivial predictions, but it also has to provide meaningful explanations of the relations and predictions it proposes.* . . . The model is an *empiric generalization* that is not even fully supported by the empirical results; it is *not a theory.* (1973, p.375)

The contingency model merely suggests a set of relationships without exploring the basic dimensions of those relationships. Such considerations as the class basis of organizations and the ideological legitimation of organizational hierarchies are conveniently avoided, implying an acceptance of the power status quo. The recent research of Wilkinson and Smith (1984) has emphasized that management does not implement and stress 'humanistic' ideas like leadership for the benefit of all members of the organization, but that the implementation of these ideas

> is purely for reasons of motivating the workforce; it is not to do with 'looking after the other side'. . . . The . . . managers, then, according to personnel officer Pat Thomas, see themselves as 'people people'. Being a person person means looking for a new way of inculcating a solidarity in the workforce amenable to management but antithetical to the union. (Wilkinson and Smith, 1984, p.105)

Even apart from the above considerations Ashour concludes that:

> Fiedler's contingency model and its related research have serious empirical, methodological and theoretical problems.
>
> [Any] attempt to improve the empirical validity of the model and its meaningfulness would have to start with solving the methodological and theoretical problems. (1973, p.376)

It is clear that the contingency model of Fiedler is far from perfect. In particular it presents a static picture of the leader's followers. The followers are acted upon, they are led. There is no hint of contestation or resistance which would being about an ongoing dialectic of change. In short, people are presented as mere ciphers without any hint of real, vibrant human agency (Giddens, 1979). In the light of the evidence, anyone attempting to use it to measure leadership in schools would be left with uncertain and dubious results. Indeed, Graen *et al.* (1970, 1971) claim that their two studies 'cast grave doubt on the plausibility of the contingency model of leadership-effectiveness' (1970, p.295). While

Shiflett and Nealey's findings 'give one little confidence in the ability of the contingency model . . .' (1972, p.381).

Perrow sums up his discussion of Fiedler's work by arguing that

> One is tempted to say that the research on leadership has left us with a clear view that things are far more complicated and 'contingent' than we initially believed, and that, in fact, they are so complicated and contingent that it may not be worth our while to spin out more and more categories and qualifications — if we wish to learn about organizations. Already the task of either training leaders to fit the jobs or designing jobs to fit the leaders, a position Fiedler is led to advocate, appears to be monumental. If leadership techniques must change with every change in group personnel, task, timing, experience, and so on, then either leaders or jobs must constantly change. (Perrow, 1979, p.107)

Such an absurd situation reflects the predicament in which much of the traditional leadership work finds itself. However, Fiedler (1987) has endeavoured to salvage what he can of the contingency model of leadership through developing a new theory of leadership which blends his contingency model with a new cognitive resource theory. This new theory appears to be a variant of the old trait theory. 'The theory says that in the best of all best possible worlds the leader's intellectual abilities are the major source of the plans, decisions and strategies that guide the group's actions' (1987, p.105). The development of this new theory is a response to some of the harshest criticism of the contingency model which highlighted the lack of explanation that could explain its underlying processes. 'As a consequence cognitive resource theory attempts to fill this gap' (1987, p.7). However, the startling conclusion which Fiedler arrives at after much discussion of this new theory is that 'directive leaders who are stupid give stupid directions, and if the group follows these directions, the consequences will be bad' (1987, p.199). Such a finding would appear to be obvious, and has led Perrow to suggest that 'at the extremes, we can be fairly confident in identifying good or bad leaders, but for most situations we will probably have little to say' (1986a, p.92).

It should be clear from the traditional literature reviewed here that most of the conventional approaches to leadership are under attack on all fronts. Yet amazingly this highly questionable material is still included in standard texts. The reasons for this would seem to be based on ideological concerns and an attempt to maintain the power status quo in organizations. These reasons will be discussed in the next section, which presents a critique of the traditional approach to power. The actions of those in designated leadership positions, that is, in positions of authority, are best understood in terms of power. Consequently the next section will explore some of the dominant ideas of power in traditional organization texts.

Power: A Critique of the Traditional Views

At the beginning of this chapter it was argued that leadership should be considered as a subset of power. Consequently similar criticisms to those raised against theories of leadership can be levelled at the traditional functionalist approach to power as presented by such writers as French and Raven (1959), Etzioni (1961) and Blau (1964). Their view has not only been critized as static, indifferent towards historical forces and ignorant of moral and political dimensions, but also 'if power is analyzed at all, it is in terms of influence or authority, the legitimized-based power of management or organization elites. Almost never are domination, subjugation, coercion, manipulation or extortion of one group or class of organization members by a more powerful group or class analyzed' (Zey-Ferrell and Aiken, 1981, p.16). To demonstrate the deficiencies in the traditional view of power two of the most influential views will be examined. The first explores the bases of power, the second analyzes power through exchange theory.

Bases of Power

Perhaps the most influential writers on power have been French and Raven (1959), who suggested that there were five bases of power. *Expert power* is based on the perception that the power wielder has superior knowledge and information. *Reward power* is based on the perception that the power wielder has the ability to mediate rewards. *Coercive power* is based on the perception that the power wielder has the ability to mediate punishments. *Legitimate power* is based on the belief that the power wielder has the right to prescribe certain behaviour and opinions. *Referrent power* is based on a feeling of identification or a feeling of 'oneness' with the power wielder. For French and Raven authority is seen in terms of legitimate power, while power is generally seen in terms of potential influence.

Etzioni (1961) narrowed down the bases to three categories: normative, remunerative and coercive. *Normative power* relates to the ability to allot and manipulate symbolic rewards especially in areas which carry esteem and prestige. *Remunerative power* is based on the ability of the organization to hand out rewards or prized resources to particular people. In contrast *coercive power* depends on fear of the application or threat of application of various sanctions. However, Etzioni relates these bases of power to the structure of the organization, and so in essence he has developed a structuralist-functionalist approach.

Clegg (1977) has criticized the formulation of bases of power not only because of their a priori nature but also because there is an underlying assumption that particular 'resource' bases will have the same utility in all situations. To do this is to overlook the fact that historical circumstances are perpetually in a state of flux and that social sites do not have uniform characteristics but differ in marked ways. In addition Clegg charges that:

> The assumption of 'resource' based explanations of 'power' ought also to entail an exposition of how some people come to have access to these 'resources' while some others do not. The prior possession of resources in anything other than equal amounts is something which a theory of 'power' has to explain. It may presume equilibrium, but it ought to justify its presumption in some way. (1977, p.25)

The proponents of power bases within organizations have taken for granted that resources in organizations should or will be distributed in some way, and that any distribution of resources will be of an unequal nature.

Kipnis *et al.* (1984) also have criticized the limiting nature of the power bases approach to the study of power in organizations. They suggest that 'the problem here . . . is that this theoretical approach does not help us identify all the strategies actually used by managers — that is, managers use strategies not mentioned by French and Raven' (1984, p.59). One of these strategies has been suggested by Bachrach and Baratz (1962), who argue that by focusing on bases of power the deliberate suppression or overlooking of issues by dominant groups within organizations can be obscured. Further, an approach which centres on bases of power cannot allow for a situation or a circumstance where the inherent bias of the organization results in a particular outcome without any overt activity from the dominant members of the organization (see Bourdieu and Passeron, 1977). Indeed, such traditional studies gloss over the moral and political dimension of administrative action and 'how this action may both preserve and conceal what is problematic within organizations and society' (Willmott, 1987, p.250).

The Exchange Theory of Power

Etzioni's typology can also be viewed as a variant on exchange theory. The non-instigation of sanctions or threats, the offer of rewards, or the conferring of symbolic rewards are exchanged by the dominant members of the organization for the compliance of subordinates. Exchange theory, however, has been more fully developed by Blau (1964, p.118) from the 'power-dependence' formulation put forward by Emerson (1962).

Blau argued that the power relationship should be inherently unequal. This inequality creates a dependence relationship where the subordinate is dependent on the dominant person either not to impose sanctions or to supply certain rewards. Thus for Blau the most potent form of power results from an unequal exchange. So 'if an individual has much power over others . . . they will be eager to do his bidding and anticipate his wishes in order to maintain his good will, particularly if there are still others who compete for the benefits he supplies them' (Blau, 1964, pp.134-5). This inequality of power in turn develops an organizational structure, which arises from the accumulation of resources by the dominant to maintain their position within the organization and their power over subordinates. In this way roles within the organization are defined and patterns of authority relations become routinized.

A major shortcoming of this approach is that Blau does not justify why inequality of power permeates organizations and how this inequality relates to and reflects the inequalities of the wider society. For if it is accepted that organizations are socially constructed, then it must be realized that there is an inherent political element in the structuring of organizations which reflects the political processes evident in the workings not only of the organization but also of the wider society. Because exchange theory neglects this political element as well as factors such as the influences of self-interest, values and social biases, Clegg and Dunkerley have dismissed exchange-based theories of power as basically superficial (1980, pp.450-1).

When reading these influential texts by Blau and Etzioni, which are now over twenty years old, one is struck, especially in Blau, by the sexist language and the patriarchal ideology underpinning the arguments. It is taken for granted that the leaders and the most powerful people in the organization are men. Powerful men and their wives are discussed (e.g., Blau, 1964, p.276), but there is little hint of powerful women and their husbands. (For a more detailed argument on patriarchy and power see Blackmore, this volume.)

The tendency for traditional approaches to power to simplify structure and human action into a dualism whereby one aspect is either ignored or taken for granted overlooks the duality of structure and agency where structure is conceived as both the medium and the outcome of social practices (Giddens, 1979). This dialectic relationship has been well caught by Lukes:

> Social life can only properly be understood as a dialectic of power and structure, a web of possibilities for agents, whose nature is both active and structured, to make choices and pursue strategies within given limits, which in consequence expand and contract over time. Any standpoint or methodology which reduces that dialectic to a one-sided consideration of agents without . . . structural limits or structures without agents, or which does not address the problem of their interrelations, will be unsatisfactory. No social theory merits serious attention that fails to retain an ever-present sense of the dialectic of power and structure. (Lukes, 1977, p.29)

If we are to treat people as anything other than mere ciphers or automatons blindly following a superior who has been designated or who has been taught to be a leader, then we must incorporate a view of human agency (Giddens, 1979, 1981; Watkins, 1985) whereby people are seen to conduct their lives not as 'cultural dopes' but as knowledgeable human beings. Giddens suggests that human agency is a crucial concept in any social analysis: 'we should not conceive of the structures of domination built into social institutions as in some way grinding out "docile bodies" who behave like the automata suggested by objectivist social science' (1984, p.76). Human beings live out their daily lives and socially construct their reality through the negotiations, contestations and resistances of the rules and resources within which their lives are entwined. Through this ongoing dialectic people both influence and are influenced by the structures in which they find themselves.

A more realistic, demystified approach is to view leadership in terms of power relations within the ongoing dialectic of human agency (Giddens, 1982). In such a context leadership becomes a metaphoric symbol through which human beings construct the social reality in which they carry out their daily struggle for existence (Denhardt, 1981; Morgan, Frost and Pondy, 1983). Based on the above critique of conventional approaches to leadership and power, this chapter presents two alternative views of leadership. Firstly a critical approach centring on ideas of class, power and human agency will be discussed. Secondly leadership will be presented as a dialectical relationship which reflects the cultural symbols and metaphors of an organization.

An Alternative Approach

This alternative viewpoint has two aspects which constitute elements of the same view. The first of these aspects will be discussed under the heading of class, power and human agency, while the second will be analyzed through the notions of dialectics, symbols and metaphors.

Class, Power and Human Agency

Critical scholars such as Apple (1982), Bernstein (1977a, 1977b) and Bourdieu (1977) have sought to investigate the part power plays in educational and other social institutions. As Bernstein argues, one of the main considerations of educators should be to resolve how 'power relationships . . . penetrate the organization, distribution, and evalua-tion of knowledge through the social context' (1977a, p.68). But important in this consideration is how the class structure, which reflects society's power distribution, impinges on organizational relationships and hierarchies of control. In this context Bernstein argues that the origins of power and control in educational systems reside in the basic class structure of society.

> Class structure and relationships constitute and regulate both the distribution of power and the principles of control; that is, constitute and regulate the relationships between categories, the hierarchical form of their constitution *and* regulate the realization of the categories — that is, the principles of control. (1977b, p.181)

Gender is also an important factor in power relations. The recent work of Apple (1985), Arnot and Weiner (1987) and Weiner and Arnot (1987), for instance, has highlighted the importance of gender issues in the way schools are organized. Taking account of such considerations as class and gender, any discussion of educational leadership within an educational organization should be situated in its historical and social milieux. To avoid the stable, functionalist approach which minimizes the historical forms of organization, we need to examine the interaction between human practice and social structures. The latter are the generative rules and power relations which are embedded in a specific historical locale. But the rules and power relations of social institutions not only constrain and enhance human action and practice, they also emerge in time and space out of those very acts (Giddens, 1979). Through such a structurationist view the functionalist position embodied in the traditional concept of leadership can be unmasked to reveal its basic class nature and the inequality of power, for in class societies class domination becomes the structural principle of those societies, of their organizations and the basis of state power (see Giddens, 1981).

Moreover, the structurationist approach emphasizes that power is a process, refuting any implication of a static relationship. People are knowledgeable and active with some insight into the forms which dominate them. They exercise choices and options in the way they work, their actions and reactions in the complex nature of relationships which constitute an organization. As Giddens puts it:

> Power relations in social systems can be regarded as relations of autonomy and dependence; but no matter how imbalanced they may be in terms of power, actors in subordinate positions are never wholly dependent and are very often adept at converting whatever resources they possess into some degree of control over the conditions of reproduction of the system. (1982, p.32)

In the production and reproduction of social structures power processes are a central factor. By examining these through a critical approach the question of whose interests are served in creating certain structures of power and domination might be answered.

Giddens stresses that power is a relationship not a resource. Power is the transformative capacity through which people are capable of achieving certain outcomes (1979, p.88). In this way power is tied closely to any notion of human agency. If the use of power is characteristic of all human action, then, Giddens claims, power is not a resource. Instead he argues that 'resources are media through which power is exercised, as a routine element of the instantiation of conduct in social reproduction' (1984, p.16). Moreover, any consideration of power, Giddens suggests, should be seen in the context of the duality of structure. In this perspective resources should be approached as structural elements which are utilized by human agents at particular moments of interaction. Thus 'the power relations sustained in the regularised practises constituting social systems can be considered as *reproduced relations of autonomy and dependence in interaction*' (Giddens, 1981, p.50).

Fundamental in applying this approach to leadership in education is the conception that people are active and knowledgeable. These agents create and transform processual power relations through the ongoing interplay which exists between the actions of people and social institutions' structures of domination (Giddens, 1984, p.16). In such a relational situation the structures of domination are dependent as much on the actions of subordinates as on the use of power by superordinates.

Even if one recognizes that there may be large disparities in the availability of resources between the parties, the relational notion of power ensures that subordinates have some measure of autonomy while superordinates have some measure of dependency. In this way 'a relation of power binds and constrains the activities of both parties, and each party defines its purposes and range of alternatives partly in terms of the other' (Burbules, 1986, p.103).

A critical approach to the concept of leadership, then, focuses on the power dimensions that underlie the process of reality construction and which give force to the human agency of people in organizations. Forester (1982a, 1982b, 1986), for instance, has explored this critical aspect of leadership and power by looking at the way people in positions of power utilize a form of leadership to mould, channel and guide expressions of popular sentiment along particular paths. In this way popular under-standings and political argument within an organization may be shaped not only to establish an apparent factual position but also to reinforce the legitimacy of those exercising the power of their hierarchical position. As Forester argues:

> those already in positions of power may make practical claims and offers about factual conditions, normative rightness, social interests, and particular needs that may be conventionally established but simultaneously *removed from criticism* — by invoking precedent, incentives, sanctions, exclusion, ostraciza-tion, stigma, threat and so forth. Under such conditions, popular beliefs, consent, trust and attention are appropriated through conditions of social interaction — influenced by policy initiatives — that discourage critical discourses. (1982b, p.46)

The important point of the above argument is that rather than examining organizations and their designated leaders in simplistic functionalist terms of merely operating in order to solve particular problems, organizations should instead be viewed as containers holding people in relations of power. In these containers power is continuously being exercised to shape the attention of participants, to channel information and selectively construct agendas. Put in a critical context, the organizational aims and rationales put forward by the designated leaders of an organization should consequently be subject to close scrutiny, with the realization that they are political solutions which can be reassessed and reformulated in different ways. To sum up, a critical perspective of leadership and power is necessary 'so that we can examine the way systemic rationalizing or commodifying forces obliterate or dominate the popular voice, so that we can examine particularly the ways that citizens are (or are not) able to speak and act politically, to question facts, rules, stereotypical identities' (Forester, 1986, p.202).

The critical paradigm outlined above offers the possibility of a view of educational administration which will help the school community to understand how the most 'efficient' and elaborately devised organizational planning often turns out to be a manipulative trap from which organizational members may have difficulty extricating themselves. The traditional school principal with a disproportionate degree of power was often able to create and implement such manipulative traps through the ability to shape much of the language, direct much of the discourse and guide much of the practice within the educational community. By adopting a critical view of leadership within schools, by recognizing that all human agents have some degree of knowledge, by unmasking manipulative, deceptive tactics, school administration would be founded on a more equal power basis. As a consequence many administrative practices would become demystified as the school community gained a critical understanding of those processes central to the reshaping of school administration on a more participatory, collaborative basis.

Dialectics, Symbols and Metaphors

A second approach which might constitute another dimension of structuration theory would be to view leadership as a dialectic relationship in the social construction of reality. In a recent study of leadership Smircich and Morgan (1982) move away from the traditional functionalist literature to present a picture of leadership as a distinctive form of social practice. Such practice arises out of the constructions and actions of both the leaders and the followers. Thus leadership is a social construction of reality which involves an ongoing interaction. From this argument the relationship is necessarily a dialectical one. As Smircich and Morgan put it, 'the phenomena of leadership in being interactive is by nature dialectical. It is shaped through the interaction of at least two points of reference i.e. of leaders and of led' (1982, pp.258-9). When seen as a dialectic, leadership implies the presence of considerable tensions and contradictions which, when resolved, lead to the continual transformation of the relationship. Thus people in the school community may turn to a particular person to frame and give substance to their sense of reality. However, in turn they may reject, resist or discard that view of reality as put forward. This notion of leadership avoids the static, functionalist view presented in much of the literature.

In contrast to the functionalist position leadership should be seen as a processual dialectical relationship. This view can offer insights on the production, reproduction and demise of certain organizational practices and structures. Such a processual perspective implies that there is not one preordained or designated leader within the organization, but that at any time any one member of the organization can come to the forefront to provide guidance in resolving the tensions and contradictions that beset organizations. As a consequence a dialectic view of the leadership process focuses on the human agency of all members of the organization as that agency interacts with the constraining or enabling structure of the institution. This ongoing dialectical relationship between individuals and institution means that both are continuously 'becoming' in time and space as the dialectics of practice and structure unfold. Thus a dialectic perspective of leadership within a school involves the consideration of all human agents, pupils, parents, teachers, support staff as well as the principal in the formation of social institutions whose structured properties are simultaneously the medium and outcome of social acts (Giddens, 1979). As a consequence 'the social world is in a continuous state of becoming — social arrangements which seem fixed and permanent are temporary, arbitrary patterns and any observed social patterns are regarded as one among many possibilities' (Benson, 1977, p.5). With such an ongoing, flowing dialectic of transformative human action, leaders become followers and followers become leaders in the ebb and flow of organizational interaction. This view is similar to Perrow's recent comments on principal-agent relationships. Perrow sees the relationship 'as a reflexive one that oscillates, dissolves and is born again, making it difficult and arbitrary to designate who is agent and who is principal' (1986b, p.41).

The tensions and contradictions which provide the thrust within any dialectical relationship are the basis of what Morgan (1981) terms a schismatic metaphor. This metaphor, in contrast to the traditional mechanical or organic metaphors applied to organizations, presumes that organizations have a tendency towards disintegration. In turn the resolution of these organizational tensions and contradictions may give rise to a new unity. The consequent ongoing dialectic embodied in the schismatic metaphor provides an understanding of the patterns of social relationships and the forms that organizations take.

Cohen (1976) has pointed to the dialectical relationship between power and symbols. Myths, stories, symbols, rituals and the other facets which may make up an organization culture are there as an indication of power. However, 'symbols are not mechanical reflections or representations of political realities' (1976, p.35). Rather the power order and the symbolic order are autonomous, although 'interdependent in such a way that a change in the one is likely to affect the relation between the two even if the other remains apparently unchanged' (1976, p.36). Cohen suggests that the relationship between power relations and symbolic categories operates in a dialectical fashion. The rejection of a mechanical fitness between the power order and the symbolic order can clarify the way, in certain situations, 'old symbolic forms perform new symbolic functions and new symbolic forms perform old symbolic functions' (1976, p.39).

Thus in the study of leadership in organizations a critical examination can attempt to discern whether myths, rituals and the symbolic order are being manipulated to attain and legitimate a particular political position. For instance, an authoritarian school principal may be able to manipulate the new symbolic, participatory, collaborative school council in an attempt to maintain the dominant position within the school. 'There is thus a continuous process of action and counteraction between the symbolic order and the power order' (1976, p.135), as those of greater power capacity struggle with those of lesser capacity to shape the symbolic order for either reproduction or transformation.

Moreover, in the resolution of these tensions symbolic, mythical heroes or heroines may arise to guide the organization into new paths (Denhardt, 1981). Indeed, Denhardt argues that leadership in organizations is often 'a modern ritualised hero system' (1981, p.94). A symbolic hero/heroine may be created or recreated when organizational members vest elements of their world, beliefs and great significance in one particular person (see Morgan, Frost and Pondy, 1983). This interpretation and production of social reality is often associated with the military metaphor (Pondy, 1983). Thus our symbolic hero/heroine leads members in the struggle against difficult odds: ground is won or lost; new lines of attack are formulated and different strategies are planned. If successful, the metaphor of emancipation may be conjured up (see also Lakoff and Johnson, 1980). This use of symbol and metaphor exemplifies the rich and complex patterns of cultural activities which are to be found within all social institutions. Coupled with a dialectic perspective, culture may be studied as an ongoing process as people continually construct and reconstruct their reality. The study of such shared symbolic and metaphoric cultural processes can bring about the recognition 'that organizations are not simple systems like machines or adaptive organisms; they are human systems manifesting complex patterns of cultural activity' (Morgan, Frost and Pondy, 1983, p.4).

Conclusion

This chapter commenced with a brief survey of some of the major theoretical perspectives on leadership and power. This survey indicated a number of serious shortcomings which are manifest in the traditional functionalist view of these concepts. In particular the functionalist account was charged with being simplistic, ahistorical, static and lacking in a sense of human agency, while neglecting basic concepts such as the class structure of society. In short, as Perrow has bluntly stated, 'the history of research in this area is one of progressive disenchantment' (1986a, p.86). This position has been endorsed by Stogdill, long one of the doyens of the field, who has stated that 'the endless accumulation of empirical data has not produced an integrated understanding of leadership' (1974, p.vii).

In order to avoid the deficiencies inherent in the traditional views of leadership and power it has been suggested in this chapter that they should be looked at as relational concepts developing over lengthy periods of time. In this sense they should be understood as processual in character, in a constant state of flux, where human agents both constitute and are constituted by the structures in which they find themselves. As Giddens indicates, while explaining the dialectical nature of his theory of structuration, 'all human action is carried on by knowledgeable agents who both construct the social world through their actions, but yet whose action is also conditioned or constrained by the very world of their creation' (Giddens, 1981, p.54).

The study of leadership and power as relational concepts highlights the argument of critical scholars such as Giddens (1981) and Smircich and Morgan (1982), which conceptualizes organizational structure and human action and conduct as not separate entities but rather as a duality in which people both shape and are shaped by the continually emerging power relationships within an organization. But such shaping also helps to create the culture of an organization. The management and channelling of meaning within an organization are frequently an outcome of the dialectical relationship between power and symbols as new power relations come into tension with pre-existing cultural and symbolic orders. The resolution of these tensions through the manipulation and construction of beliefs, discourse and new symbolic forms gives rise to a form of leadership which:

> is associated with a set of myths serving to reinforce a social construction of meaning that legitimates leadership role occupants, provides the belief in potential mobility for those not in

leadership roles, and attributes social causality to leadership roles, thereby providing a belief in the effectiveness of individual control. (Pfeffer, 1978, p.31).

The critical approach to leadership and power outlined in the latter part of this chapter stresses their relational, dialectical dimensions which underlie the process of reality construction and give force to the human agency of people in organizations.

If one looks at more basic underpinnings of social relations, the charge might be avoided that too often leadership concepts have become tainted by the manipulative overtones implicit in much of the research discussed in this chapter. In schools also the facile employment of a 'motherhood' term like leadership can obscure the seduction and subversion carried out in the name of administration. In such a context leadership can be reduced to the exploitation of the school community through the manipulative and subversive tactics of those in powerful management positions. Gronn (1984), for instance, has detailed the techniques of a school principal who saw his role of so-called leadership in terms of manipulating people whom, it seems, he saw essentially as 'cultural dopes' (Giddens, 1979). However, behaviour of this type would seem to be inappropriate for contemporary school administrators in a period of increasing community involvement in the running of schools, of collaborative decision-making, and a concern by some people to redistribute power on a more equal basis in the educational community, particularly in the state of Victoria in Australia.

In the collaborative rhetoric which underlies the Victorian Ministry of Education's Ministerial Papers and the recent Victorian Education Department guidelines on the 'role of the principal' the emphasis is that the principal should not perceive his or her position as that of the all-dominating leader but rather as a facilitator. Administrative action would not arise from manipulation and direction but from the facilitation of collaborative, participatory decision-making processes involving, and unfolding from, the dialectical interaction of the school community. Thus in Victorian schools the principal should, according to the rhetoric of the guidelines:

> facilitate effective communication and collaboration between staff, students, parents and the wider community; . . . facilitate links between the school community and the wider community for the benefit of the school; . . . foster collaborative and collective decision making among staff; . . . facilitate an effective working environment for staff members. (*Education Gazette*, 5 July 1984, p.444)

However, the collaborative approach embodied in the Ministerial Papers and guidelines has come under attack from those senior administrators seeking to set in place a corporate management structure. Indeed, the recent document *The Structure and Organization of the School Division* (1987) advocates the withdrawal of these guidelines while labelling principals as *line-managers* (see Watkins, 1988).

The case for facilitating leadership has also been advocated by Barber in presenting his case for strong democracy (Barber, 1984). Through strong democracy Barber envisages the implementation of fully participatory and collaborative decision-making in all institutional settings. In this context the leader or 'facilitator is responsible to a process rather than specific outcomes — to the integrity of the community rather than to the needs of particular individuals' (1984, p. 240). The facilitator in schools would ease the way for others in the school community to emerge as leaders within a participatory environment. Instead of offering and setting specific goals or aims for the school community, the principal as facilitator assists the school community to find and develop its own goals. Vern Wilkinson (1987), a former Victorian primary school principal, has suggested that in the current concern for democratic decision-making the principal has been relocated from the apex of the pyramid to the centre of the school community, operating essentially as a change catalyst and resource. As a consequence 'the new model of collaborative decision making . . . has upset the traditional model of hierarchical decision making and responsibility of principals' (Wilkinson, 1987, p. 19).

This changed view of the principal, as mainly operating as a facilitator, has been emphasized by Sergiovanni (1987) in a recent address to the Victorian Association of Principals of Secondary Schools. Sergiovanni contrasts transactional leadership, as typified by traditional views of leadership and power, with transformative leadership, which can be equated with facilitating leadership. Sergiovanni explains that transformative leadership is a means to empower the school community:

> Transformative leaders are more concerned with the concept of power to than power over. They are concerned with how the power of leadership can help people become more successful, to accomplish the things that they think are important to experience a greater sense of efficacy. They are less concerned with what people are doing and more concerned with what they are accomplishing. (Sergiovanni, 1987, pp. 18-19)

From the administrative perspective the aim of the facilitating or transformative leader would be to help foster an organizational community in which all the members of the organization have the capacity and opportunity to be leaders and where there is a common concern for empowerment and the betterment of the human condition.

References

Apple, M.W. (1982) *Education and Power,* London, Routledge and Kegan Paul.

Apple, M.W. (1985) 'Teaching and "women's work": A comparative historical and ideological analysis,' *Teachers College Record,* 86, 3, pp.455-73.

Arnot, M. and Weiner, G. (1987) *Gender and the Politics of Schooling,* London, Hutchinson.

Ashour, A.S. (1973) 'Further discussion of Fiedler's contingency model of leadership effectiveness,' *Organizational Behavior and Human Performance,* 9, pp.369-76.

Bachrach, P. and Baratz, M. (1962) 'The two faces of power,' *American Political Science Review,* 56, pp.947-52.

Barber, B. (1984) *Strong Democracy: Participatory Politics in a New Age,* Berkeley, Calif., University of California Press.

Benson, J.K. (1977) 'Organizations: A dialectical view,' *Administrative Science Quarterly,* 22, 1, p.3-21.

Bernstein, B. (1977a) 'Education cannot compensate for society,' in B. Cosin, I. Dale, G. Esland, D. Mackinnon and D. Swift (Eds), *School and Society,* London, Routledge and Kegan Paul.

Bernstein, B. (1977b) *Class, Codes and Control,* Vol.3, London, Routledge and Kegan Paul.

Blau, P. (1964) *Exchange and Power in Social Life,* New York, John Wiley.

Bourdieu, P. (1977) 'Symbolic power,'in D. Gleeson (Ed.), *Identity and Structure: Issues in the Sociology of Education,* Driffield, Nafferton Books.

Bourdieu, P. and Passeron, J. (1977) *Reproduction,* London, Sage.

Bramel, D. and Friend, R. (1981) 'Hawthorne, the myth of the docile worker and class bias in psychology,' *American Psychologist,* 38, 8, pp.867-78.

Burbules, N.C. (1986) 'A theory of power in education,' *Educational Theory,* 36, 2, pp.95-114.

Burrell, G. and Morgan, G. (1979) *Sociological Paradigms and Organizational Analysis,* London, Heinemann.

Campbell, J.P., Dunnette, M.D., Lawler, E.E. and Weick, K.E. (1970) *Managerial Behavior, Performance and Effectiveness,* New York, McGraw-Hill.

Clegg, S. (1977) 'Power, organisation theory, Marx and critique.' in S. Clegg and D. Dunkerley, *Critical Issues in Organizations,* London, Routledge and Kegan Paul.

Clegg, S. and Dunkerley, D. (1980) *Organization, Class and Control,* London, Routledge and Kegan Paul.

Cohen, A. (1976) *Two-Dimensional Man,* Berkeley, Calif., University of California Press.

Deetz, S., and Kersten, A. (1983) 'Critical models of interpretive research,' in L. Putnam and M. Pacanowsky (Eds), *Communication and Organizations,* Beverley Hills, Calif., Sage.

Denhardt, R. (1981) *In the Shadow of the Organisation,* Lawrence, Regents of Kansas.

Emerson, R. (1962) 'Power-dependence relations,' *American Sociological Review,* 27, pp.31-40.

Etzioni, A. (1961) *A Comparative Analysis of Complex Organizations,* New York, Free Press.

Fiedler, F. (1967) *A Theory of Leadership Effectiveness,* New York, McGraw-Hill.

Fiedler, F. (1970) 'Leadership experience and leader performance,' *Organisational Behaviour and Human Performance,* 5, pp.1-14.

Fiedler, F. (1972a) 'The effects of leadership training and experience: A contingency model interpretation,' *Administration Science Quarterly,* 17, pp.453-70.

Fiedler, F. (1972b) 'Personality: Motivational systems and behaviour of high and low LPC persons,' *Human Relations,* 25,5, pp.391-412.

Fiedler, F. (1987) *New Approaches to Effective Leadership,* New York, John Wiley and Sons.

Fishbein, M., Landy, E. and Hatch, G. (1969a) 'A consideration of two assumptions underlying Fiedler's contingency model for prediction of leadership effectiveness,' *American Journal of Psychology,* 82, pp.457-73.

Fishbein, M., Landy, E. and Hatch, G. (1969b) 'Some determinants of an individual's esteem for his least preferred co-worker,' *Human Relations,* 22,2, pp.173-88.

Forester, J. (1982a) 'Planning in the face of power,' *Journal of the American Planning Association,* 48,1, pp.67-80.

Forester, J. (1982b) 'A critical empirical framework for the analysis of public policy,' *New Political Science,* 3/4, 9/10, pp.33-61.

Forester, J. (1986) 'Critical theory and public life: Only connect,' *International Journal of Urban and Regional Research,* 10,2, pp.185-206.

French, J.R.P. and Raven, B. (1959) 'The bases of social power,' in D. Cartwright (Ed.), *Studies in Social Power,* Ann Arbor, Mich., University of Michigan Press.

Giddens, A. (1976) *New Rules of Sociological Method,* London, Hutchinson.

Giddens, A. (1977) 'Functionalism: apres la lutte,' in A. Giddens (Ed.), *Studies in Social and Political Theory,* London, Hutchinson.

Giddens, A. (1979) *Central Problems in Social Theory: Action, Structure and Contradictions in Social Analysis,* London, Macmillan.

Giddens, A. (1981) *A Contemporary Critique of Historical Materialism,* London, Macmillan.

Giddens, A. (1982) 'Power, the dialectic of control and class structuration,' in A. Giddens and G. MacKenzie (Eds.), *Social Class and the Division of Labour,* Cambridge, Cambridge University Press.

Giddens, A. (1984) *The Constitution of Society,* Cambridge, Polity.

Goldman, P. (1978) 'Sociologists and the study of bureaucracy: A critique of ideology and practice,' *Insurgent Sociologist,* 8, pp.21-30.

Graen, G., Alvares, K., Orris, J. and Martella, J. (1970) 'Contingency model of leadership effectiveness: Antecedent and evidential results,' *Psychological Bulletin,* 74, pp.285-96.

Graen, G., Alvares, K., and Orris, J. (1971) 'Contingency model of leadership effectiveness: Some experimental results,' *Journal of Applied Psychology,* 55,3, pp.196-201.

Graen, G., Dansereau, F. and Minami, T. (1972) 'Dysfunctional leadership styles,' *Organisational Behaviour and Human Performance,* 7, pp.216-36.

Graham, W. (1973) 'Leader behaviour esteem for the least preferred co-worker and group performance,' *The Journal of Social Behaviour,* 90, June, pp.59-66.

Greenfield, T.B. (1979) 'Ideas versus data: How can the data speak for themselves? in G. Immegart and W. Boyd (Eds), *Problem Finding in Educational Administration,* Lexington, Mass., Heath.

Gronn, P. (1984) '"I have a solution . . .": Administrative power in a school meeting,' *Educational Administration Quarterly,* 20,2, pp.65-92.

Halpin, A.W. (1955) 'The leader behaviour and leadership ideology of educational administrators and aircraft commanders,' *Harvard Educational Review,* 15, Winter, pp.18-32.

Halpin, A.W. (1969) 'How leaders behave,' in F. Carver and T. Sergiovanni (Eds), *Organisations and Human Behaviour: Focus on Schools,* New York, McGraw-Hill.

Harmon, M. (1981) *Action Theory for Public Administration,* New York, Longman.

Janda, K. (1960) 'Toward the explication of the concept of leadership in terms of the concept of power,' *Human Relations,* 12, pp.345-63.

Kipnis, D., Schmidts, S., Swaffin-Smith, C. and Wilkinson, I. (1984) 'Patterns of managerial influence: Shotgun managers, tacticians and bystanders,' *Organizational Dynamics,* 12,3, pp.58-67.

Knights, D., and Willmott, H. (1982) 'Power, values and relations,' *Sociology,* 16,4, pp.578-85.

Korman, A. (1966) '"Consideration" "initiating structure" and "organisational criteria" — A review,' *Personnel Psychology,* 19, pp.349-61.

Lakoff, G. and Johnson, M. (1980) 'Conceptual metaphor in everyday language,' *Journal of Philosophy,* 77,8, pp.453-86.

Leavitt, H.J. (1964) 'Applied organization change in industry: Structural, technical and human approaches,' in W.W. Cooper, H.J. Leavitt and M. Shelly (Eds), *New Perspectives in Organization Research,* New York, John Wiley.

Lowin, A. (1968) 'Participative decision making,' *Organisational Behaviour and Human Performance,* 3, pp.68-106.

Lukes, S. (1977) *Essays in Social Theory,* London, Macmillan.

McCall, M. and Lombardo, M. (1978) 'Where else can we go?' in M. McCall and M. Lombardo (Eds), *Leadership: Where Else Can We Go?,* Durham, N.C., Duke University Press.

McMahon, J.T. (1972) 'The contingency theory — logic and method revisited,' *Personnel Psychology,* 25, pp.697-710.

Macpherson, R.J.S. (1984) 'A Hitch-Hikers Guide to the Universe of Tom Greenfield', *The Australian Administrator,* 5,2, pp.1-6.

Manz, C.C. and Sims, H.P. Jr. (1984) 'Searching for the "Unleader": Organizational member views on leading self-managed groups,' *Human Relations,* 37,5, pp.409-24.

March, J., and Simon, H. (1958) *Organizations,* New York, Wiley.

Merton, R. (1968) *Social Theory and Social Structure,* New York, Free Press.

Ministry of Education (1987) *The Structure and Organization of the Schools Division,* Melbourne, Ministry of Education.

Mitchell T.R., Bilgan, A. Oncken, G. and Fiedler, F. (1970-71) 'The contingency model: Criticism and suggestions,' *Academy of Management Journal,* 13-14, pp.253-67.

Morgan, G. (1981) 'The schismatic metaphor and its implications for organisational analysis,' *Organisational Studies,* 2,1, pp.23-44.

Morgan, G., Frost, P. and Pondy, L. (1983) 'Organisational symbolism,' in L. Pondy, P. Frost, G. Morgan and T. Dandridge (Eds), *Organisational Symbolism,* Greenwich, JAI Press.

O'Brien, G. (1969) 'Group stucture and measurement of potential leader influence,' *Australian Journal of Psychology,* 21,3, pp.277-89.

Perrow, C. (1979) *Complex Organizations: A Critical Essay,* 2nd ed., Glenview, Scott Foresman.

Perrow, C. (1986a) *Complex Organizations: A Critical Essay,* 3rd ed., New York, Random House.

Perrow, C. (1986b) 'Economic theories of organization,' *Theory and Society,* 15, pp.11-45.

Pfeffer, J. (1978) 'The ambiguity of leadership,' in M.W. McCall and M.M. Lombardo (Eds), *Leadership: Where Else Can We Go?* Durham, N.C., Duke University Press.

Pondy, L. (1983) 'The role of metaphors and myths in organisation and the facilitation of change,' in L. Pondy, P. Frost, G. Morgan and T. Dandridge (Eds), *Organisational Symbolism,* Greenwich, JAI Press.

Salaman, G. (1981) *Class and the Corporation,* London, Fontana.

Sample, J. and Wilson, T. (1965) 'Leader behaviour, group productivity and rating of least preferred co-worker,' *Journal of Personality and Social Psychology,* 3, pp.266-70.

Sayles, L.R. (1979) *Leadership: What Effective Managers Really Do . . . And How They Do It,* New York, McGraw-Hill.

Sayles, S.M. (1966) 'Supervisory style and productivity: Review and theory,' *Personnel Psychology,* 19, pp.275-80.

Sergiovanni, T.J. (1987) 'Leadership for quality schooling: New understandings and practices,' Paper presented at the Victorian Association of Principals of Secondary Schools Annual Leadership Conference, August, Geelong, Australia.

Shiflett, S. and Nealey, S. (1972) 'The effects of changing leader power: A test of "situational engineering",' *Organisational Behaviour and Human Performance,* 7, pp.371-82.

Smircich, L. (1983) 'Implications for management theory,' in L. Putnam and M.E. Pacanowsky (Eds), *Communication and Organizations: An Interpretive Approach,* Beverley Hills, Calif., Sage.

Smircich, L. and Morgan, G. (1982) 'Leadership: The management of meaning,' *Journal of Applied Behavioural Science,* 18,3, p.257-73.

Steiner, I. (1959) 'Interpersonal orientation and assumed similarity between opposites,' Mimeo, Urbana, Illinois.

Stogdill, R.M. (1970) 'Personal factors associated with leadership: A survey of literature,' in C.A. Gibb (Ed.), *Leadership,* Harmondsworth, Penguin.

Stogdill, R.M. (1974) *Handbook of Leadership: A Survey of Theory and Research,* New York, Free Press.

Teulings, A.D. (1980) 'Structure and logic of industrial development: Philips and the international electronics industry,' in D. Dunkerley and G. Salaman (Eds), *The International Yearbook of Organization Studies,* London, Routledge and Kegan Paul.

Tinker, T. and Lowe, T. (1982) 'The management of science of the management sciences,' *Human Relations,* 35,4, p.331-47.

Watkins, P. (1983) *Class Control and Contestation in Educational Organisations,* Geelong, Deakin University Press.

Watkins, P. (1985) *Agency and Structure: Dialectics in the Administration of Education,* Geelong, Deakin University Press.

Watkins, P. (1986) *A Critical Review of Leadership Concepts and Research: Implications for Educational Administration,* Geelong, Deakin University Press.

Watkins, P. (1988) 'The transformation of educational administration: The hegemony of consent and the hegemony of coercion,' Mimeo, Deakin University.

Weiner, G. and Arnot, M. (1987) *Gender under Scrutiny,* London, Hutchinson.

Weissenberg, P. and Gruenfeld, L. (1966) 'Relationships among leadership dimensions and cognitive style,' *Journal of Applied Psychology,* 50, pp.392-5.

Wilkinson, B., and Smith, S. (1984) 'From old school hunches to departmental lunches,' *Sociological Review,* 32,1, pp.92-115.

Wilkinson, V. (1987) 'Human agency and educational administration,' in F. Rizvi, P. Watkins and R. Bates (Eds), *Working Papers in the Theory and Practice of Educational Administration,* Geelong, Deakin University.

Willmott, H. (1987) 'Studying managerial work: A critique and a proposal,' *Journal of Management Studies,* 24,3, p.249-70.

Wright, E.O. (1979) 'Intellectuals and the class structure of capitalist society,' in P. Walker (Ed.), *Between Labor and Capital,* Brighton, Harvester Press.

Wrightsman, L., and Deaux, K. (1981) *Social Psychology in the 80's,* Monterey, Calif., Brooks/Cole.

Yukl, G. (1970) 'Leader LPC scores: Attitudes dimensions and behavioural correlates,' *Journal of Social Psychology,* 80, pp.207-12.

Yukl, G. (1971) 'Towards a behavioural theory of leadership,' *Organisational Behaviour and Human Performance,* 6, pp.414-40.

Zey-Ferrell, M. and Aiken, M. (1981) *Complex Organizations: Critical Perspectives,* Glenview, Ill., Scott Foresman.

Chapter 2

Toward a Critical Practice of Leadership

William Foster

Leadership as a construct and a practice has considerable currency in contemporary thought. Whether one looks at academic disciplines, practical fields or the popular press, the term 'leadership' figures prominently in the attempt to describe a particular set of relationships among people. There are undoubtedly a number of reasons for this position of significance given to the idea of leadership: these would certainly include the romanticized elements of leadership as well as the more realistic effect that 'leaders' have on our social and natural world. Perhaps a good deal of interest in the concept can be traced to a certain malaise about our interactions with and within organizations and the routine and determined nature of life that organizations tend to impose. Facing an uncertain future where a mistake can have deadly and unknown ramifications, we ask that *somebody* be prescient enough to guide us. Whether the concern is with questions of a global nature or with questions of a more local character, and whether the concern is with improving an organization or improving chances of survival, it is clear that the idea of leadership meets some kind of modern need, a deep desire both to be in control of our circumstances and to alter them for the better.

But what exactly is meant by the term 'leadership'? Like other such labels, the term covers a great deal and seems to mean whatever the user intends. It is, as Burns (1978) has noted, one of the most misunderstood concepts in our language, and the misunderstanding is a conceptual one. There remains, however, a sense that leadership *is* a real phenomenon, one that does make a difference. But before the term can be utilized meaningfully, it is necessary to try to tease out the various ways in which it has been used and to try to come to an agreement on its essential aspects.

To accomplish this, this chapter examines, first, various contemporary accounts of leadership with a critical eye. It then proposes some alternative considerations which may be important to a more precise analysis of leadership. Finally, it attempts to examine the significance of leadership within the modern context.

The Two Traditions of Leadership Research

In contemporary usage there are essentially two different traditions which have informed social scientific definitions of leadership. One tradition comes from the political-historical disciplines; the other from business management and public administration.

The political-historical model of leadership has a long history and tends to focus on the role of significant individuals (from Machiavelli's Prince to modern presidents) in shaping the course of history. Leadership, in this sense, is largely the story of events and actions, of ideas, and of how individuals transformed their social milieux. The other major model of leadership is drawn from the sociology of organizations and the administration/management literature. Here leadership tends to mean the authority of office and is dependent on a variety of strategies designed for goal accomplishment. Neither approach, as we hope to show, is completely satisfactory to an understanding of the complexity of leadership. Yet both need to be analyzed in order to demonstrate the contemporary focus in leadership studies.

The Political-Historical Model

The study of leadership done through the lenses provided by this model is a study of power, politics and historical fact. Leaders are individuals who 'make' history through their use of power and resources, and leadership is exemplified by familiar names: Ghandi, Churchill, Roosevelt and so on. Their stories, their history, tell us in a retrospective fashion what qualities, machinations and visions were of value in accomplishing a new and different social order.

This model of leadership, however, is not solely biographic, though it depends on biography for its sustenance. That an abstract and theoretical formulation of leadership can be derived through the study of individual biographies is demonstrated by James McGregor Burns' book (1978), *Leadership*. By analyzing the life stories of such individuals as Ghandi and Roosevelt, Mao Tse Tung and Lenin and Hitler, Burns arrives at the conclusion that there are essentially two basic types of leadership. These he labels 'transactional' and 'transformational'.

Transactional leadership is largely based on exchange relationships between leader and follower. Much of political leadership is transactional; a series of exchanges between politician and voter is characteristic. In exchange for the voter's support, the leader adopts a programme of promises designed for those particular groups. This type of leadership is representative of lay definitions of the term and is often what we think of when we consider politicians.

For schools, transactional leadership is seen in the superintendent's or governor's relationship with unions, with individual teachers and with parents. Concessions and negotiations need to be made, accommodations worked out, and a more or less popular support for the leader developed through the manipulation and interplay of various social forces.

Transformational leadership is cut from a different cloth entirely. Here Burns addresses what in the popular imagination might be termed 'real leadership'. Transformational leadership is the ability of an individual to envision a new social condition and to communicate this vision to followers. The leader here both inspires and transforms individual followers so that they too develop a new level of concern about their human condition and, sometimes, the condition of humanity at large. Ghandi, for Burns, is perhaps the exemplar of transformational leadership; his ideas and actions served to liberate minds as well as bodies.

Burns writes that transformational leadership requires that 'leaders engage with followers, but from higher levels of morality; in the enmeshing of goals and values both leaders and followers are raised to more principled levels of judgment. . . . Much of this kind of elevating leadership asks *from* followers rather than merely promising them goods' (1978, p.455). Leaders thus are essentially involved in the creation of *new* social realities, and their role is largely to convince followers that the current realities are not cast in concrete but can indeed be changed for the better.

Burns' work has been a significant advance in leadership studies. He has looked at the idea of leadership from a moral and value-driven basis, and has not accepted a view of leadership as simply a managerial tool. In his formulation history and politics become a driving force, shaped by individual action. In this way Burns' work rescues leadership from the more technocratic interpretations of the concept. His work, however, has not been without some criticism.

Tucker (1981), for one, has contended that Burns provides an inadequate distinction between the concept of leadership and that of simply wielding power. Burns suggests that these are two very different animals; leadership involves a moral dimension which requires that leaders elevate followers to new moral heights, whereas power wielding (demonstrated, for example, by Hitler) does not and, therefore, using Burns' definition, is not leadership at all. Tucker contests this distinction, suggesting that an evil leader is still a leader. Tucker provides an alternative formulation for leadership; leadership, simply put, is politics. What leaders do, for Tucker, is to 'define the situation authoritatively . . . prescribe a course of group action . . . [and engage in a] mobilizing function . . .' (Tucker, 1981, pp. 18-19). Leaders, in this view, are not so much transformational as they are goal-setters and mobilizers. Clearly, this robs the concept of transformational leadership of a great deal of its power, and reduces the idea of leadership to the politics of group management.

Tucker's contribution is of value in pointing out the political and group dimensions of leadership; Burns' contribution is of value in stressing the moral and value base of leadership. Both, however, falter in their highly voluntaristic and individualistic treatment of the issue. Both continue to see leadership as residing in an individual, only to be brought out voluntarily by circumstances. While Burns does stress the fact that leadership occurs in a relationship between leader and led, he nevertheless tends to see leadership as something of a trait that certain individuals possess.

Such a view neglects two crucial aspects. First, leadership is always context bound. It always occurs within a social community and is perhaps less the result of 'great' individuals than it is the result of human interactions and negotiations. Roosevelt and Churchill, to take two often cited examples, took advantage of what might be called a 'corridor of belief' which already existed in followers. Each leader did not so much create a new and idiosyncratic universe so much as enter these corridors and open various doors. Leadership then is an entering into the currents of mainstream consciousness and changing it through a dialectical relationship.

It is also not particularly voluntaristic, where given individuals can volunteer for leadership roles and, by virtue of their charisma, achieve them by convincing others of the rightness of their ideas. Undoubtedly this occurs, but the more common path involves mutual negotiations and shared leadership roles. Leadership cannot occur without followership, and many times the two are exchangeable: leaders become followers and followers become leaders. The voluntaristic aspect of leadership found in the political-historical model tends to neglect the dialectical character of leadership. Leaders normally have to negotiate visions and ideas with potential followers, who may in turn become leaders themselves, renegotiating the particular agenda.

This genre of political and historical studies of leadership also tends to lack a critical focus. Even the leadership of a Ghandi or a Martin Luther King is seen more as a way of convincing followers to join a cause than as the trenchant social critique that it was. Certainly a major part of these individuals' appeal lay in personal magnetism and the strength of their message. However, it is not wise to downplay the basic role of critique within leadership. Critique is not only a result of leadership practices but is constitutive of those practices: leadership always has one face turned towards change, and change involves the critical assessment of current situations and an awareness of future possibilities.

In summary, the political-historical model emphasizes the following ideas:

- leadership is a construct describing relationships between individuals;
- such relationships involve dimensions of power, in the sense that the desire for power and for empowerment is a fundamental feature of social life;
- certain types of (transforming) leadership involve the 'leader' and the 'follower' in a cognitive redefinition of social reality;
- understanding leadership is best approached through historical study.

The Bureaucratic-Managerial Model

A second and more influential model (at least by the number of pages devoted to it in business texts and journals) is the bureaucratic-managerial one. As the label implies, this model of leadership normally describes the way business and other managers, and scholars of management, talk about the concept of leadership. This model contains a number of prime assumptions. Among them is the assumption that leadership is a function of organizational position; the 'leader' is the person of superior rank in an organization. This assumption is almost universally held among management writers and forms the basis for the various models of leadership which have been developed in the last thirty years. A related assumption is that leadership is goal-centred *and* that the goals are driven by organizational needs. Thus the reason for exerting leadership at all is not social change, or meeting followers' needs, but achieving certain organizational goals. The leader is a conduit between organization and labour, and has a clearly defined role of motivating and producing. Indeed the production function is the legitimation of the exercise of leadership.

Each of these assumptions stands out clearly in an analysis of the major models of leadership in this area. If one examines, for example, the popular treatises on leadership, such as 'situational leadership' or Fiedler's (1967) contingency model of leadership, the entire thrust is towards developing effective management skills. In these approaches one needs to be concerned with the nature of the task assigned to employees, with their level of ability and maturity, and with the leader's own position in the firm. Leadership essentially becomes getting the employees to do what management wants them to do.

The idea of the 'leader' in these presentations depends on the *prior* context of an organization. Leaders can only exercise their powers within an environment bounded by certain task responsibilities, and the leader's role is assumed to be one of determining how these tasks can be accomplished most effectively and efficiently. The strong assumption here is that leadership *only* occurs as a result of position. Top executives control their organizations through the manipulation of power designed to make individuals perform (task) and feel good about performing (consideration) at their level of competency (maturity).

The origins of all this, of course, lie in a brand of Taylorism, with a healthy respect for the volatile possibilities of 'human relations' thrown in for good measure. Taylor suggested how we could design the workplace to be error-free, through the development of ever more specific tasks which even the most unorganized amongst us could accomplish. Human relations, the title given the series of research studies undertaken at the Western Electric plants in the late 1920s, cautions us, however, about the reflexivity that social groups tend to display, and that they might, indeed, penetrate the nature of the system and thus prove to be recalcitrant to even the harshest of managerial measures.

These two staples of industrial relations, Taylorism and human relations, form the core of contemporary leadership approaches in management. As appealing as they have been to industrial managers, with their assurance of providing a modicum of control over the production process, it was only a matter of time before they spilled over into all other areas of life, from 'domestic management' to 'educational management'. Not only is the situational leader ensconced in the boardroom, but now he or she 'leads' in the school and the bedroom.

If one accepts the assumption of leadership as position, then it is necessary to accept the other assumption that was discussed: leadership is dedicated to organizational goal-achievement. The bureaucratic-managerial model of leadership ties the exercise of leadership closely with performance, and performance is defined by goal-achievement, whether those goals have to do with productivity or other organizational concerns.

At this point the administrator might object to the discussion, claiming that achieving organizational goals, assuring productivity and achieving standards of performance are indeed the stuff of leadership; these are what leaders *do*. Failure to exert some measure of control over the organization and its membership is an assurance of failure, and with failed organizations nobody wins.

This is a telling objection only if we continue to confuse leadership with management (See Rost, 1985). Leadership is not organizational management, and it is of no use to the concept of leadership continually to equate it with position or managerial effectiveness. It is crucial to understand that while leadership may occur in organizational settings, and may be exercised by position holders, there is no necessary or logical link between the two concepts. Yet this conflation of terms persists, and the most obvious culprits are those writing in the administrative/ management literature. The lack of distinction between management and leadership has become such a common feature of our language that we are often hard pressed to recognize that leadership can be unorganized, little concerned with production, uncaring of feelings and still be effective if the power of ideas is commanding. The effects of this confusion will be examined next.

The 'Translation' of Leadership

In many ways the concept of leadership has been chewed up and swallowed down by the needs of modern managerial theory. The idea of leadership as a transforming practice, as an empowerment of followers, and as a vehicle for social change has been taken, adapted and co-opted by managerial writers so that now leadership appears as a way of improving organizations, not of transforming our world. What essentially has happened is that the language of leadership has been translated into the needs of bureaucracy.

One finds scholars such as Bennis (1984) talking about the leader's transformational role, the need for vision and for the empowerment of employees. The transformational leader is now a popular concept for organizations (Tichy and Devanna, 1986). But the concept has been denuded of its original power; transformational leaders are now those who can lead a company to greater profits, who can satisfy the material cravings of employees, who can achieve better performance through providing the illusion of power to subordinates. Transformational leadership has gone from a concept of power to a how-to manual for aspiring managers.

It would be welcome news if the words above prove to be too harsh an appraisal of the current condition of leadership study. The indications are, however, that they are not. This is not to say that those prescriptions which use the idea of transformational leadership as their base do not offer good advice to managers; assuredly they do, and in doing so may increase the attractiveness of the workplace for many. However, this is not to say that this is leadership in practice. To repeat some of our claims, leadership is and must be socially critical, it does not reside *in* an individual but in the relationship between individuals, and it is oriented toward social vision and change, not simply, or only, organizational goals.

The reasons for and consequences of the translation of the language of leadership into the language of management are aptly if severely described by MacIntyre, a philosopher, and it will be useful to review his claims here.

MacIntyre (1981) has identified three 'characters' which are archetypes in twentieth century culture. His three characteristic types *define* in a sense contemporary life: these are the Rich Aesthete, the Therapist and the Manager. These three are 'characters' in that they are more than roles people play; rather, they are symbols of a culture, carriers of a history and representatives of current social consciousness. In MacIntyre's words, these characters:

> are, so to speak, the moral representatives of their culture and they are so because of the way in which moral and metaphysical ideas and theories assume through them an embodied existence in the social world. *Characters* are the mask worn by moral philosophies. (MacIntyre, 1981, p.27)

The last two are of immediate relevance to leadership: the Therapist and the Manager are of such common currency in our language that they have come to dominate our way of thinking about certain issues, such as leadership. Each character can be readily seen in many of our social situations: the teacher, for example, acts as a therapist in the one instance and as a manager in the next. The therapist is, of course, interested in *adjustment,* the adjustment of the individual to the current social condition. The manager is interested in *control,* the control of the social environment for personal and organizational gain. Each character seems to be endemic to our modern form of highly routinized and organized life — one to manage it for us and the other to accommodate us to it. The relationship of these two concepts to the task-consideration dichotomy prevalent in leadership studies is quite clear.

This concept of characters is an attempt to delineate the central moral philosophies of the age, as these are carried by everyday actors and agents. The manager and the therapist are not simply social roles but symbols of our major beliefs, presuppositions and ways of acting. Yet these characters are based on a false sense of control over human nature. At best the therapist and the manager can provide only a temporary security: therapy ultimately leads to resignation or acceptance, while management never really knows whether the decisions made have had the effects intended. MacIntyre talks about management as follows:

> It is specifically and only managerial and bureaucratic expertise that I am going to put in question. And the conclusion to which I shall finally move is that such expertise does indeed turn out to be one more moral fiction, because the kind of knowledge which would be required to sustain it does not exist. But what would it be like if social control were indeed a masquerade? Consider the following possibility: that what we are oppressed by is not power, but impotence; that one key reason why the presidents of large corporations do not, as some radical critics believe, control the United States is that they do not even succeed in controlling their own corporations; that all too often, when imputed organisational skill and power are deployed and the desired effect follows, all that we have witnessed is the same kind of sequence as that to be observed when a clergyman is fortunate enough to pray for rain just before the unpredicted end of a drought; that the levers of power — one of managerial expertise's own key metaphors — produce effects unsystematically and too often only coincidentally related to the effects of which their users boast. (MacIntyre, 1981, p.73)

Such a conclusion about managerial effectiveness and bureaucratic expertise is not idiosyncratic to MacIntyre, although he does put it so well; rather a whole host of organizational studies carry the same theme. Weick's (1976) concept of loose coupling certainly carries an implicit suggestion that rational and goal-oriented control of organizations is an illusion; in this world events are only loosely coupled to each other and causality (read power) is both multiple and recursive. March and Olsen (1976) address the fundamental ambiguities in the manager's job, observing that rationality tends to take place largely as post hoc rationalization, and that organizations simply do not function in the efficient, Tayloristic view promulgated by a self-labelled 'management science'. Lincoln (1985) similarly questions the rational, cause-effect view of management, arguing that a new 'paradigm' is well underway. Benson (1977) suggests that the goal-seeking, rational model of management and organization is a popular fiction. Various other views of managerial behaviour, such as that contained in the 'organizational culture' school of thought (Smircich, 1983), and in those schools concerned with the analysis of 'sensemaking' in organization (Weick, 1979) further reflect the variability, not to say ineffectiveness, of managerial authority.

If we accept MacIntyre's concerns with managerial power, then what implications are there for leadership? The first is that to let the concept of leadership be captured by management is to emasculate any power the idea of leadership offers to us. To see it as a managerial virtue is to see it as a powerless attempt to control and predict human action. Yet this is probably the main thrust of most authors on leadership: any discussion of leadership seems to dissolve into a discussion of effective management techniques. Burns' work, which, as we noted above, served at first to define the idea of leadership and to show its relevance to the political arena, has now been condensed, changed and otherwise manipulated to justify and in many ways shore up extant power relationships existing in organizations.

If leadership cannot be reduced to management, then it must involve somethimg more than management. We will make the claim here that leadership is fundamentally addressed to social change and human emancipation, that it is basically a display of social critique, and that its ultimate goal is the achievement and refinement of human community.

The Creation of Community

It is an enduring feature of human life to search for community; to attempt to establish patterns of living based on mutual need and affection, development and protection. But this communitarian impulse is never 'accomplished'; rather it is an ongoing and creative enterprise in which actors or agents continually re-create social structure, and it is this which allows us to identify 'communities'. Giddens (1984) has proposed a theory of 'structuration' which takes as an essential focus the *duality* of structure: that 'the structural properties of social systems are *both medium and outcome* of the practices they recursively organize' (Giddens, 1984, p.25, emphasis added). Individuals, in other words, engage in social practices which are the foundation for social structure, yet social structure limits and enables the type of practices that can be engaged in.

Giddens provides this analysis:

> According to structuration theory, the moment of the production of action is also one of reproduction in the contexts of the day-to-day enactment of social life. This is so even during the most violent upheavals or most radical forms of social change. It is not accurate to see the structural properties of social systems as 'social products' because this tends to imply that pre-constituted actors somehow come together to create them. In reproducing structural properties . . . agents also reproduce the conditions that make such action possible. Structure has no existence independent of the knowledge that agents have about what they do in their day-to-day activity. (1984, p.26)

This property of social structures, and thus of communities, is why leadership can be effective and important. Certain agents can engage in transformative practices which change social structures and forms of community, and it is this that we label leadership. But for leadership to exist in this capacity requires that it be critical of current social arrangements and that this critique be aimed at more emancipatory types of relationships; any other type of 'leadership' is basically oriented toward the accumulation of power and, while this is certainly a feature of all relationships within social structures, such accumulation indicates a personal rather than communitarian impulse. Emancipation, it should be stressed, does not mean total freedom; rather, the concept as it is used here means the gradual development of freedoms, from economic problems, racial oppression, ethnic domination, the oppression of women and so on (each of which has its own heroes and heroines: Roosevelt, Churchill, Ghandi, King, Anthony are just some examples).

Emancipatory leadership, however, is not just the property of enlightened individuals. The idea that leadership occurs within a community suggests that ultimately leadership resides in the community itself. To further differentiate leadership from management, we could suggest that leadership is a communal relationship, that is, one that occurs within a community of believers. Leadership, then, is not a function of position but rather represents a conjunction of ideas where leadership is shared and transferred between leaders and followers, each only a temporary designation. Indeed, history will identify an individual as the leader, but in reality the job is one in which various members of the community contribute. Leaders and followers become interchangeable.

Certain Conceptual Demands for Leadership

When leadership is separated from a simple legitimation of a managerial philosophy, it then adopts certain characteristics which particularly define it as a subject of attention. These serve as distinguishing criteria for leadership, whether practised in business, education, the arts or elsewhere. Leadership, in this sense, is to be quite differentiated from decision-making, from goal-setting, or from authority: in other words, it serves in a different way than the type of authority necessary to run an organization, build cars or accumulate real estate. There are, in this new way of thinking about leadership, at least four criteria for the definition and practice of leadership:

1　leadership must be critical;
2　leadership must be transformative;
3　leadership must be educative;
4　leadership must be ethical.

Leadership as Critical

Leadership as a critical practice depends largely on one's worldview of human activity: whether one conceives of human activity as essentially 'received,' passed down from generation to generation without much change, or as 'constructed', passed down but reinterpreted and re-created in that passing. If one conceives of human activity in the latter sense, then it becomes clear that a particular aspect of leadership is to examine the previous conditions of social life and subject them to critique; to find, indeed, that there are possibly various conditions of domination which have been resisted.

Seeing human practice as constructed allows us to see humans as agents who can intervene in their affairs. This is an important distinction because it suggests that humans are not just objects of scientific inquiry; that they use social scientific knowledge to change and reorder their particular universes, and that each is his or her own sociologist (see Giddens, 1984).

Theories of leadership are essentially based in the social science disciplines. As must be the case with all such disciplines, the theory itself must be critical. Giddens (1984, p.xxxv) observes that 'the formulation of critical theory is not an *option*.' This is because all social science knowledge is, first, dependent on the commonsense constructions of those being observed, in the sense that a social scientific statement, such as the fictitious 'Birth order will determine success in school', depends for its understanding on commonsense notions of schooling, birth, the timing of children and particular formulas for school success. Even if this principle could be reduced to a formula, such as Bo=S.Su, that formula itself would in turn depend for its interpretation on the preunderstandings of the social scientific community, which in turn depend on lay agents' understandings.

It is because of this first feature that the second feature comes into play. This is, secondly, that social science findings ultimately reflect back upon previous commonsense knowledge in a reflective and critical manner. In this example the critical aspect is suggesting that our previous commonsense knowledge of the relationship of order of birth to school success is faulty to some extent; that recent findings suggest other conclusions, and so on. All social science is critical in some sense, and cannot be anything other than critical; as social science moves into more theoretical and less empirical studies, this becomes even more pronounced.

This feature is a circular one. The findings of social science are circulated among the lay agents (because it is for them that the entire enterprise takes place), and these agents adopt those findings and incorporate them into their new sets of common knowledge, which in turn becomes the foil for social science critique, and in this way a progressive spiral is born.

At the heart of social science is its critical aspect. As Giddens says:

> The point is that reflection on social processes (theories, and observations about them) continually enter into, become disentangled with and re-enter the universe of events they describe. No such phenomenon exists in the world of inanimate nature, which is indifferent to whatever human beings might claim to know about it. (Giddens, 1984, p.xxxiii)

This critical aspect suggests for leadership research in particular that it must always be a critical *practice*. Grob (1984) tells us the following:

> In pointing to the critical spirit as the ground of all leadership, my intent has been to argue that without that willingness to examine one's life, alleged leaders in any and all areas of human endeavor must, of necessity, become identified with their purposes, purposes which inevitably congeal into fixed doctrines or dogma. In short, potential leaders *without this ground* find themselves in the service of fixed ideas or causes, and thus agents of the use of power in their behalf. *No longer nourished by a*

wellspring of critical process at its centre, leadership 'dries up' and becomes, finally, the mere wielding of power on behalf of static ideals. (p.270, emphasis in original)

Leadership is at its heart a critical practice, one that comments on present and former constructions of reality, that holds up certain ideals for comparison, and that attempts at the enablement of a vision based on an interpretation of the past. In being critical, then, leadership is oriented not just toward the development of more perfect organizational structures, but toward a reconceptualization of life practices where common ideals of freedom and democracy stand important.

Leadership as Transformative

The critical spirit of leadership leads naturally to the notion of transformation. Leadership is and must be oriented toward social change, change which is transformative in degree. That leadership is transformative is easily demonstrated by human history: there have been periods of progress and development which have transformed the course of human events, and these have been called leadership. Burns' view of transformational leadership documents many of these; Ghandi is one example, Martin Luther King another. Transformation of *consciousness* is what took place, and as a result of that, a transformation of social conditions. But this required a community of believers, not just a 'leader'. Certainly one person helped to serve as a catalyst, but if the full story be known, such transformations occurred because of a community of leaders.

Transformation though is not a special or unique occurrence, one that is found only in certain grand moments of human history. Rather, it happens in everyday events, when 'commonplace' leaders exert some effect on their situations. Bhaskar (1975, p.196) has commented that 'it is not necessary that society should continue. But if it is to do so, then men must reproduce (or more or less transform) the structures (languages, forms of economic and political organization, systems of belief, cultural and ethical norms, etc.) that are given to them.' Transformation of social relations is a basic feature of all our social living; such transformation may occur as reproduction, wherein social structures may be changed but slightly, or as a true transformation, where structures are changed significantly. It is in the latter case that we claim that leadership has been exerted.

Transformation does involve social change. But this does not necessarily mean *societal* change. Social change can be accomplished without the complete restructuring of any given society; in fact, social change occurs frequently, in small doses, in the actions and activities of various groups and individuals who hope to make some sort of difference. A number of movements, from feminism to racial awareness, can make a claim to transformative leadership and accomplished social change. In some instances this is societal in nature; in others it is much more regionalized. Nevertheless, the balance to the critical aspect of leadership is indeed transformation and change.

Leadership as Educative

If leaders are both critical and transformative agents when engaged in their leadership capacity, so too are they educators. Fay (1987, p.9) has observed that 'humans are not only active beings, but they are also embodied, traditional, historical, and embedded creatures: as a result their reason is limited in its capacity to unravel the mysteries of human identity and to make the difficult choices with which humans are inevitably faced; and their will to change is circumscribed in all sorts of ways.' Human agents are, in other words, *located* in a specific history and set of circumstances, one which to some degree controls their behaviour, ways of seeing and options for acting. This history is their tradition, a tradition which suggests how one is to live, what one is to value and often how one is to think. We are both victims and beneficiaries of this tradition: on the one hand, it closes down many options for living free and independent lives; on the other hand, it provides meaning and a sense of place for those lives we do live.

But while tradition can provide meaning, it can also be oppressive. This is why education is such an important part of leadership. To the degree that leadership can critique traditions which can be oppressive, and aims for a transformation of such conditions, then it must be educative.

But what does being educative mean for a leader? In this context it means that a leader can present both an analysis and a vision. The analysis means that the leaders enable self-reflection to occur; in an organizational context this means devoting some time to talk about organizational history, organizational purpose and the distribution of organizational power. Such analysis represents the concerted efforts of various members of the organization to deal with the received structures that orient their working lives. This is not to say that such analysis takes place in the context of commitments to massive organizational change; rather the purpose remains simply to reflect upon institutional arrangements, to reveal the 'taken-for-granted' features of institutional life, and to allow for commentary on the ways and means that the institution either restrains or promotes human agency.

Vision is another aspect of education. It is not enough to reflect on current social and organizational conditions; in addition, a vision of alternative possibilities must be addressed. Such a vision pertains to how traditions could be altered, if necessary, so that they meet human needs while still providing a sense of meaningfulness. This is perhaps the most crucial and critical role of leadership: to show new social arrangements, while still demonstrating a continuity with the past; to show how new social structures continue, in a sense, the basic mission, goals and objectives of traditional human intercourse, while still maintaining a vision of the future and what it offers.

Vision involves what both MacIntyre (1981) and Fay (1987) have discussed as narratives, stories of human lives, stories that have a sense of meaning and continuity, and which provide to future generations a degree of connectedness to the past. Narratives provide a community with its history, its unique place in the course of human events, its significance in the world order. Each community, and each organization, must have some kind of narrative in order to remain cohesive as a community and organization. But the re-telling of narratives is hardly enough; vision describes the telling of possible narratives and the presentation of new narratives. It is here in particular that one can see how leadership is a shared, communitarian role, one in which different narratives are presented by different individuals, each presenting a possibility for a new narrative and interpreting the previous narratives in their own fashion.

This analysis and envisionment obviously results in education; this educative aspect of leadership is intended to have citizens and participants begin to question aspects of their previous narratives, to grow and develop because of this questioning, and to begin to consider alternative ways of ordering their lives. The educative aspect, in other words, attempts to raise followers' consciousness about their own social conditions, and in so doing to allow them, as well as the 'leader', to consider the possibility of other ways of ordering their social history.

Leadership as Ethical

A final dimension to leadership is its ethical commitment. This occurs in two ways: the first is the individual ethical commitments of various leaders; the second is the overall ethical commitments to a community of followers.

In regard to the first, we are concerned with the use of leadership to attain various objectives through the use of power. Leadership will involve power relationships, and these can in turn be used in a positive or negative fashion. A negative power relationship involves the use of power to achieve those ends desired by the 'leader', what Burns (1978) would label 'power wielding'. This means that the individual entrusted with some position of power uses that position to achieve objectives that are not of communal benefit, but of benefit to the aspirations of only that individual. Burns would not, and we agree, consider this leadership at all.

This use of power to achieve an individual's ends only often results in treating people as means rather than as ends-in-themselves. Treating people as means is to dehumanize them, yet this is often the result of 'leadership' training programmes which see the task as the end and the person as the means to accomplish that end. Here, there is an ethical slide: from a type of Kantian idealism found, for example, in Burns' work, to a form of utilitarianism found, for example, in the work of most management-oriented writers on leadership. In utilitarianism the focus is on achievement, and 'what works' is 'what's right'.

But leadership is founded on the fact of moral relationships; it is intended to elevate people to new levels of morality. This is because of what leadership means to a community of followers: it critiques social conditions, and the followers' role in maintaining such conditions; offers new possibilities for social arrangements, and the followers' role in making such arrangements; and in so doing helps to raise the level of followers' moral consciousness regarding their received situation.

However, the ethical aspects of leadership go further than the particular leader's relationship with given followers, and how he or she demonstrates a morality. Rather, leadership in general must maintain an ethical focus which is oriented toward democratic values within a community. This has to do with the meaning of ethics historically — as a search for the good life of a community; an attempt to come to some understanding regarding the various options available for living that life. Ethics here refers to a more comprehensive construct than just individual behaviour; rather, it implicates us and how we as a moral community live our communal lives.

Consider for a moment Sullivan's (1982) comments on how a liberal philosophy in modern society contributes to an erosion of community:

Liberal thinkers rightfully decry the encroachment on individual life of the administrative state, and, though less often, the bureaucratic corporation and mass media. But they see no relationship between willful abnegation of an ethics of mutual concern, announced as freedom, and weakening of social solidarity outside those encroaching structures. Yet, as some thinkers sympathetic to the liberal tradition have come to see, if personal dignity and self-determination are to survive the constraints and potentiality for social control found in modern society, it can only be through the political action of citizens joined in active solidarity. (p. 155)

His argument, also expressed in such places as Bellah *et al.* (1985), is that such factors as individualism, arising out of the shattering of tradition caused by the Enlightenment and its search for non-mystical and objective knowledge, also parade as freedom in contemporary societies. There is also a tendency toward a shunning of community and a concern with utilitarian self-aggrandizement. Lost is the precious community connection wherein *ways* to live figure prominently; where the search for the good and the right life predominates; and where leadership turns into the development of strategies for success. The result is an atomistic citizenry which acquiesces to even the most irresponsible of governments if only they are left alone.

Sullivan (1982) points out a possible solution: 'the achievement of maturity, or moral virtue, consists in a genuine transformation of motives, not simply their combination. And this takes place only through a certain kind of educative social interaction. Civic moral education is, then, natural in that it fulfils humanity's distinctive need to be at once self-reflective and yet interdependent members of a community' (p. 170). This, in particular, is constitutive of the social and generative aspect of leadership, as a moral undertaking. Leadership carries a responsibility not just to be *personally* moral, but to be a *cause* of 'civic moral education' which leads to both self-knowledge and community awareness. This is a central, defining aspect of leadership; leadership which is ethically-based takes on the task — indeed, a shared task among community members and leaders — of critique and vision: critique in the sense that it remains unsatisfied with social conditions which are either dehumanizing or threatening, and vision in the sense of searching for a kind of life which realizes more closely the Aristotelian ideal.

Some Concerns for Leaders

We have outlined above some aspects of leadership which seem important to the intellectual consideration of the subject. We can summarize some of these ideas and attempt to present them in a way which might have an impact on individuals who hope to be leaders in their own fashion.

1   Leadership and management are not interchangeable concepts. Leadership comes in a number of forms: it has been exerted intellectually, charismatically, modestly, passively, actively. What these forms share in common is a commitment to social change and development, not to control and production. While management might be an essential tool for modern society (and then again it may not be), leadership occurs as a form of communal life concerned with how lives should be lived, not how they should be controlled.

2   Leadership is communal and shared. This has come up a number of times in this chapter, yet has never been addressed completely satisfactorily. The issue is that *leaders* are embodied individuals, while *leadership* is a shared and communal concept. This means that while leaders occur in a certain time-space context, it is neither necessary nor sufficient that leadership be identified for all of time and space with these individuals. One of the generative aspects of leadership is that leaders exist only because of the relationship attained with followers, and that this relationship allows followers to assume leadership and leaders, in turn, to become followers. Leaders, in short, create other leaders, and it is in this fashion that leadership becomes a shared and communal process.

3   Leadership involves self-criticism and self-clarity. While the need for each of these should by now be apparent, it will help to cast them in the terms that Fay (1987) has used. Self-criticism and self-clarity lead to what he calls 'genuine narrative'. A critical theory, of the self or the society, 'will see the lives of its audience as composed of two levels of being: the manifest, in which there is confusion and frustration; and the latent, in which there is an underlying order which is the mainspring of their behavior' (p.69). The genuine narrative addresses the latent level, the underlying unity of human consciousness and human activity: 'This narrative depicts the underlying principle of change at work in the emergence and disappearance of the

57

numerous forms of human life and the countless welter of human activities and relationships' (Fay, 1987, p.69).

Developing a genuine narrative means for leadership to be both clear and critical regarding the circumstances of its influence and the circumstances of its followers. A genuine narrative is a story of human history and how it is accomplished; a story of the basic drives, wants and needs of a people. In modern life such a narrative becomes clouded and opaque, not the least because a market-centred economy dominates our relationships and a utilitarian philosophy controls our goals.

Leadership and leaders can and should be concerned with the discovery of this narrative: Is there, indeed, an underlying, thematic unity to the lives of followers? Are there wants and needs which lie beyond the surface of conscious awareness? Is there a search for a sense of place and a sense of meaning? Finding the genuine narrative in our lives could be the major contribution of leaders to their community. At the same time traditions can be oppressive: a cursory look at racial and gender traditions in various countries certainly reveals this. This is why leaders and leadership need to be critical of those same traditions. Leadership thus turns into a dialectic: it must in turn strive for a sense of community based in tradition, while still based in a search for justice, freedom and equality, those guiding beacons which help to reorient our daily lives to issues of major humanitarian concern.

Conclusion: Implications for Education

Bellah and his colleagues (1985) have written:

> The tension between private interest and the public good is never completely resolved in any society. But in a free republic, it is the task of the citizen, whether ruler or ruled, to cultivate civic virtue in order to mitigate the tension and render it manageable.
>
> As the twentieth century has progressed, that understanding, so important through most of our history, has begun to slip from our grasp. . . . The citizen has been swallowed up in 'economic man'. (pp.270-1)

This is why leadership has become both so rare and so crucial in different world communities. Indeed, where people gather to conduct commerce, to educate each other, to watch each other's performances, to evaluate each other's artistic abilities, to gather in friendship or debate, there is a need for a leadership conscious of civic responsibility.

We live in an age of instrumentalities, where people themselves become instruments for the achievement of organizational goals; where people are driven by the need to achieve, with achievement defined by economics; and where the individual, rootless and guide-less, strives for a sense of identity and meaning. If we are to climb out of this valley of depression, then we certainly do need leaders, but leaders who are not managers, leaders who can see beyond the immediate needs of the organization, and leaders who can provide a 'genuine narrative' for our lives.

How can such leadership exert itself in a community? Think, for example, of a school, but a school as a community of agents, not as an organization of members. Rather than seeing children as individual products being processed through the system, certified according to their achievement test scores, what would it be like to consider the children and the adults as participants in a practising democracy, where each has the chance to live out a meaningful narrative of their own lives, and where all can exert leadership?

Such a situation seems, perhaps, too idealistic, and to a certain degree it might be. Yet it appeals to all of us in a fundamental way: it suggests that our experiments with democracy might well be lived ones, occurring beyond just the voting booth; it suggests, further, that republican ideals can be reproduced in everyday settings, and this reinforces our belief in a polity where each one can have a say; and finally it suggests that the vital spark which keeps democracy alive, and which prevents a benign government from deciding for us, is that spark which occurs in a specific community of believers. (For a discussion of how participatory democracy can be accomplished in school settings see White, 1983.)

Such experiments in democracy are not unknown, however, and thus not completely idealistic. Certain guidelines do pertain. First, it is leadership that contributes to the development of such a situation. This is to say that the existing administration, if it is concerned with leadership ideas, will adopt a programme of self-critique, ethics, transformation and education. Secondly, this attempt at democratization does not mean that every decision is open to full community participation: rather, adjustments have to be made for the type of decision and its importance to the community. In addition, recognition has to be given to the fact that students, and their parents, have to be educated to the responsibilities of participation in a democratic regime; it is the responsibility of participation in a *government* as opposed to participation in an *anarchy*. Thirdly, recognition must be given to the words of those with experience and with wisdom; a community requires its elders, those with a sense of the past and a vision for the future.

Leadership in such a situation is concerned with the meeting of followers' concerns, and with transforming the values of followers so that they too exert leadership. In a school setting it should be recognized that followers come in all sizes, ages and shapes; that each of these, from students to teachers to administrators, can in fact be leaders with respect to their influence over others. Nicoll (1986) has put this well. Asking about the relationship between followers and leaders, he finds that:

> Our answer — if we ever are going to find one that is satisfactory — will require leaders to accept and believe that *followers use leaders to make a path*. This is fundamental. Our leaders must allow themselves — and us — to believe that followers are *not* passive, reactive tools of charismatic power figures. They are, instead, the creators of energy. They are the architects of the open moments into which some people must be the first to step. As followers, they are the agents who show their leaders where to walk. They are the ones who validate their leaders stepping out in a direction that has meaning for all of us. (1986, p.34)

It must be admitted that there are two major issues which make the achievement of a true democracy in education difficult to achieve. The first is the issue of size; the second, that of values.

Size pertains, of course, to the basic structure of schooling in many countries, where the sheer size of the institution makes it difficult if not impossible for administrators to exert the degree of influence over school processes that might be desired. The move toward comprehensive schools, with rigidly departmentalized faculty, curricula and students, argues against the establishment of a community of students, each with the possibility of some input into the way things are organized and reproduced in that setting.

The second issue is concerned with values. In modern society the guiding principles have had to do with the provision of equality and liberty. These are, indeed, *public* values, ones that cut across a number of various groups and interests. Yet for a strong public value system to exist, Strike (1982) claims that it is *private* values that must be taught. Private values have to do with a sense of important religious and ethical beliefs, the same beliefs that a fully public system may have trouble addressing because of its diversity and accommodation of various beliefs. Thus a democratic regime depends on the inculcation of various values which are ethical in degree, and which depend often on religious belief.

Public schools, however, cannot be overly dependent on the presence of private values in their students; they must to some degree be neutral in their acceptance of various values, treating each as equally worthy.

These two issues pose a basic problem for leadership in education, yet neither is unsolvable. Smaller schools are certainly an option, but so are schools within schools, and schools with differentiated representation patterns so that all students can feel that they can participate in some fashion in the formulation of important policy. The second problem is a harder one. Yet leadership is concerned with the transformation of values, and here school leaders can address basic social end values such as democracy, justice and liberty. These are, indeed, public values in the sense that a society will depend on their formulation for its success as a caring society.

Finally, leadership can surmount such problems by its concern with establishing a true narrative for all participants. This is not something given, but rather something searched for. It suggests that *conscious* attention be paid to the way the organization serves its members, to the stories and even culture that have evolved, to the levels of participation in the formation of new policy, and to the meanings that have evolved in the organizational context.

Leadership, in the final analysis, is the ability of humans to relate deeply to each other in the search for a more perfect union. Leadership is a consensual task, a sharing of ideas and a sharing of responsibilities, where a 'leader' is a leader for the moment only, where the leadership exerted must be validated by the consent of followers, and where leadership lies in the struggles of a community to find meaning for itself.

References

Bellah, R.N., Madsen, R., Sullivan, W.M., Swidler, A. and Tipton, S.T. (1985) *Habits of the Heart: Individualism and Commitment in American Life,* Berkeley and Los Angeles, University of California Press.

Bennis, W. (1984) 'The 4 competencies of leadership,' *Training and Development Journal,* August, pp.15–19.

Benson, J.K. (1977) 'Innovation and crisis in organizational analysis,' in J.K. Benson (Ed.), *Organizational Analysis: Critique and Innovation,* Beverly Hills, Calif., Sage Press.

Bhaskar, R. (1975) *A Realist Theory of Science,* Leeds, Leeds Books.

Burns, J.M. (1978) *Leadership,* New York, Harper and Row.

Fay, B. (1987) *Critical Social Science,* Cambridge, Polity Press.

Fiedler, F. (1967) *A Theory of Leadership Effectiveness,* New York, McGraw-Hill.

Giddens, A. (1984) *The Constitution of Society,* Berkeley and Los Angeles, University of California Press.

Grob, L. (1984) 'Leadership: The Socratic model,' in B. Kellerman (Ed.), *Leadership: Multidisciplinary Perspectives,* Englewood Cliffs, N.J., Prentice-Hall.

Lincoln, Y. (Ed.) (1985) *Organizational Theory and Inquiry: The Paradigm Revolution,* Beverly Hills, Calif., Sage Press.

MacIntyre, A. (1981) *After Virtue,* Notre Dame, Ind., University of Notre Dame Press.

March, J.G. and Olsen, J.P. (1976) *Ambiguity and Choice in Organizations,* Bergen, Universitetsforlaget.

Nicoll, David (1986) 'Leadership and followership,' in J.D. Adams (Ed.), *Transforming Leadership: From Vision to Results,* Alexandria, Va., Miles River Press.

Rost, J. (1985) 'Distinguishing leadership and management: A new consensus,' Paper presented at California Principals Conference, Anaheim, Calif., November.

Smircich, L. (1983) 'Concepts of culture and organizational analysis,' *Administrative Science Quarterly,* 28, September, pp.339-58.

Strike, K.A. (1982) *Educational Policy and the Just Society,* Urbana, Ill., University of Illinois Press.

Sullivan, W.M. (1982) *Reconstructing Public Philosophy,* Berkeley and Los Angeles, University of California Press.

Tichy, N. and Devanna, M.A. (1986) *The Transformational Leader,* New York, John Wiley.

Tucker, R.C. (1981) *Politics as Leadership,* Columbia, Mo., University of Missouri Press.

Weick, K. (1976) 'Educational organizations as loosely coupled systems,' *Administrative Science Quarterly,* 21, pp.1-19.

Weick, K. (1979) *The Social Psychology of Organizing,* 2nd ed., Reading, Mass., Addison-Wesley.

White, P. (1983) *Beyond Domination: An Essay in the Political Philosophy of Education,* London, Routledge and Kegan Paul.

Chapter 3

'New' Leadership and the Possibility of Educational Reform

Lawrence Angus

There seems to be broad agreement in Western education systems that educational reform at the school level is urgently required. Much of the recent literature in educational administration posits particular styles of leadership as being an appropriate means for achieving school reform and improvement. This chapter argues, however, that the predominant conception of 'new' leadership as a moral and cultural enterprise is inadequate because it tacitly assumes a functionalist perspective within which the nature of school relationships is misunderstood. Moreover, an undue emphasis upon the role of administrative leaders in schools suggests that it is possible to reduce complex educational problems to administrative issues that are represented as being soluble at the school level. Many educational problems, however, can only be understood in relation to the broad social, political and cultural context of which education is a part. An alternative conception of leadership, one which appreciates educational complexity and facilitates critical scrutiny of school problems such that connections are explicitly made between the educational sphere and other spheres, is required.

The chapter begins with a review of some recent literature and concepts that have been influential in the formulation of revised notions of leadership in education. Many of these concepts have arisen in the area of business administration and have been incorporated into the educational sphere under the rubric of school effectiveness which, among other things, asserts a strong role for principals in schools. Secondly, revised views of leadership are criticized for their limited understanding of the concept of culture, which is regarded as a property that is appropriate for managerial manipulation. Thirdly, the representation of leadership in recent literature is argued to constitute a 'moral fiction' as it is found that none of the bases upon which claims to leadership are founded can be unequivocally supported. Fourthly, the new models of leadership are criticized for their continuing reliance upon bureaucratic assumptions, and for their silence regarding the ideological context of leadership and education. Finally, a view of leadership as agency is tentatively suggested as overcoming some of the limitations of conventional leadership models, and as offering some possibilities for more substantial educational reform which connects education to broader social and political spheres.

Renewed Calls for Leadership

There has been great interest, even fascination, in leaders and the subject of leadership in recent years. Captains of commerce have published biographies that have featured well in the best seller lists (Iacocca, 1984; Pullan, 1986; Denton, 1986), American studies of the best performing companies conclude that effective leadership is essential to business success (Peters and Waterman, 1982; Deal and Kennedy, 1982), and management texts continue the tradition of extolling chief executives to be not merely managers but leaders (Mintzberg, 1973; Kotter, 1982). One of the more recent and more fervent of this last category seems to regard renewed leadership as being connected to the very survival of Western industry. Bennis and Nanus (1985) claim that the need for new leaders and a 'comprehensive strategic view of leadership' (p. 2) across all levels of politics and business has never been so great. They are so convinced of the appropriateness of their own view of leadership that they conclude their book with this emotive appeal:

> Without leadership of the kind we've been calling for, it is hard to see how we can shape a more desirable future for this nation or the world. The absence or ineffectiveness of leadership implies the absence of vision, a dreamless society, and this will result, at best, in the maintenance of the status quo or, at worst, in the disintegration of our society because of lack of purpose and cohesion.
>
> We must raise the search for new leadership to a national priority. We desperately need women and men who can take charge, and we hope that you, the reader, will be among them. What can be more consequential and inspiring? (Bennis and Nanus, 1985, pp. 228-9)

In this view the emphasis is upon organizational change and improvement rather than merely the maintenance of mediocre levels of performance. Progress and the pursuit of excellence require reforms that can be brought about by inspiring purposeful activity on the part of organization members and harnassing this within the leader's 'vision' of what is possible. The notion of 'vision' is to the forefront in calls for leadership in education also. There, too, there is a perceived need for people of vision to take charge. The educational literature draws on the language of both business (Duignan, 1985) and school effectiveness (Purkey and Smith, 1983) in an attempt to define a form of educational leadership that will weld schools and their cultures into successful, or even excellent, educational enterprises (Dunlap, 1985; Peterson *et al.*, 1987; Duignan, 1986).

This new literature advocates a particularly influential role for principals in schools. Strong leadership is demanded of them as part of 'the new catechism for school effectiveness' (Brandt, 1982). Principals are at the top of the agenda for educational reform (Zirkel and Greenwood, 1987). They are expected to develop effective schools, to assert a productive organizational culture, and to get the best out of staff and students. As a Canadian study of the demands made upon principals concluded, 'In short, they are expected to perform with the verve, vigour and elan of administrative prima donnas' (Allison, 1983, p.23). Such expectations may be rather too ambitious, not only because a much more interventionist style of leadership is required, but also because the construct of leadership employed in most of the literature still assumes that 'leaders' are those who have been appointed to positions of formal authority.

As part of an overly demanding job description, principals, who have traditionally been encouraged to see their role as part of a largely unproblematic top-down bureaucratic structure, are expected to exercise educative leadership of a type described by Duignan and Macpherson. According to these directors of an Australian Educative Leadership Project:

> . . . we envisage an educative leader as one who communicates a sense of excitement, originality and freshness in an organisation. We believe that an educative leader is a person who challenges others to participate in the visionary activity of defining 'rightness' and preferred ways of doing and acting in education. Finally, we see an educative leader as a person who challenges educators to commit themselves to approaches to administration and professional practices that are, by their nature, educative. (Duignan and Macpherson, 1987, p.51)

These are high expectations, far removed from the traditional view of the principalship which is reflected in the conventional approach to the selection of principals. Appointees are typically experienced teachers who have achieved a degree of seniority and demonstrated competence in various teaching and administrative areas. The most pressing expectations of principals that are set out in the school effectiveness literature are rather less esoteric and more utilitarian than those that might be associated with inspirational 'educative leaders'.

School Effectiveness and Educational Leadership

Even a cursory examination of the literature on school effectiveness reveals that, while there are some differences of approach, the active leadership of the principal is regarded as essential to school improvement and the most essential ingredient of educational reform (Purkey and Smith, 1983; Murphy *et al.*, 1985). To be regarded as 'effective', the principal, the key educational leader, must ensure that other effectiveness factors are put in place. In a review of this literature Duignan (1986) identifies a number of characteristics that are thought to constitute effective educational leadership. These include 'setting an atmosphere of order, discipline and purpose, creating a climate of high expectations for staff and students, encouraging collegial and collaborative relationships and building commitment among staff and students to the school's goals, facilitating teachers in spending maximum time on direct instruction, encouraging staff development and evaluation, and being a dynamic instructional leader' (Duignan, 1986, p.67).

In this largely North American literature schools are generally deemed to be effective or not on rather narrow grounds, and this in turn suggests a rather limited appreciation of problematic aspects of both leadership and education. Essentially, schools and classrooms are measured to be effective if student scores on standardized tests of a range of basic skills (usually reading, vocabulary, grammar, number operations, and definitions and facts in science) improve over a particular period of time relative to state-wide norms. The complex nature of education is therefore reduced to particular problems that are represented as being capable of direct solutions. School administration and teaching are reduced to a narrow range of techniques for improving test results in areas where there are clearly non-controversial, right or wrong answers. As Cuban (1984, p.132) points out, 'school effectiveness research and programs ignore many skills, habits and attitudes beyond the reach of paper-and-pencil tests.'

In the more instrumental accounts of school effectiveness, a traditional and limited notion of 'what counts' as education is reinforced by the repetition of mundane, low-level skills which ignore the interests of pupils, richness of the mind, or a spirit of inquiry. Although this literature enthuses about effective principals and strong leadership, it would appear that educational administrators, rather than stimulating critical and reflective thinking, social inquiry and creative activity on the part of pupils and teachers, are being encouraged to value control, predictability and efficiency in their schools. While such views of leadership appear somewhat simplistic, a number of scholars (e.g., Duignan, 1985; Dunlap, 1985) make strong connections between recent developments in business administration and the findings of research on school effectiveness. According to one of these authors:

> One of the most successful compilations of recent theory and practice in the business world is the best-selling book *In Search of Excellence* (Peters and Waterman, 1982). Many of the basic principles discovered by the authors in their study of forty-three successful companies will look familiar to readers of the school effectiveness literature. What is found in successful companies is also often found in successful schools. (Dunlap, 1985, p. 1)

Many researchers have concluded that a principal's leadership is essential to initiate and sustain school improvement efforts (e.g., Rutter *et al.*, 1979; Glasman, 1984). Shrewd leaders are expected to manipulate people and situations so that the leader's 'vision' is willingly shared by followers; teachers in schools will work earnestly and purposefully to do well that which the leader of vision wants them to do.

Such leadership is thought to be especially important in much of the current literature that treats schools as loosely coupled systems in which teachers in semi-autonomous classrooms are not able to be directly controlled in a bureaucratic framework. They therefore require less obvious regulation. The originator of the metaphor of organizations as loosely coupled systems explains the more subtle form of control in this way:

> In a loosely coupled system, you don't influence less, you influence differently. The administrator . . . has the difficult task of effecting perceptions and monitoring and reinforcing the language people use to create and coordinate what they are doing. A loosely coupled system requires strong leadership of the kind where administrators model the kind of behaviour they desire. (Weick, 1986, p. 10)

Such an approach, while it recognizes the virtual impossibility of direct, authoritarian leadership in which subordinates unquestioningly obey orders, assumes only a limited sense of agency or personal autonomy on the part of organization members.

Revised Views of Leadership

Given the enormous recent literature on leadership, especially that linking business practices to recommendations for school principals, it is obviously important that critical perspectives on school leadership are not content with criticizing ghosts of the past. Some years ago Stogdill's (1974) massive analysis of leadership research identified both the problem of conceptualizing an adequate definition of leadership, and the difficulty of progressing beyond a two-dimensional model of leadership based on a task/relationship dichotomy. Even more alarming, Stodgill found no consistent correlation between any presumed leadership behaviours and organizational success. These findings were later confirmed by Bass (1981). Some recent studies, however, claim to have identified somewhat broader, more productive and substantive ways of understanding leadership.

Many of these later studies are in large part in the tradition of the human relations school of management. This approach originated in the researches of Elton Mayo and his colleagues at the Hawthorne works of the Western Electric Company in the late 1920s and early 1930s (Wood, 1985). Mayo's work failed to confirm the scientific management theories of F.W. Taylor, which had predicted that plants would become more productive as workers and machinery were made more efficient through the scrupulous application in the workplace of the results of rigorous time and motion studies. Under Taylorism workers were regarded more or less as appendages to their machines; people who could be made to be more efficient through increased specialization and by altering work practices to increase the pace of work. This approach had a significant impact, especially in the United States, in the emergence of educational administration as a specialist career and area of academic study in the first half of this century (Callahan, 1962). The significance of Mayo's findings was in his conclusion that the productivity of workers was influenced as much or more by social conditions as by the physical nature of the workplace.

Mayo's work launched the development of a school of management studies that regarded people as humans rather than work units. This human relations approach, informed by organizational psychology and sociology, asserted that happy employees would be more productive employees, and that it was the job of management to stimulate and motivate their workers through appropriate expectations of them (McGregor, 1966), attention to motivation factors such as responsibility and recognition (Herzberg, 1972), and involvement of employees in forms of participatory management (Likert, 1976). While critics argue that this approach did little to give employees any measure of control over workplaces (e.g., Braverman, 1974), it nonetheless led to the reduction in many organizations of impersonal, mechanical forms of management.

Recent developments in the human relations school continue to emphasize heavily the responsibility of administrators to control the well-being of employees. This work also introduces a new emphasis on active and personal leadership, and on organizational change and renewal, rather than merely competent and sensitive management. This is required not merely to keep employees satisfied but also to incorporate their desires and needs into a corporate agenda that is set by the leader. In this much more active and interventionist role the leader is responsible for organizational change in positive, productive ways. The approach draws heavily upon the work of scholars such as Weick (1976, 1986), Burns (1978), Vaill (1984) and Deal and Kennedy (1982).

Burns' (1978) work is particularly important for its distinction between transactional and transformative leadership. The former describes what Burns regards as conventional leadership, which is characterized by a form of exchange between leader and subordinates. In return for effort, productivity, loyalty and so on, leaders offer rewards of one kind or another to subordinates. These may be tangible payments, promotion or improved conditions, or may be in the form of less obvious but especially important matching of respective needs such that both leaders and followers get some satisfaction (or at least a reduction of antagonism) out of the exchange. While such transactions may lead to more harmonious and efficient workplaces, however, the efficiency is achieved in an environment that remains essentially static.

Transformative leadership, by contrast, is concerned with exploring conventional relationships and organizational understandings such that there is involvement between persons in which 'leaders and followers raise one another to higher levels of motivation and morality' (Burns, 1978, p.17). Leaders must engage followers such that there is mutual commitment to the shared purpose of building the best of organizations. Followers, it is claimed, can be motivated to give more of themselves such that, for instance, in schools:

> . . . teachers decide to exceed the limits of the traditional work
> relationship. Here they give more than can reasonably be

> expected and in return are provided with rewards and benefits that are of a different kind. In a sense they are drawn to higher levels of performance and commitment. Following Burns the leadership that evokes [such a] performance investment is that which transforms one's needs state from lower to higher by arousing different dimensions of human potential. Ultimately this leadership becomes moral in its tone and direction enhancing both significance and meaning of work and life for both leader and followers. (Sergiovanni, 1987, pp.9-10)

In this way leaders are thought to bring about a negotiated order that accords by and large with their own definitions and purposes. This is especially important in organizations, such as schools, which are generally loosely coupled culturally. In such cases transformative leadership may achieve a state of order by 'seeking to "domesticate" the "wild" cultural system to which teachers are tightly aligned' (Sergiovanni, 1987, p.11). That is, although the literature is drenched with a rhetoric of change and reform, it seems that such change is to be directed into reasonable, predictable channels by the overriding moral force of the leader.

The heavy responsibility of leaders, in Burns' approach, to draw upon the best of motives of their subordinates and to direct these towards the best interests of the organization, is in some ways matched by Vaill's notion of 'purposing' (Vaill, 1984). This amounts to the leader's capacity to define the institutional mission and role of the organization and to come to embody the institution's purpose. Through 'purposing' the leader conveys a sense of mission to other organization members by means of a 'continuous stream of actions . . . which have the effect of inducing clarity, consensus, and commitment regarding the organization's basic purposes' (Vaill, 1984, p.91). With a sense of shared meaning and purpose, Sergiovanni claims, 'people respond to work with increased motivation and commitment' (1987, p.17). By asserting and defending particular values, it is argued, leaders so strongly articulate and endorse their vision that it becomes also the vision of followers, and so bonds leader and followers together in a shared covenant (Bennis and Nanus, 1985), which incorporates what then comes to be the non-negotiable core values and beliefs of the organization (Sergiovanni, 1987; Starratt, 1986). This core, according to the argument, amounts to an organizational culture in which effective leaders can utilize particular rituals and values 'to mobilize and focus the energy and commitment of employees on organizational goals' (Starratt, 1986, p.11).

The notion of an organizational culture that can be in a sense manufactured and manipulated, and the influence upon it of leaders, derives in this literature largely from the work of Deal and Kennedy (1982), and has been influential in attempts to define educative leadership. According to Duignan and Macpherson, for instance:

> . . . educative leadership is part of the process of modifying or maintaining an organizational culture. . . . Educative leadership helps to articulate, define and strengthen those endearing values, beliefs and cultural characteristics that give an organization its unique identity in the minds of participants . . . educative leaders use the tools of culture to build an ethos, to create shared assumptions about responsibilities and relationships, and to gain the commitment of groups to the achievement of tangible and intangible goals and objectives. (1987, pp.51, 55)

As Bates (1987) points out in criticism of the growing emphasis in administration literature on the importance of culture in the management of organizations, successful management has become as much a matter of getting the culture right as it is of getting the technology right. As he also points out, the particular notion of culture being applied is regarded in this literature as curiously unproblematic. There is virtually no sense, for instance, of an anthropological concern with culture as a shifting and contested concept which is continually being constructed and reconstructed and which must be subjectively understood. Instead, there is only a managerial concern with the manipulation of and intervention in culture to shape it in ways that enhance the efficiency of the organization (Bates, 1987). Not only is there a lack of appreciation of the importance and complexity of cultural politics, but also there is a taken-for-granted assumption that the appropriate cultural expectations of those associated with the organization will be embodied in the particular values of the leader.

Leadership as a Moral Fiction

It is a little ironic that calls for new forms of leadership have come at a time when many commentators have discerned a lack of faith in public and private institutions and their leadership in Western nations (Mitchell and Scott, 1987; Habermas, 1975; Weiler, 1983; *The Age Saturday Extra,* 27 February 1988). In another sense, however, the contradiction here is perhaps symptomatic of broader contradictory messages within the literature. In Australia, for instance, in times of economic uncertainty, calls from particular quarters for so-called 'entrepreneurs' to enter federal politics (*The Age,* 23 February 1988) are balanced against revelations of scandals in a financial world that seems rife with insider share trading and other scams, as well as the fall from grace of financiers and risk-takers during and after the October 1987 share market crash. Events like these, along with the enforced departure from office of senior politicians, illustrate the point that before leaders can 'lead' they must have some claim to legitimate authority. Yet, according to Mitchell and Scott:

> . . . the underlying notions of legitimate authority are grounded today in the ideas of expertise, entrepreneurship, and steward-ship. These legitimizing concepts may also be the great moral fiction of our age as they apply to the personal qualities of administrators as a class. That is, while they may want others to believe that they are expert, visionary, and trustworthy, little theoretical or empirical evidence supports these claims. (1987, p.446)

Prevailing theories of administration and leadership, according to a number of extensive reviews, have little predictive power (Peters *et al.,* 1985; Cameron, 1986). Certainly, few law-like generalizations have been produced by the so-called administrative sciences. Despite this, traditional theories are extremely influential in that they have largely become accepted as orthodoxy. As such they act as ideologies, legitimating particular managerial concepts and forms of organization, while constraining the conceptualization of alternatives.

In relation to leadership, this ideology, or what MacIntyre (1981) prefers to call 'moral fiction', has in the past been manifested in claims of leaders (and the advocates of organizational leadership) to particular expertise and skills of effectiveness. But after an extensive review of relevant literature, Mitchell and Scott (1987) could only conclude that there is little evidence to support the view that administration can be based on claims to expert authority:

> Part of the problem is that neither expertise nor effectiveness are defined very well. The literature on leadership suggests that there is simply no consensus about what attributes make an adminis-trator an expert or effective. . . . [F]actors such as the internal organizational design, the external economic and competitive environment, and other chance events are aften as important as anything that is done by the organization or its leaders. (Mitchell and Scott, 1987, p.447)

Only part of the strength of the new leadership literature, however, rests on claims of administrative expertise and effectiveness. Also important is the rhetoric of entrepreneurship and moral vision.

The term 'entrepreneur' once referred to especially innovative and progressive individuals who were able successfully to exploit ideas, inventions or gaps in the market to produce new and valued goods and services. Renewed calls for entrepreneurship from governments and business journals are applied to both private and public organizations which are urged to become more productive. In the case of schools, entrepreneurial leaders are called upon to arrest enrolment decline, attend to the school's public image, take charge and lead with skill and vision. This last point is especially important in the new literature on leadership because, as Mitchell and Scott (1987, p.447) point out, the rhetoric of entrepreneurship implies that only a few have the requisite skill or vision to be leaders.

This flattering notion of 'an administrative elite inspiring progress within large organizations' (Mitchell and Scott, 1987, p.447) is essential to the approaches to leadership of Burns (1978) and Vaill (1984), both of whom regard genuine leadership as being in the capacity of leaders to transmit their vision to others. Such a view is also central to the work of Deal and Kennedy (1982), who regard skill in shaping organizational culture as the essence of leadership. The elitist implication in this literature is that not only are leaders more visionary than anyone else but also, given the new emphasis on moral leadership, more trustworthy as well.

Despite the current popularity of notions of entrepreneurship, Mitchell and Scott (1987) have little doubt about the limited value of this concept: 'Empirical work on entrepreneurship is in utter disarray. There is simply no empirical support for the idea that certain traits (such as vision or risk taking) lead to either innovation or success' (p.447). Indeed, although there are problems even in the definition of success, especially regarding public service and educational institutions, where success *can* be identified it is usually associated with chance events such as being in the right place at the right time (Kent *et al.*, 1980). When this happens, the leader is able to appear expert and visionary, but scholars such as Ramos (1981) and MacIntyre (1981) have raised serious doubts about the claims of administrators to such qualities.

If these authors are correct, all that is left to justify the special status and power of leaders are the sorts of claims made in the new leadership literature to the moral rectitude of genuine leaders who exercise what Mitchell and Scott (1987, p.448) call 'stewardship'. These would demonstrate themselves to be 'more ethical, trustworthy, honorable and accountable . . . than any other hypothetical group' (Mitchell and Scott,

1987, p.448). Yet the continuing sagas of business fraud, tax evasion, cheating on government contracts and the diversion of funds from asset stripping and windfall profits into personal wealth rather than productive investment, as well as scandals amongst evangelist preachers and the indications of corruption at the highest levels of police, politics and the judiciary, make one wonder about the degree of trust and honourableness displayed by those who claim to be legitimate leaders or 'stewards'. Clearly, one cannot automatically assume that holders of positions of administrative leadership are necessarily honourable, despite the tendency in the literature to place leaders on a pedestal. The abundance of such scandals involving three-piece-suited bushrangers also makes one wonder whether the various theories of leadership drawn from the business world are at all appropriate for educational institutions that should above all be concerned about the well-being of their pupils.

Criticism of New Leadership

While clearly an improvement upon mechanistic models of leadership which emphasized direct control over employees and the maintenance of a restricted organizational paradigm, the new theories of leadership are not without problems. They can generally be regarded as following in the tradition of human relations reforms that attempt to secure the consent of subordinates and build it into otherwise largely unchanged forms of control (Clegg and Higgins, 1987; Wood, 1985; Braverman, 1974). The shift from managerial to ideological means of control is particularly well illustrated by the expectation that leaders will create and sustain an appropriate organizational culture. In schools, as we have seen, the leader's moral vision and sense of purpose in this regard should be sufficiently strong to 'tame' the existing 'wild' culture of the loosely coupled school (Sergiovanni, 1987; Starratt, 1986). In this way the rhetoric of moral vision, purpose, organizational covenant and the like begin to sound like the reduction of complex issues, contested and contradictory demands, and essentially problematic questions about appropriate social formation and quality of life as well as education, to a rather simplistic and conservative slogan system.

Like the earlier human relations approach, the new leadership models contain certain built-in assumptions that are flattering to the leaders and generally consistent with conservative approaches to organization. One of these is the assumption that the particular 'vision' that is appropriate and that should prevail in any school or organization is that of the leader. Given the above shortcomings of the stewardship of many in leadership positions, one is prompted to wonder why the dreams or vision of the leader should be somehow 'better' than the dreams or vision of any other organization member. Moreover, as Simon (1987) correctly points out, '. . . dreams are never neutral; they are always SOMEONE'S dreams and to the degree that they are implicated in organizing the future for others they always have a moral and political dimension' (p.372). This point is particularly relevant for two reasons: firstly, the new literature on leadership, like most of its predecessors, still assumes the appropriateness of traditional bureaucratic bases of power that are thought to be apolitical; and secondly, the literature rests upon functionalist assumptions which largely ignore political and ideological influences on organization and administration.

New Leadership and Traditional Bureaucracy

It is important to re-emphasize that the notion of leadership that is generally employed in the literature refers to formal, appointed positions that are part of the organizational structure. The leader is a formal leader, one who is expected to exercise clear and unambiguous leadership, rather than a person who may have emerged in an informal sense from within the group and so achieved some influence over colleagues. Other organization participants, such as teachers in schools, are generally viewed as essentially passive recipients of the leader's vision or purpose. It is assumed that they can be drawn into a convenant which embodies shared goals and a common value system that is shaped by the leader's management of the organization's culture (Bates, 1987). In other words, despite some appreciation in this literature that superior-subordinate relationships are more complex than organizational charts suggest, and an understanding that the phenomenon of leadership and the nature of organization requires a more interpretive, interactive perspective (Burrell and Morgan, 1979; Deal and Kennedy, 1982; Griffin *et al.*, 1987), there is still an expectation that particular leadership tasks can be ascribed to a hierarchical position and that these will be instrumental in the realization of organizational goals. Such is especially the case with the literature on leadership and education, particularly the effective schools literature.

Within the currently popular but still overly uni-directional approach to leadership, in which the role of leader is attributed to a particular individual, Griffin *et al.* point out that

> The position [of leader] is a symbol of rights and responsibilities to the followers. The actions performed by the leader also become

> symbolic and are the leader's interpretation of the situation, giving meaning to actions. In this sense, the leader becomes responsible for instilling meaning in organization action and events. More specifically, Pfeffer (1981) states that it is the function of the leader to construct reality for the followers. (1987, p.202)

The leader is regarded as being personally powerful in being able to determine the definition of reality that is to prevail in the organization. In contrast to the view of leader as sole decision-maker and source of both authority and even organizational reality, however, it needs to be recognized that the actions and beliefs of followers also influence the situation and the leader. This has been demonstrated time and again in ethnographic studies of schools on several continents (e.g., Angus, 1988; Ball, 1986; Smith *et al.*, 1987).

Leadership is interactive in multiple directions such that in schools, for instance, the principal is largely shaped by the teachers, the reputation and history of the school and the expectations that have become institutionalized over time within the school and its community (Angus, 1988). Such is particularly the case in public schools in Victoria where, in a formal manner, as part of an industrial agreement between the Ministry of Education and the teacher unions, principals must consult with an administrative committee comprising administrative staff and teacher unionists. Yet, even in the absence of such formal arrangements, leadership, like all other aspects of organizational life, is a dynamic, interactive and emergent process as organization members act within a specific context that must continually be interpreted and understood (Griffin *et al.*, 1987, p.203). Leaders and followers learn from their ongoing interactions with each other and with the situation, and such learning influences subsequent actions. While various organization members may learn to cooperate within a broad framework, this does not disguise the ongoing, contested nature of school organization (Ball, 1986).

Some appreciation of the interactive nature of leadership and organizational change is apparent in the work of Schein (1984). He argues that leadership is often legitimated retrospectively as leaders claim credit for decisions that may have been stumbled upon but which later can be incorporated into an apparently coherent and logical interpretation of organizational success. Such are the origins, it is argued, of many of the myths, legends and sagas that are incorporated into the life of the organization and which can be drawn upon to legitimate further adjustments (Starratt, 1986). But regardless of such backgrounds, it is clear that leaders cannot assume the unproblematic obedience or followership of subordinates. Even instances that appear as loyalty or followership may in fact be instances of ingratiating tactics. Alternatively, what appears superficially as order and harmony in organizations such as schools, and which may be interpreted as consensus, may in fact be an example of compliance that is gained by forms of coercion in which superiors view subordinates in an instrumental fashion (Knights and Roberts, 1982).

Principals and administrators, in the belief that they are maintaining traditions of strong and effective leadership, may cross the boundary between the advocacy of a particular vision or value system and the exercise of arbitrary power. Principals may view their power, for instance, not as something that arises out of the quality of their relationship with staff but as a property simply of position in a hierarchy of control. When principals are expected actively to supervise the work performance of teachers, as is recommended in the effective schools literature and suggested in reforms to educational governance in Victoria (Ministry of Education, 1987), tensions arise as bureaucratic accountability conflicts with teacher professionalism. Such tension is likely to become manifest in the internal industrial politics of the school (Seddon and Connell, 1987).

Moreover, despite a tendency in much of the 'soft' organizational literature to deprecate rigid forms of bureaucracy, all of us are so familiar with bureaucracies and ways of thinking about bureaucracy that we are likely to take bureaucratic forms of organization for granted. The ideology of bureaucracy is strong and pervasive. Most of us work in bureaucracies and encounter others virtually every day. As Johnston (1985) explains, we are part of a social formation that is characterized by 'an evaluative/belief orientation toward existing bureaucratic structural arrangements as generally efficient, proper and, if not inevitable, at least highly resistant to intervention and transformation' (p.336).

Bureaucratic thinking amounts to an ideology because the rhetoric and logic of bureaucracy structure the way participants talk and think about organization and appropriate ways of operating. Bureaucratic ideology provides structures for interpreting what count as problems and for conceptualizing possible solutions to them. In these ways, bureaucratic structures and modes of thinking encourage compliance with established interests and the expectations of administrators. There is a tendency for individuals to define themselves in relation to the organization in such a way that subsumes the self into the larger bureaucratic structure. Rather than empowering participants, the new models of leadership encourage them to adapt to the established institutional identity, which seems larger than life, in ways that do not disturb established patterns of relationships.

Such bureaucratic thinking holds that organizations should be led by experts whose task it is to apply instrumental solutions to practical problems. This helps to explain the wide acceptance by teachers, principals and public of the supposed 'neutrality' of schooling. Indeed, a 1986 study by Gunn and Holdaway found that Canadian principals had little to say about leadership or the nature of their influence on the school because their preoccupation was with more mundane, utilitarian matters that are consistent with impartial bureaucratic administration:

> . . . many of the principals who were interviewed saw themselves as occupants of 'middle management' appointments rather than as organizational leaders. Many perceived the school leadership role as one of 'institutional maintenance' in which the primary function is merely to maintain the status quo. This attitude of 'keeping the ship afloat' contrasts sharply with the metaphor that portrays the administrator as the 'captain of the ship', who must set and stay on course — that is, as an assertive, effective organizational leader. (Gunn *et al.*, 1988, p.3)

To the pressure for institutional maintenance can be added the inheritance of past meanings, traditions, folklore and entrenched expectations and understandings about the principalship, school organization and teaching, all of which have strongly influenced current perceptions of schooling.

In their concern to be good teachers and administrators, therefore, and in the face of a range of problems in day-to-day schooling (including problems of discipline and control, assessment, the allocation of time and space, diverse abilities and attitudes of pupils, pressure from administrators and parents) teachers and administrators are likely to 'do their jobs' in ways that largely ignore the social and cultural aspects of education in favour of 'practical' concerns. This point connects with the second major criticism of the new leadership literature — its underdeveloped sense of the broader social and ideological context within which leadership, organizations and education must be interpreted.

The Social and Ideological Context of Leadership

The important point here is that leadership is not only contingent upon the particular context in which superior-subordinate relationships are continually being negotiated and renegotiated, but also, and in terms of the argument of this chapter more importantly, leaders and others operate within a broader social, cultural and political context which influences the nature of choices available to them. Yet the general approaches to leadership that are currently influential in educational administration seem to neglect both the complexity of teacher and administrator roles and the context in which they work.

From this point of view the most startling weakness of human relations theories, and current approaches to controlled participation and purposeful leadership in education which are consistent with human relations, is that, in keeping with the functionalist perspective from which they have only rhetorically and not substantively departed, they assume rather than demonstrate the harmony and functionality of education within the social system. Conversely, these theories underplay both instability and disorder (Tinker, 1986, p.376). Conflict is generally regarded as dysfunctional and must be controlled or channelled towards creative ends. While the existence of conflict is at least recognized, such conflict 'may be intra-individual, intragroup and intergroup; but it is never social structural' (Tinker, 1986, p.377).

The Complexity of School Relationships

Even in terms of the local context of schools the complex and somewhat contradictory nature of education and teaching needs to be emphasized. Teachers are more than biddable, servile, altruistic individuals who are amenable to being either directed or led. Indeed, any close direction or interference in the work of professional employees such as teachers is likely to cause conflict and possibly industrial action (Blackmore and Spaull, 1986; Sorenson and Sorenson, 1974). School organization is a contested and uncertain process in which teachers and administrators variously struggle with, support or ignore each other. Conflicts are played out as various personal, industrial and educational issues such as conceptions of appropriate schooling, subject affiliations, union membership, gender, age and ideology influence various forms of group affiliation and identity (Angus, 1988; Ball, 1986; Connell, 1985).

Most approaches to leadership do not fully appreciate this complexity, because they present leadership and school organization essentially in terms of interpersonal relationships within a general value consensus in which stability is the natural order of things such that goals may feasibly be shared and unproblematic. In schools individual teachers are expected to respond to the particular vision of the principal. Such an individualistic perspective overlooks the prevailing and enduring

79

structure of schooling which bears down upon all school participants in manifold ways to shape and limit their possibilities for action (Britzman, 1986). Moreover, this perspective accounts for the success or otherwise of schools and school reforms in terms of the motivation, enthusiasm and visionary appeal of individual teachers and administrators, who are deemed to be individually responsible for their inclination and capacity to engage in new and valued practices. Such an exaggeration of the notion of individual responsibility for school outcomes cloaks the nature of social relationships that are embedded in school structure.

This is consistent in one way with the predominant liberal reformist strategy in education which for several decades has stressed objective and technical means of school improvement that accord with the principle of meritocracy. Yet any number of scholars working within various conflict perspectives have demonstrated that apparently neutral school practices, which have usually been regarded as fair, open and meritocratic, contribute to the reproduction of existing social and economic arrangements (e.g., Grace, 1985; Bowles and Gintis, 1976; Bourdieu and Passeron, 1977).

The most interesting thing about the liberal reform programme, however, is that while the principle of meritocracy remained its cornerstone, its most pressing concern was with the amelioration of disadvantage which was seen to hinder the chances of children from particular groups of being able to compete on equal footing with their more socially advantaged peers (Angus, 1986a). It is this aspect of liberalism that seems to have particularly suffered in the current press for tighter, more efficient leadership and effective schools that has been a marked feature of recent educational reports (Angus, 1986b), such as the *Report of the Quality of Education Review Committee* (1985), *A Nation at Risk* (National Commission on Excellence in Education, 1983) and *The Organisation and Administration of the Schools Division* (Ministry of Education, 1987). While speaking particularly of Britain, Broadfoot outlines the situation that is broadly applicable to the Western democracies:

> The creeping tide of economic recession which brought in its wake the twin spectres of monetarism and structural youth unemployment effectively obliterated the liberal, sixties concern with improving the quality of educational content as such and replaced it with much more instrumentally-inspired policies, heavily vocational in focus and aimed at fostering what was conceived as almost an umbilical cord between school and work. . . . From its pre-eminent position as the inspiration of most of

the major post-war educational reforms, the issue of social inequality and educational opportunity no longer appears as an overt concern on the policy agenda. (Broadfoot, 1986, p.207)

Education is seen as the performance of teaching tasks as efficiently as possible within the constraints of a given structure. This approach is typified by the publication in the United States of the extremely popular and influential *What Works: Research about Teaching and Learning* (United States Department of Education, 1986), a booklet which purports to offer to teachers and administrators sure-fire strategies for teaching success that have been confirmed by educational researchers. The booklet confidently asserts that strong instructional leadership is one of the most important requirements for effective schools.

Education and Inequality

This is not to say that the current push for school leadership and school effectiveness ignores totally issues of social justice. Indeed, it is important to recall that the early research on school effectiveness in Britain and in the United States was directed towards identifying school-level practices that were associated with improved student learning in schools in areas of social disadvantage (Rutter *et al.*, 1979; Edmonds, 1979). While there were problems with this early work in terms of its conception of equity (Ashenden, 1981), there are now serious and growing concerns that the effect of current reforms which emphasize accountability, effectiveness and excellence is unlikely to promote social justice (Apple, 1986; Shapiro, 1986; Broadfoot, 1986). Given the emphasis in the American reforms on standardized achievement tests that are used as 'the absolute authority for promotion, graduation, admission and evaluation', argue Yeakey and Johnston, 'We cannot take comfort in the old myth that only ability matters in our highly competitive achievement-oriented society, for the very high correlation between achievement and family income remains unaltered' (1985, p.162). While the language of school effectiveness is replete with enthusiastic references to effective leadership, instructional supervision, time on task, direct instruction, monitoring of teacher and student performance and the like, it does not address educational issues and concepts such as the hidden curriculum which, as Yeakey and Johnston point out, is uncritically and unknowingly moved 'to center stage' (1985, p.167).

The tendency of the work on effective schools to ignore the historic association between education and inequality is illustrated by the way in which, as Ashenden points out in relation to the early research of Rutter *et al.*, 'The complex task of analysing social and historical processes is collapsed into picking and choosing from a shopping list of "variables" and "factors". . . . The book has no way of understanding the school as a political and cultural system, or of tracing its powerful and complex relations with the political and cultural system beyond' (1981, p.100). This approach lacks not only theoretical sophistication but also a sense of reality in that there is no appreciation of '"the school" as real people, pushing and shoving, feeling, shaping and forming, being shaped and formed. There is little sensitivity to the way people treat each other, of their common needs, problems and experiences, of their differences and conflicts and the way these are handled' (Ashenden, 1981, p.100). Pupils and teachers are largely reduced to abstractions, with a clear expectation that teachers occupy a limited role in conceptualizing what education could be. The essentially functionalist assumptions that are inherent in such a conception amount to a bias in favour of the status quo and a disregard for political and power differentials in both schools and society.

Education and Power

Inequality in power relationships in education also tends to be disguised by the rhetoric of new leadership, for it assumes that opportunities for participation are offered in an education structure which is legitimate and neutral, and free from power. That is, the moral legitimacy of education's formal structures is taken as given, and followers are invited to contribute to educational governance within the accepted paradigm. In keeping with the distinction between power and authority that is derived from a particular reading of Weber (1947), power is thought to be exerted only when officials or properly elected representatives attempt to exceed their legitimate authority. Maintaining the agreed rules and given structure is an exercise of proper authority. Forcing through changes involves power.

As Clegg and Dunkerley (1980, p.436) point out, this artificial distinction between legitimate authority and self-interested power has the important effect of taking for granted, as legitimate and appropriate, the prior and possibly inequitable arrangements within which leadership and followership are exercised. Power is apparent only when conflict arises within these arrangements. But as Lukes' perceptive analysis of power makes clear, 'the most effective and insidious use of power is to prevent such conflict arising in the first place' (Lukes, 1974, p.23). Conflict is contained as power is subtly and invisibly exercised through systematic biases that are 'not sustained simply by a series of individually chosen acts, but also, more importantly, by the socially structured and culturally determined patterned behaviour of groups and practices of institutions' (Lukes, 1974, pp.21-2).

Organization members need not be aware when their interests are not being served because, although their formal participation may give them the authority to intervene, the effect of this subtle power is to 'prevent people, to whatever degree, from having grievances by shaping their perceptions, cognitions and preferences in such a way that they accept their role in the existing order of things, either because they can see or imagine no alternative to it, or because they see it as natural and unchangeable' (Lukes, 1974, p.24). This notion of power, as being institutionalized in existing relationships and organizational arrangements, helps us to understand power as a conserving and stabilizing force, as a way of maintaining unequal relationships, despite increased participation, because of 'the inherence of power in certain institutions regardless of anyone's actively choosing or directing them' (Burbules, 1986, p.96).

It is this conserving use of power that is ignored in the new leadership and school effectiveness literature. Although the cooperation of diverse participants is to be invited by transformative, purposing or visionary leadership, the participation is to be shaped quite blatantly in this perspective by the larger-than-life leader. But the influence upon participation of the ideological context and background power relationships, within which such channelled participation is invited, is generally overlooked.

At a quite fundamental level, in all realms of social life including education, people have always participated in shaping the conditions, structures, organizations, rules and agreements that shape their lives (Giddens, 1984). But, because in many situations participants may have a limited awareness of, or limited opportunities to exert, their agency, participation may be of an utmost minimal kind. It may take the form merely of passive consent. It is important to realize, as Srivastva and Cooperrider correctly point out, 'People participate in the construction of social reality even through the act of "non-participation". "Non-participation" itself must be recognised as a form of participation' (1986, p.685). The important point here in relation to new models of leadership is whether the form and nature of the involvement in schooling that already existed for various participants, including teachers, administrators, students and the public, has substantially altered and had substantial effects on education. It is likely that such change will be limited because of a number of ideological and structural factors which hinder rather than facilitate new forms and levels of understanding and involvement.

The way people participate in education has been influenced by prevailing structures and the associated pattern of power relationships. Despite a rhetoric of reform, these are sustained in often subtle ways that involve the culturally and historically constituted dispositions of particular groups. Amongst the strongest of these are institutionalized expectations about the nature of education and educational administration, and the entrenched roles of education participants. Because of such widely shared, historical understandings, participants in educational governance tend to shape themselves to fit the pattern of established, neutrally defined role positions. There is a fairly common set of expectations, therefore, of people who occupy the roles of pupil, teacher, parent, principal, school administrator and so on.

The context in which educational reform is promoted in the new leadership and school effectiveness literature is confined and pragmatic. Schools remain detached from politics and economics, and from historical changes in the social context. Reforms, in keeping with generalized conceptions of good and effective schooling, are seen as something to be applied to schools to make them fit more closely with the expectations of an anxious public, or better to fit students to take their places in society without any critical appraisal of the appropriateness of that matching or of that society.

Leadership and the Possibility of Educational Reform

Substantial educational reform requires that school participants penetrate the level of immediacy of everyday actions and consider the practices of schooling in relation to the social, cultural, political and economic context of education. Otherwise, reforms that rely on a renovated notion of leadership, or the type of prescription inherent in models of school effectiveness, can be characterized as 'dynamically conservative' rather than 'reformist' in Linblad's (Wallin, 1985) terms. That is, because '"reforms" entail a change in the goals and basic values underlying school activities, ANY STRUCTURE OF CHANGE THAT DOES NOT TAKE THESE GOALS AND VALUES INTO ACCOUNT HAS A FUNDAMENTALLY WRONG APPROACH' (Wallin, 1985, p.344). Established and taken-for-granted goals and values are unlikely to be confronted within the current press for leadership and school effectiveness because its advocates, despite the limited insights that they provide into the nature of schooling and educational administration, generally propose these from the perspective of administrators. Administrators are to be 'leaders' whose role is still to manage the various interests that impinge upon schools, but to do this in a way that is detached from politics and ideology. It is a view of administration that fails to see any connections between the administrator (or schooling) and inequalities of power within both the education sphere and the broader social context.

The type of change that is likely to emerge from this perspective, despite strong, purposeful, educative leadership, will occur largely within what Kallos and Lundgren (1979) call 'proximal frames' — within the constraints of day-to-day, practical understandings, knowledge and expectations of the nature of schools, teaching and administration. This is particularly the case with much of the school effectiveness literature which still sees school leadership as part of a largely unproblematic top-down bureaucratic structure.

Recent research on school leadership within this literature posits an interventionist role for principals and other officials in securing particular reforms at the school level (Murphy et al., 1985; Edmonds, 1979; Peterson et al., 1987; Murphy et al., 1986). But, while it is particularly important to search for school-level solutions to educational problems, this approach is limited by its narrow emphasis on improvement of test scores and by its orientation towards linear educational change involving the close supervision of lower-order participants and of the process and product of education (e.g., Peterson et al., 1987). Such controlled change, and the reliance upon the inspiration and strength of leaders, is unlikely to penetrate the 'higher order frames' (Kallos and Lundgren, 1979). These are 'distal' frames which constrain action and change in schools, and which emanate from the framework of decisions of an apparently neutral educational bureaucracy; one which is actually located within a political and ideological context of which the education 'system' is a part (Smith, 1985).

The tendency to attend to the immediate rather than the broader social context of schooling raises one of the inherent dilemmas encountered by educational reformers who have attempted to grapple with issues of equity (Berlak and Berlak, 1981; Rizvi and Kemmis, 1988). As Rizvi and Kemmis explain in relation to a series of reform attempts in Australia, educationalists have begun to realize that

> reforms within schools cannot alone produce transformations in the distribution of inequalities in Australian society, that schools do, however, play a part in the production and reproduction of inequalities and therefore must change if they are to contribute to transforming the distribution of social inequalities, and there

> must be changes outside schools if the contemporary inequalities
> of Australian society are to be overcome. (1988, p.223).

Therefore, while the greatest opportunities for educational reform may be identified at the school level, an appreciation of the school's social and political context requires that our notions of both leadership and educational change be reformulated to accommodate powerful barriers to reform in the thinking and practices of administrators and teachers. These include traditional notions of hierarchical leadership, and of the roles of administrators and teachers which, along with entrenched organizational paradigms and the pervasiveness of bureaucratic rationality in largely taken-for-granted assumptions about educational administration, allow school participants to regard pressing educational problems as 'system' problems to be accommodated within proximal frames.

If leadership is to contribute to educational reform that goes beyond offering more of the same in disguise, it will be necessary to conceive of school leadership as something other than part of a top-down hierarchy. Leaders are not necessarily those in 'positions of leadership', and people may exercise leadership or perform an act of leadership on some occasions but not on others. From a broad social and political perspective an act of leadership would be one that was influential or potentially influential, and which contained a degree of penetration or potential penetration of the broader social and political context so that some aspect of education might be seen more clearly within that context. The type of leadership suggested here is one that celebrates human agency (Giddens, 1981, 1984) and the possibility of participants in education having a sense of control over the practices and 'rules' of education. Education would become better understood within 'distal' a well as 'proximal' frames (Kallos and Lundgren, 1979), as knowing participants would make connections between their everyday actions and the organizational and social structures that both shape and are shaped by human agency.

The connection between leadership and agency is important in two ways. Firstly, the exercise of agency in the face of taken-for-granted assumptions and expectations about education, power relationships and patterns of operation is itself a significant act of leadership. Secondly, those who hold administrative positions would need to realize that their best contribution to educational reform may be to use the authority of their position to facilitate the exercise of agency of those on their staff who, for one reason or another, have begun to examine critically, and engage in dialogue about, educational issues and educational purposes so that they are rendered problematic and subjected to scrutiny. Such administrators would feel less need to defend their own expertise, and would be prepared instead to canvass considered input from all quarters in open discourse in which the aim would be to assist all participants — teachers, parents, administrators and others — to regain power over their lives and their schooling processes. Power and leadership would then necessarily be more free-floating and could be appropriated by any participants as they exercise their human agency in self-determining ways to challenge the entrenched orthodoxy.

It is important, however, that the difficulties of bringing about fundamental change in schools are not underestimated. Much more work needs to be done on conceptualizing ways in which a reconstructed understanding of leadership might suggest new possibilities for educational reform. Individual dissatisfaction with and penetration of conventional expectations of schooling must be regarded as 'only an initial condition for the realization of the existing alternative social possibilities' (Wexler, 1982, p.176). This is not necessarily a pessimistic position regarding educational and social change, as current examples of dissatisfaction and resistance, while they do not constitute a collective reform movement, do indicate a potential for organizational transformation. Hence, although relatively stable meanings and understandings have become largely taken-for-granted in schools as particular organizational and social structures have become institutionalized, these have been sustained by the creative actions and interpretations of school participants. The apparent permanence and stability of such structures should therefore be regarded as illusory as they are open to continual transformation and re-creation by organizational actors.

It is through the dialectic of human agency and social structure that relations of cooperation, consent or coercion are actively constructed, and institutional understandings of what may be treated as problematic are shaped. Equally importantly, the capacity to exert human agency and engage in communicative interaction can lead to individual leadership acts being translated into collective rather than individual responses to pressing educational problems. School leaders, including principals, would seek to break from the bureaucratic rationality that encourages uncritical acceptance of established norms of organizational behaviour. Within this perspective, power and authority would be regarded as reciprocal, relational concepts. This allows recognition of the wide web of social and political relationships in which individuals and organizations are located, but also recognizes that some have power in such relationships because they are empowered by others. Such a recognition further implies that, despite the apparent resilience of entrenched relationships, reform can be asserted from below by participants.

There is much that teachers and administrators can do to make schools more humanitarian, equitable, educative and socially critical institutions. However, any discussion of the possibilities of school reform needs to be aware of the complexities of school practices and of the web of ideological, economic and social relationships of which teachers and schools are a part. This suggests that much more attention needs to be given to the constraints, ideological and otherwise, upon teachers and administrators in their workplaces. For members of school communities can exercise their own creative human agency in ways that both support and undermine conventional definitions of school reality. The critical movement from critique to change may come when it becomes clear to participants that current social and educational arrangements, and the relationships between schooling and society, are neither neutral nor natural.

None of this is to deny that there are massive external constraints upon what even the most perceptive and creative teachers and administrators can do in devising and implementing substantial reforms in a society in which hierarchy and inequality appear to be institutionalized. But the emergence of collective reform efforts at the school level is more feasible if there is facilitative educational leadership in which many school participants have access to forms of self-determining power within a context of participative democracy. Such an approach can be theoretically understood from the dialectical perspective offered by Giddens (1981, 1984; see also the chapters by Foster and Watkins in this volume). This would see educational reform as an ongoing process that is both enabled and constrained by organizational and social structures and also by conceptions of leadership and agency.

References

Age, The (1988) 'Elliot, MP, still an option if Liberals lose,' 23 February, p.1.
Age Saturday Extra, The (1988) 'The year of lying dangerously,' 27 February, p.7.
Allison, D. (1983) 'The principal: Prince, pawn or prima donna?' *The Yellow Papers* (OISE), 3,1, pp.18-23.
Angus, L. (1986a) *Schooling for Social Order: Democracy, Equality and Social Mobility in Australian Society,* Geelong, Deakin University Press.
Angus, L. (1986b) *Schooling, the School Effectiveness Movement, and Educational Reform,* Geelong, Deakin University Press.
Angus, L. (1988) *Continuity and Change in Catholic Schooling: An Ethnography of a Christian Brothers College in Australian Society,* Lewes, Falmer Press.
Apple, M. (1986) 'National reports and the construction of inequality,' *British Journal of Sociology of Education,* 7,2, pp.171-90.

Ashenden, D. (1981) 'Fifteen thousand facts,' in Course Team EED 433, *Management of Resources in Schools, Reader 1,* Geelong, Deakin University Press.

Ball, S. (1986) *The Micro-politics of Schooling,* London, Methuen.

Bass, B. (1981) *Stogdill's Handbook on Leadership: A Survey of Theory and Research,* New York, Free Press.

Bates, R. (1987) 'Corporate culture, schooling, and educational administration,' *Educational Administration Quarterly,* 23,4, pp.79-115.

Bennis, W. and Nanus, B. (1985) *Leaders: The Strategies for Taking Charge,* New York, Harper and Row.

Berlak, H. and Berlak, A. (1981) *Dilemmas of Schooling: Teaching and Social Change,* London, Methuen.

Blackmore, J. and Spaull, A. (1986) 'Australian teacher unionism: New directions,' Unpublished manuscript, Monash University.

Bourdieu, P. and Passeron, J. (1977) *Reproduction in Education, Society and Culture,* London, Sage.

Bowles, S. and Gintis, H. (1976) *Schooling in Capitalist America,* London, Routledge and Kegan Paul.

Brandt, R. (1982) 'Overview: The new catechism for school effectiveness,' *Educational Leadership,* 40, p.3.

Braverman, H. (1974) *Labour and Monopoly Capital,* New York, Monthly Review Press.

Britzman, D. (1986) 'Cultural myths in the making of a teacher: Biography and social structure in teacher education,' *Harvard Educational Review,* 56,4, pp.442-56.

Broadfoot, P. (1986) 'Assessment policy and inequality: The United Kingdom experience,' *British Journal of Sociology of Education,* 7,2, pp.205-24.

Burbules, N. (1986) 'A theory of power in education,' *Educational Theory,* 36, pp.95-114.

Burns, J. (1978) *Leadership,* New York, Harper and Row.

Burrell, G. and Morgan, G. (1979) *Sociological Paradigms and Organizational Analysis,* London, Heinemann.

Callahan, R. (1962) *Education and the Cult of Efficiency,* Chicago, Ill., University of Chicago Press.

Cameron, K. (1986) 'Effectiveness as a paradox: Consensus and conflict in conceptions of organizational effectiveness,' *Management Science,* 32.

Clegg, S. and Dunkerley, D. (1980) *Organization, Class and Control,* London, Routledge and Kegan Paul.

Clegg, S. and Higgins, W. (1987) 'Against the current: Organizational sociology and socialism,' *Organization Studies,* 8,3, p.201-22.

Connell, R. (1985) *Teachers' Work,* Sydney, George Allen and Unwin.

Cuban, L. (1984) 'Transforming the frog into a prince: Effective schools research, policy, and practice at the district level, *Harvard Educational Review,* 54,2, pp.129-51.

Deal, T. and Kennedy, A. (1982) *Corporate Cultures: The Rites and Rituals of Corporate Life,* Reading, Mass., Addison-Wesley.

Denton, P. (1986) *Elliott: A Biography of John D. Elliott,* Sydney, Little Hills Press.

Duignan, P. (1985) 'Near enough is not good enough: Developing a culture of high expectations in schools,' *Studies in Educational Administration,* 37.

Duignan, P. (1986) 'Research on effective schooling: Some implications for school improvement, *Journal of Educational Administration*, 23,1, pp.54-73.

Duignan, P. and Macpherson, R. (1987) 'The educative leadership project,' *Educational Management and Administration*, 15, pp.49-62.

Dunlap, D. (1985) 'New ideas for school improvement,' *OSSC Report*, 23,3.

Edmonds, R. (1979) 'Effective schools for the urban poor,' *Educational Leadership*, 37.

Giddens, A. (1981) *A Contemporary Critique of Historical Materialism*, London, Macmillan.

Giddens, A. (1984) *The Constitution of Society*, Cambridge, Mass., Polity Press.

Glasman, N. (1984) 'Student achievement and the school principal,' *Educational Evaluation and Policy Analysis*, 6, pp.283-96.

Grace, G. (1985) 'Judging teachers: The social and political contexts of teacher evaluation,' *British Journal of Sociology of Education*, 6,1, pp.3-16.

Griffin, R., Skivington, K. and Moorhead, G. (1987) 'Symbolic and interactional perspectives on leadership: An integrative framework,' *Human Relations*, 40,4, pp.199-218.

Gunn, J., Holdaway, E. and Johnson, N. (1988) 'The power of principals,' *The Canadian Administrator*, 27,4.

Habermas, J. (1975) *Legitimation Crisis*, London, Heinemann.

Herzberg, F. (1972) *Work and the Nature of Man*, London, Staples Press.

Iacocca, L. (with W. Novak) (1984) *Iacocca: An Autobiography*, New York, Bantam Books.

Johnston, B. (1985) 'Organizational structure and ideology in schooling,' *Educational Theory*, 35, pp.333-43.

Kallos, D. and Lundgren, U. (1979) 'The study of curriculum as a pedagogical problem,' in *Curriculum as a Pedagogical Problem*, Stockholm, GWK Gleerup.

Kent, C., Sexton, D. and Vesper, K. (Eds) (1980) *New Ventures Strategies*, Englewood Cliffs, N.J., Prentice-Hall.

Kotter, J. (1982) *The General Managers*, New York, Free Press.

Knights, D. and Roberts, J. (1982) 'The power of organization or the organization of power,' *Organization Studies*, 3,1, pp.47-63.

Likert, R. (1976) *The Human Organization*, New York, McGraw-Hill.

Lukes, S. (1974) *Power: A Radical View*, London, Macmillan.

McGregor, D. (1966) *Leadership and Motivation*, Cambridge, Mass., MIT Press.

MacIntyre, A. (1981) *After Virtue*, London, Duckworth.

Mintzberg, H. (1973) *The Nature of Managerial Work*, New York, Harper and Row.

Ministry of Education, Victoria (1987) *The Structure and Organisation of the Schools Division*, Melbourne, Government Printer.

Mitchell, T. and Scott, W. (1987) 'Leadership failures, the distrusting public, and prospects of the administrative state,' *Public Administration Review*, November/December, pp.445-52.

Murphy, J., Hallinger, P. and Mesa, R. (1985) 'School effectiveness: Checking progress and assumptions and developing a role for state and federal government,' *Teachers College Record*, 86, pp.615-41.

Murphy, J., Peterson, K. and Hallinger, P. (1986) 'The administrative control of principals in effective school districts: The supervision and evaluation functions,' *The Urban Review*, 18,3, pp.149-75.

National Commission on Excellence in Education (1983) *A Nation at Risk,* Washington, D.C., US Government Printing Office.

Peters, L., Hartke, D. and Pohlman, J. (1985) 'Fiedler's contingency theory of leadership: An application of the meta-analysis procedures of Schmidt and Hunter,' *Psychological Bulletin,* 79, pp.274-85.

Peters, T. and Waterman, R. (1982) *In Search of Excellence,* New York, Harper and Row.

Peterson, K., Murphy, J. and Hallinger, P. (1987) 'Superintendents' perceptions of the control and coordination of the technical core in effective school districts,' *Educational Administration Quarterly,* 23,1, pp.79-95.

Pfeffer, J. (1981) 'Management as symbolic action: The creation and maintenance of organizational paradigms,' in L. Cummings and B. Staw (Eds), *Research in Organizational Behaviour,* Vol.3, Greenwich, Conn., JAI Press.

Pullan, R. (1986) *Bob Ansett: An Autobiography with Robert Pullan,* Melbourne, John Kerr.

Purkey, S. and Smith, M. (1983) 'Effective schools: A review,' *Elementary School Journal,* 83, pp.335-51.

Quality of Education Review Committee (1985) *Quality of Education in Australia,* Canberra, Australian Government Printing Service.

Ramos, A. (1981) *The New Science of Organization,* Toronto, University of Toronto Press.

Rizvi, F. and Kemmis, S. (1988) *Dilemmas of Reform,* Geelong, Deakin Institute for Studies in Education.

Rutter, M. *et al.* (1979) *Fifteen Thousand Hours,* Cambridge, Mass., Harvard University Press.

Schein, E. (1984) 'Coming to a new awareness of organizational culture,' *Sloan Management Review,* Winter, pp.3-16.

Seddon, T. and Connell, R. (1987) 'Teachers' work,' in T. Postlethwaite and T. Husen (Eds), *The International Encyclopedia of Education Supplement,* New York, Pergamon Press.

Sergiovanni, T. (1987) 'Leadership for quality schooling: New understandings and practices,' paper prepared for the Southwestern Bell Conference, "Restructuring Schooling for Quality Education: A New Reform Agenda", Trinity University, Texas, 18-21 August.

Shapiro, S. (1986) 'Education, the welfare state and Reaganomics: The limits of conservative reform,' *Urban Education,* 20,4, pp.443-71.

Simon, R. (1987) 'Empowerment as a pedagogy of possibility,' *Language Arts,* 64,4, pp.370-82.

Smith, L., Prunty, J. Dwyer, D. and Klein, P. (1987) *The Kensington Trilogy,* Lewes, Falmer Press.

Smith, R. (1985) 'The policy of education change by changing teachers: Comments on the "democratic curriculum",' *Australian Journal of Education,* 29,2, pp.141-9.

Sorenson, J. and Sorenson, T. (1974) 'The conflict of professionals in bureaucratic organizations,' *Administrative Science Quarterly,* 19, pp.98-106.

Srivastva, S. and Cooperrider, D. (1986) 'The emergence of the egalitarian organization,' *Human Relations,* 39, pp.290-301.

Starratt, R. (1986) 'Excellence in education and quality of leadership,' Occasional Paper No. 11, Geelong, Institute of Educational Administration.

Stogdill, R. (1974) *Handbook of Leadership: A Survey of Theory and Research,* New York, Free Press.

Tinker, T. (1986) 'Metaphor or reification: Are liberal humanists really libertarian anarchists?' *Journal of Management Studies,* 23,4, pp.363-83.

US Department of Education (1986) *What Works: Research about Teaching and Learning,* Washington, D.C., US Government Printing Office.

Vaill, P. (1984) 'The purposing of high performing systems,' in T. Sergiovanni and J. Corbally (Eds), *Leadership and Organizational Culture,* Urbana, Ill., University of Illinois Press.

Wallin, E. (1985) 'To change a school: Experiences from local development work,' *Journal of Curriculum Studies,* 17,3, pp.321-50.

Weber, M. (1947) *The Theory of Social and Economic Organization,* London, Routledge and Kegan Paul.

Weick, K. (1976) 'Educational organizations as loosely coupled systems,' *Administrative Science Quarterly,* 21,1, pp.1-19.

Weick, K. (1986) 'The concept of loose coupling: An assessment,' *Organizational Theory Dialogue,* December, pp.8-11.

Weiler, H. (1983) 'Legalization, expertise and participation: Strategies of compensatory legitimation in educational policy,' *Comparative Education Review,* 27,2, pp.259-77.

Wexler, P. (1982) 'Body and soul: Sources of social change and strategies of education,' *Journal of Curriculum Theorizing,* 4,12, pp.166-80.

Wood, S. (1985) 'Work organization,' in R. Deem and G. Salaman (Eds), *Work, Culture and Society,* Milton Keynes, Open University Press.

Yeakey, C. and Johnston, G. (1985) 'High school reform: A critique and a broader construct of social reality,' *Education and Urban Society,* 17,2, pp.157-70.

Zirkel, P. and Greenwood, S. (1987) 'Effective schools and effective principals: Effective research?' *Teachers College Record,* 89,2, pp.255-67.

Chapter 4

Educational Leadership: A Feminist Critique and Reconstruction

Jill Blackmore

We now have fewer women heads of educational institutions than we had in the first two decades of this century. . . . When women move into male areas, they remain clustered at the lower levels, marginally represented at the middle levels and absent from the top other than the occasional deviant, nonconformist, articulate, pioneer. On a national scale there are fewer than 3% women heads of mixed institutions in education. (Byrne, quoted in Sampson, 1983, p. 52)

The structural barriers can be seen in the cultivation of young male teachers in appropriate administrative and organisational tasks, while in the first five years of teaching, many women teachers concentrate on child centred tasks. In this way, authority in schools becomes linked with masculinity and leadership in education takes on a masculine image. (Sampson, 1983)

This chapter constitutes a marking out of territory which has significance for education and educational administration. Leadership is a concept central to theories of how organizations such as schools and educational bureaucracies work since, historically, schools have been organized in hierarchical ways. Authority is seen to be legitimately accorded to the principal, generally a male. Increasingly the ways in which schooling and school knowledge are defined and organized have been contested. The implications of the gendered and hierarchical division of labour within education for pedagogy and organizational life have been recently theorized about and questioned (Connell, 1987; Apple, 1985). Similarly organizational theory, the source of many central concepts of educational administration, has only begun to be criticized for its gender-blindness (Hearn and Parkin, 1983). Emphasis in this criticism has been on the masculinist model which has been assumed to portray all experience. The assumption of the universality of the male experience has been the consequence of a privileging of positivist knowledge claims and research approaches. It is this positivist research paradigm which has informed the liberal interventionist policies of equal opportunity during the 1970s and early 1980s. Premised upon sex role socialization theory, such policies sought to facilitate individual women taking on 'leadership roles' in schools in order to create a more equitable gender balance, and in so doing establish role models for girls and other women as 'leaders'. But the reduction of women in such positions over this period suggests that the issue is more complex than merely a matter of numbers.

This paper argues that whilst the conceptualization of leadership in education is seen to be unproblematic, there is little hope for education becoming a site for emancipatory change. A particular view of leadership premised upon liberal theories of abstract individualism and bureaucratic rationality, and supported by positivistic theories of knowledge which privilege universal laws of administration and human behaviour, has become dominant in educational administration. The universal individual central to this perspective of leadership is modelled upon men's experience. Hierarchical relationships are considered to be the 'givens' of 'rational' organizational life. Leaders display attributes and behaviours, possess moral virtues and principles, which are generally associated with 'masculinity'. It is a view which has effectively displaced women in educational thought, and therefore rendered women invisible in administrative practice (Martin, 1984). Currently it is epitomized in the view of school principals as corporate managers.

It is necessary, therefore, to reconstruct a view of leadership which counters the emphasis on individualism, hierarchical relationships, bureaucratic rationality and abstract moral principles. I propose, therefore, elements of what would constitute a feminist reconstruction of the concept of leadership. These would include a view of power which is multi-dimensional and multi-directional. Leadership is seen as being practised in different contexts by different people and not merely equated to formal roles. Leadership looks to empower others rather than have power over others. Such a view assumes a relational view of morality in which moral practice is rational within given contexts and social and political relations and not according to abstract moral laws or principles. Leadership is concerned with communitarian and collective activities and values. Thus the process of leading is both educative and conducive to democratic process, and, one would hope, consistent with education.

Problems and Explanations: The Liberal Interventionist Approach

During the last fifteen years federal and state governments have introduced affirmative action and recognized the principle of equal opportunity through both legislative and policy initiatives. Despite this, the number of women in 'leadership positions' in education in Australia, Great Britain and the USA has decreased (Yeakey, Johnson and Adkinson, 1986). In the state of Victoria, Australia, in the period 1971-1983 the percentage of female principals in the secondary system fell from 20 to 11 per cent, whilst the percentage of female teachers increased from 45 to 52 per cent of all teachers. In the adjoining state of New South Wales the percentage of female primary principals decreased from 28 to 19 per cent of all principals (Sampson, 1987). This phenomenon can be partially explained as a consequence of the declining school population, the reclassification of staff appointments, and major educational and administrative restructuring in most state systems since the early 1980s. Opportunities for advancement in the promotional stakes are often reduced in a contracting system, particularly for latecomers, as many women are, to long-term careers. But economic conditions and structural impediments alone are inadequate explanations of another feature of what is a re-emerging pattern of masculine dominance. This second feature is the tendency for many women who have the qualifications, expertise and aptitude often not to apply for positions of leadership in schools as principals. Furthermore, those women who do apply indicate a 'preference' for more democratic styles of school organization and administration (State Board, 1986). This 'problem' is the focus of this chapter.

There are a number of conventional explanations which have dominated the social science research over the past two decades which suggest reasons for this 'failure' of women to possess those aspirations, behaviours and attributes for leadership so readily displayed by their male counterparts. Women, it would be construed from such research, 'fear' success and lack 'self-esteem', are passive and non-aggressive. These explanations, it will be shown later, imply a female 'deficiency' in terms of 'leadership' skills, attributes and vision. At this stage I wish to suggest that there will be little change in the historical dominance of males in educational administration whilst policy-makers and many liberal feminists merely look to increase the numbers of women in educational administration, in what I call the 'liberal interventionist' approach. It is necessary to 'go beyond the numbers game', in which gender equity is assumed to result purely from the better 'representation' of women in positions of authority, and to question the very concept of leadership itself, how it is portrayed in the literature, and how it is perceived by women and the community in education. It is the continuing association of masculinity with a particular view of leadership, especially in education where women constitute over half the occupation, which is problematic. How the particular notion of leadership dominant in educational administration has been socially and historically constructed in a way that connects so-called 'masculine' characteristics to leadership will be a theme of this paper. The deconstruction of this 'masculinist notion of leadership' will largely be at a theoretical and conceptual level, in laying out and displaying the assumptions underlying the dominant notion of leadership, although the policy ramifications will not be totally ignored.

Whilst I would argue that liberal feminism, in supporting this 'interventionist approach', has only achieved 'success' for the few, largely middle-class women by not challenging the norms, institutions and structures of masculine dominance in education, this is not to be dismissive of the achievements of liberal feminists during the past decades, or denigratory of liberal reforms as merely co-option of feminist discourse. It is necessary to record, analyze and account for the discrepancies, contradictions and failures of this period in order to create the basis for more radical change. Much of the valuable work on women in educational administration has mapped out the patterned discrimination against women, analyzed why and how it has been historically constructed and reproduced, indicating the structural, psychological and social factors influencing women's opportunities (Adkinson, 1981). Strategies have been developed and undeniably affirmative action policy has gone some way in removing the structural impediments in particular to the progression of women into 'leadership positions' (equating them at this stage with formal bureaucratic roles), whilst enforcing at least superficial change to the sexist attitudes pervading state controlled educational institutions. But it is necessary to go a step beyond having women 'represented' in administrative positions, and undertake a more radical critique from a feminist perspective of the very nature of educational administration and leadership.

Feminism as Critique

First, let me discuss my intentions in mounting a feminist critique. Although I talk of *a* feminist critique, it is necessary to remember that there is no single feminist theory, but rather a body of theories which take on different political hues ranging from liberal feminism to radical separatism. Furthermore, there is a high level of scepticism amongst some feminists about the need for theory at all because of the feminist emphasis on personal experience and understandable distrust of intellectualism. Some radical separatists urge that feminist theory must necessarily reject all that is masculine and set up a theoretical framework in opposition. I would reject both views in favour of the stance that all world views are theory-ridden. The issue is whether these theories are made explicit or not, and the level of theoretical generalization (Gatens, 1986, p.14). Nancy Hartsock expresses it well:

> We must understand that theorising is not just done by academic intellectuals but that theory is always implicit in our activity and goes so deep as to include our understanding of reality . . . we can either accept the categories given us by capitalist society or we can begin to develop a critical understanding of our world. If we choose the first alternative, our theory may forever remain implicit. In contrast, the second is to commit ourselves to working out a critical and explicit theory. (Hartsock, 1979, p.57)

It is necessary to critique the established social theories of politics, economics, philosophy and psychology in order to understand what, how and why the feminine perspective has been obliterated from social theory, and more specifically in this paper from what is construed to be 'leadership'. Barbara Johnson describes what such a critique would involve:

> It is an analysis that focuses on the grounds of that system's possibility. The critique reads backwards from what seems natural, obvious, self-evident, or universal, in order to show that these things have their history, their reasons for being the way they are, their effects on what follows from them, and that the starting point is not a (natural) given but a (cultural) construct, usually blind to itself. . . . Every theory starts somewhere; every critique exposes what that starting point conceals and therefore displaces all the ideas that follow from it. (Johnson, 1981, p.xii-xvi)

Such a critique raises epistemological, moral and political and not merely methodological questions. At the same time that social theory is reworked from a critical perspective, theory can act, in the Foucauldian sense, as a working tool, a strategy through which to critique instances and historical moments intent on reconstruction rather than construction of an alternative theoretical perspective (Morris and Paton, 1979, p.57). In constructing a 'feminist critique' of leadership in education I will be undertaking a critical analysis of and reflection on how women have been displaced from or submerged in both organizational and political theory, and how much of this invisibility of women has permeated the everyday commonsense notions of 'leadership'.

Before commencing this critique, a further consideration must be acknowledged, although it will not be developed here. Problematic to both stating theory explicitly and critiquing social theory is the nature of language and text. Sarah Fildes asserts that the traditional invisibility of women in theory can be explained partially by the conceptual language and terminology which have implicit masculinist values and models which must be questioned (Fildes, 1983, p.62). The use of certain concepts often sets the agenda and boundaries of a discourse (whether in theory, practice or policy), which in turn determines the direction and force of the final analysis. An essential aspect of feminist theory and feminism, therefore, is to question all that is 'given', to question what is not included in the discourse as much as what is, and what has been reinterpreted in a manner which displaces women's interests. Such a questioning can often commence from the dissonance between personal experience, commonsense knowledge and theory. This is the position implicit in the liberal interventionist model, which assumes that if more women can and do become 'successful' leaders, then societal behaviour and attitudes will change when personal experience 'bumps up against' myths about females in leadership roles. As to whether the success of women such as Thatcher in the particular mode of leadership I will be critiquing — that which focuses upon hierarchy, authority, individualism and claims of rationality — is desirable for women is another matter. Similarly, in a period of rampant corporate managerialism in education, whilst the rhetoric centres on notions of efficiency, skill, hierarchy and control, leadership takes on particular forms and encourages particular approaches (Ministry of Education, 1986). In this sense discourse itself is a form of 'power over others', of masking conflict, of being deployed to reinforce consensus, of constraining action and prescribing behaviours. Power therefore infuses discourse. But discourse can be an instrument of either domination or emancipatory effort (Elshtain, 1982, pp.127-9). This particular point will be elaborated in the last section, in which new elements and parameters for an alternative feminist discourse on educational leadership are offered.

Therefore, essential to a critical feminist perspective of leadership is a critique of the central concepts in the bodies of theory which inform educational administration and which control the parameters of the discourse — concepts such as rationality, individuality, competence and merit. Such a critique undermines the gendered historical and social construction of the relationship between social structures which are construed to be 'given' and 'neutral', such as bureaucracies and organizations, and the individual. Secondly, it challenges the particular views about the nature of human activity and potentiality implicit in such theories. Finally, such a critique analyzes the particular epistemological underpinnings of theories of leadership. These aspects of social structure, human agency and epistemology are interrelated and mutually reinforcing, and will be dealt with accordingly.

The next section addresses the ways in which traditional views of leadership have dominated educational administration and how leaderhip has been socially and historically constructed in a manner which looks to characteristics of 'successful' masculine leaders as those constituting leadership. The following section attempts to develop a better understanding of how liberal political theory has encouraged this hegemonic masculinist view of leadership, which is premised upon particular interpretations of rationality, morality, organization and individualism, and is typical of Western societies. In turn, other social, economic and political arrangements such as the dominance of a positivistic epistemology in social science, together with the bureaucratization of social life have supported this particular leadership perspective. The 'liberal interventionist' approach underlying many equal opportunity policy initiatives is derived largely from within this tradition. Next the notions of individual competitiveness, bureaucratic rationality and abstract morality are discussed as central to the traditional, masculinist construct of leadership. Finally, an alternative feminist perspective of leadership will be presented; one that takes into account the historical and social construction of organizations and knowledge, and which presents a view of leadership which is essentially relational and communitarian.

Leadership in Organizational Theory: A Masculinist Construct

To return to the initial question, how has the underrepresentation of women in formal leadership positions been explained in the conventional literature on leadership? Women have been cast in organizational theory as being deficient in terms of leadership skills and attributes. Theories of leadership developing within a positivistic epistemology have relied upon empirical studies of those who are or have been in formal positions of leadership; that is, men. Historical accounts of 'great men' merely substantiate what is already seen to be self-evident. The behaviours, traits and characteristics displayed by men in formal positions of authority have become the 'givens' of leadership. Therefore, leadership in organizations has been historically associated with particular characteristics which are more frequently depicted as 'masculine' than 'feminine' — aggressiveness, forcefulness, competitiveness and independence. Positivistic social science in general, and organizational and administrative theory in particular, have construed that what is masculine experience is universal across time, context and gendered subject. Theoretical work on the social construction of sexuality, from both functionalist and feminist perspectives, has rarely been related to organizational processes or theory (Hearn and Parkin, 1983, p.231).

This 'masculinist' characterization of leadership is common across the main approaches to leadership in organizational theory, whether they be trait model, the charismatic/behavioural model or the situational/contingency models of leadership central to educational administration. (For examples of such theories in a standard text in educational administration see Hoy and Miskel, 1978. For a critique see Watkins, 1986, and Foster, this volume.) Whilst trait theory considers leadership qualities or skills to be inherent attributes of the individual, the behaviourist model allows appropriate leadership behaviours or styles to be learned. More recent situational/contingency theories tend to perceive a 'match' between the individual attributes or leadership styles (innate and learned) and particular situations or contexts.

Although the 'trait' theory model of leadership has been denigrated in organizational literature for its failure to differentiate between effective and ineffective male leaders, it has been duly resuscitated as an explanation for why women are not found in leadership positions. Given that the 'traits' associated with leadership have been defined and prescribed in a gendered stereotypic manner, women are in a double bind. If a woman displays the culturally defined traits of 'femininity' (being emotional, passive, dependent, nurturing, intuitive or submissive), she is perceived to be a 'poor' leader. If she acts according to the male role definition of a leader (being aggressive, achievement-oriented, self-confident, forceful or competitive), she is condemned as being 'unfeminine' (Chapman and Luthans, 1975). More specifically, the literature on women in management focuses on three sets of personality traits: aggressiveness/dominance, emotional control/sound judgment; self-confidence and self-esteem. Women's apparent lack of such 'traits' as perceived in their behaviour is seen to make them unsuited for leadership (Bannon, 1978; Brown, 1979).

Let us consider these 'myths' in more detail. Firstly, there is little empirical evidence to support the connection between certain 'traits' and good leadership. The literature is unable to substantiate the connection, for example, between aggressiveness and various 'management' skills seen to be essential to leaders in organizations and schools, such as tackling challenges, setting achievable goals, planning, organizing, persuading, conciliating and conveying enthusiasm. The second myth that women are unsuitable leaders and decision-makers because they are too emotional and subjective is equally unfounded, both theoretically and empirically. Theoretically it assumes that decision-making is rational, logical and objective, when increasingly the irrational, subjective and illogical nature of decision-making is the basis of current revisionist theorizing within the traditional organizational research paradigm. It is increasingly accepted that decision-making is value ridden and theory laden, ideologically prescribed, generally based on inadequate and even incorrect information and consequently emotive. Therefore the dominance of a particular 'scientistic' view of what leaders do when they make decisions (as being rational and objective) and what 'traits' are required to lead (non-emotional) cannot be upheld. Ironically, more recent studies of leadership, in an attempt to produce a more balanced conceptualization of leadership, look to these very 'feminine' qualities of emotionality, sociality and caring values which traditionally imparted connotations of weakness (Sergiovanni and Carver, 1980, pp.306-26). Likewise school principals are required to become facilitators, not dominators (Chapman, 1985).

The third myth, that leadership is associated with a high level of self-confidence and self-esteem, is again highly suspect. The literature portrays women as lacking these 'qualities', whether learned or innate. For example, Antill and Cunningham's Australian study, 'Self-esteem as a Function of Masculinity in Both Sexes', argues that men have higher self-esteem than women (Antill and Cunningham, 1979. For a critique of 'self-esteem' see Putnam and Heinen, 1976; Kenway and Willis, 1988). Since 1968 a dominant theory as to why women have not gained more representation in higher levels of decision-making is that of 'fear of success' (Horner, 1972; Condry and Dyer, 1976). This 'fear' explains why women are more 'anxious' than men in leadership positions and why they lack the desire to 'take on' leadership responsibilities. Women are seen to fear success because of the negative consequences which derive from succeeding in competitive situations — social rejection and perceived loss of femininity (Sassen, 1980). Or perhaps it was fear — more of being perceived as being deviant from role models by taking on masculine behaviours (Moore and Rickel, 1980; Greenfield *et al.*, 1980).

Ironically, studies which replicated the 'fear of success' model on male subjects found that men also admitted to the same fears (Carlson, 1972, p.21). More recently the 'fear of success' model has been reinterpreted to argue that women were not so afraid of 'success', just more prepared than the male subjects to admit to the negative or 'other side of competitive success' generally ignored in the literature — the alienation, loneliness and conflict (Carlson, 1972). The effect of this research was inevitably to blame the victim. Notions of success and esteem are socially constructed and context bound. The underlying theoretical paradigm, the trait approach to leadership, therefore emphasizes innate rather than learned psychological differences between males and females, ignores the ways in which certain behaviours are developed through experience and positive reinforcement, and portrays leadership as a set of individual characteristics without regard for how behaviour is both learned and situation specific.

Whilst the trait approach assumes innate difference, the behaviourist perspective accepts the notion of learned behaviours which are gender stereotypic. The political effect is the same as that of trait theory in justifying observed behaviours as proof of difference. There are particular sets of learned behaviours which are perceived as being appropriate leadership behaviours or styles. The dominant theory to explain the lack of women in administration and leadership positions is socialization and sex role stereotypes (Adkinson, 1981). This argues that gender differentiation is constructed by the internalization of certain gender role behaviours imparted through such agencies as schools, family, work and the media (see Marshall, 1979, for an example of the argument on the need to 'socialize' female educational administrators). Thus boys learn to be rational, logical, objective and to suppress their feelings. They are encouraged to be aggressive and dominant in social situations. Girls learn to cultivate their emotions at the expense of their rationality, and are therefore more subjective. Their role is to be more dependent, nurturing and passive. This prepares each sex entrance into the public and private spheres of life, since these were the attributes required in each domain respectively. By imparting such significance to socialization, the behaviourist model assumes the passivity of the individual male and female who are 'socialized' into particular roles. At the same time this behaviourist model 'allows' women to acquire the necessary attributes. But in so doing it casts women into a deficit position in that it blames the victim when 'socialization' does not occur; it ignores resistance or the notion that an individual's socialization is partial and selective. It implies the need and precondition for women to take on masculine attributes of leadership (rationality, aggression, the ability to control and dominate) in order to succeed; it accepts the hierarchical relationship in schools and state educational bureaucracies as necessary and given; and it defines success/relevant experience in male terms (occupation, hierarchy, expertise). Ultimately particular sets of observable behaviours are valued more than others.

Finally, the recent emphasis within the traditional organizational research paradigm has been on situational or contingency theories of leadership, best represented by the work of Vroom and Yetton, Blake and Mouton and Fiedler (see Fiedler, 1978; Hoy and Miskel, 1978, for a summary; for a critique see Watkins, 1986). These theories argue that there is a package of leadership skills and behaviours ranging from democratic to authoritarian which can be learned, selected and used according to particular definable situational factors and contexts. Leaders must acquire the skill to recognize, diagnose and select the appropriate style of leadership to 'fit' the situation. No specific leadership style is given preference or more valued because of its intrinsic good. Each 'style' is selected as a means to achieve a particular organizational end most efficiently. By implication, although the gender issue is never confronted in these models, such theories assume that leadership styles and administrative contexts are gender neutral, and that such skills are context and content-free to be freely applied across a variety of 'categorizable' organizational situations. That is, any individual can assume an appropriate style provided she or he possesses this baggage of leadership skills and is able to diagnose the situation correctly. Such models ignore research from within the positivistic research paradigm on small groups and organizations (Jenkins and Kramer, 1978). Regardless of the 'appropriateness' of leadership style adopted by females, female leaders are judged differently by their colleagues and subordinates from men in like situations. Firstly, their competence is judged according to whether the task itself is perceived to be 'masculine' or 'feminine'. Success by a female at a 'masculine' task (such as leadership) is more often attributed to luck than competence by observers, whereas success by a male at a masculine task is attributed largely to competence. By contrast, success by a female at a 'feminine' task is attributed equally to competence. Thus there is different recognition for similar performance. In other words, 'what is skill for a male is luck for the female' (Deaux and Emswiller, 1974; Bayes and Newton, 1978). Secondly, the legitimacy of an action is generally associated with the legitimacy of the actor who performs it and the role he or she occupies. Since leadership is perceived largely to be a masculine role, this gives some reason why within such research paradigms there is systematic variation between males and females in similar situations (Borman *et al.*, 1978; Walker and Fennel,

1986, pp.270-1). Even the definition of task and skill, merit and competence in work situations is an historical construction which is gender biased (McNeil, 1987; O'Donnell and Hall, 1988).

Such conclusions are not surprising given the nature of the empirical research upon which the traditional construct of leadership has been premised. Because such research has focused largely upon leaders in formal positions of organizational authority, on male occupations and the achievements of men, and within a psychologistic framework, inevitably leadership attributes are perceived to be masculine attributes (Sherif, 1979; Kellerman, 1984; Sayers, 1986). Accordingly findings about male behaviours are generalized to females. Furthermore, research on women in positions of leadership is largely confined to stereotypic areas of women's work. Even when research is in comparative fields, male characteristics are more highly valued than female characteristics in linking them to 'good' leadership. Women who enter male dominated careers are therefore seen to be stigmatized as they are seen to be 'disabled, deficient or deviant' (Marshall, 1985). In such contexts rationality is seen to be a better signifier of leadership than emotionality. Consequently there is a built-in male bias in the research methodology in its assumption of homogeneity and universality of experience (Stewart, 1978; Hearn and Parkin, 1983). But it is more than a matter of methodology, since underlying such methodologies is a set of epistemic assumptions which will be discussed later.

Finally, the research in support of the various organizational theories of leadership, and some could say the 'theory movement' in educational administration per se, is inconclusive. In this field of study Foster points out the state of disarray because leadership is a 'slippery concept' (Foster, 1986). What is not disputable is that organizational and leadership theory neglects the significance of gender. Rather, it discusses authority, power and the division of labour in organizations as being both essential and neutral. It fails to recognize that there exists a gendered division of labour in organizations which historically defines women's position in a negative manner. Such divisions are justified by notions of rationality, expertise and merit. Kanter refers to how the 'masculine ethic' of rationality is found in the image of managers and in the social science models of organizations in a manner which

> elevates the traits assumed to belong to men with educational advantages to necessities for effective organisations; a tough minded approach to problems; analytic abilities to abstract and plan; a capacity to set aside personal, emotional considerations in the interests of task accomplishment; and a cognitive superiority in problem solving. (Kanter, 1975, p.43)

Performance is judged in gender biased contexts. Burton cites research which suggests that the effort of women in organizations is 'perceived as diagnostic of men's ability and compensatory of women's lack thereof' (Burton, 1987, p.429). She suggests that 'definitions of what is meritorious can undergo change depending upon the power of particular groups to define it . . . skill is a direct correlate of the sex and power of those defining it, an ideological category rather than an economic fact' (Burton, 1987, p.430).

Likewise, success can be conceived in different ways, just as self-esteem is evident in ways other than a display of uncaring aggression, competitiveness or dominance in particular social situations. Because women may value different types of success and achievement, success and actions are interpreted in negative terms for women. The construction of success is elaborated upon by Markus.

> . . . in contemporary society the organisational and technical changes in work make it increasingly difficult, if not impossible, to evaluate individual achievement, but at the same time, the work organisations and society at large, are increasingly in need of maintaining the disciplinary and legitimising function of the achievement principle. This means, then, that the evaluation of 'performing capacity' has to be accomplished symbolically. That is, based on 'extrafunctional' attitudes and ascriptive criteria of different sorts rather than effective achievement . . . as Offe points out . . . the 'achievement principle' has been transformed from an ethical attitude into 'one of the important forms of class-based power-games that rewards loyalty to dominant interests and forms of life', perpetuated cultural divisions and legitimised the existing organisational and social hierarchies. (Markus, 1987, p.104)

The manner by which authority and power in organizations are perceived and exercised is significant for women in that many do not measure their 'success' by the same external or symbolic criteria. Markus' research on female engineers in managerial positions indicates how they formulated their notion of success as being basically private. Job satisfaction was connected to internalized concrete achievements gained through personal experience (overcoming some difficulties, maintaining double roles, helping others in their work) rather than external social recognition. It was a form of success she called 'vicarious achievement' — success resulting from the contribution of the subject to the achievement of some other person. This privatized conception of success in a public arena which rewarded outward achievement (formal status, position of authority) through uniformization of success standards is thus read as indicating that women lack motivation to succeed and has the ironical effect of maintaining the inequity of their work situation (Markus, 1987, pp.101-2). They are labelled for not 'planning their careers', or 'keeping their eyes open for the next step to promotion'. Markus indicates how this is seen to be a problem particular to women, 'given the observable switch in the basic hierarchical advance within different work organisations increasingly obtained not through internal promotions, but rather through external recruitment to higher positions', as in, one could argue, the case of local selection of school principals (Markus, 1987, p.105). Thus the cultural association of masculinity and authority, of maleness and management, is reproduced by those in power who do not wish to disturb this 'natural' arrangement. Authority in organizations is judged by external and overt symbolic signs of power such as salary, space and titles rather than 'complex staff positions that involve significant discretion' (Burton, 1987, p.431). Organizations, as are all workplaces, are socially constructed along gender lines (Acker and Van Houten, 1974).

Thus the social science model utilized in organizational theory assumes that organizations such as schools are value-free, and that the social organization of schooling is neutral. It also assumes that relatively complete explanations can be found about individual behaviours within the organizations themselves and in the public domain of paid work. Little consideration is given to the private domain of human activity and how it connects to organizational situations or paid work. This distinction between the public domain of the rational and the private domain of the emotional and affective is critical to ongoing power relations in that it allows the perpetuation of the invisibility of class or gender relations in organizations (Stewart, 1978; Shakeshaft and Hanson, 1986). Furthermore, any collective activities by women to alter the ways in which organizations are structured must challenge the masculine ethic of leadership premised upon individuality, rationality and hierarchy. It is this collectivity that sociologists have failed to identify (Hearn and Parkin, 1983, p.233).

It is therefore necessary to undermine the theoretical paradigm dominant in administrative theory, which assumes that conflict is pathological and a problem to be controlled by administrators. Whilst the notion that conflict is abnormal is legitimized by administrative theory, a feminist perspective will be marginalized, controlled or dismissed as irrelevant. O'Brien aptly comments, 'The central defects of the liberal social science is that they do not treat patriarchy as an essential component of exploitation but as an accidental aberration' (O'Brien,

1986, p.96). The next two sections look to the historical contexts from which the above ideas about leadership emerged, and the political and epistemological traditions which supported and informed such a perspective.

Liberalism, Bureaucratization and the Subordination of Women in Education

So far I have laid out some of the conceptual approaches towards leadership dominating traditional administrative and organizational theory, and since the 1950s the theory movement in educational administration. The last section has indicated how organizational theory has made women 'invisible' or 'deficient' as leaders. This section examines why the particular view of leadership portrayed in administrative literature has come to be considered applicable to education. It suggests that the social formation of bureaucracies (as in education) was informed by liberal political theories which conceived of a relationship between the individual and society in a way which influenced and promoted hierarchical and individualistic views of leadership, and in turn justified patriarchal dominance in education. This is not to argue that there is necessarily some causality between bureaucracy and liberal democratic or capitalist states, as Pateman points out in her analysis of the parallel bureaucratic formation in communist states (Pateman, 1970). Rather, it is to try and understand why in liberal democracies such a view of leadership has become dominant.

The displacement of women in organizational theory is derived from their invisibility in social and political theory in general. Thiele argues that social and political theory has practised three forms or typologies by which women have become invisible: exclusion, pseudo-inclusion and alienation. Exclusion exists, for example, when Hobbes, in discussing his initial State of Nature, states that all men and women were equal, that women had natural authority over children. Yet in the civic society envisaged by Hobbes (and Locke) the Commonwealth is entirely inhabited by men. Rousseau, in his notion of the social contract, takes women into account in a pseudo-inclusive fashion, but marginalizes them by making women a 'special case'. 'What is normative is male' (Thiele, 1986, p.34). Alienation occurs when women are included as subjects, but the experience and parameters of women's lives are distorted by being 'interpreted through male categories' because the methodology and values of the theorists are androcentric' (Thiele, 1986, pp.33-4). Thus Marxist theory is both pseudo-inclusive and alienating of women in arguing that women's inequality will disappear once women enter the paid labour force. Ultimately women's perspective is rendered invisible in political and social theory firstly, by the decontextualization or abstraction of real events and people from their situation in order to make generalizations or universal statements, and secondly, by the creation of dualisms between nature/culture, public/private, mind/body, rational/emotional, which cast women into the private sphere of emotionality and men into the public, civic sphere of political and economic activity. This process of decontextualization and conceptual dualism is characteristic of liberal theory, and is focused in the notion of individuality. As Carole Pateman points out, the abstraction of the individual had unfortunate consequences for women. 'In order that the individual could appear in liberal theory as a universal figure who represents anyone and everyone, the individual must be disembodied' (Pateman, 1986, p.8). The public individual, the universal man, was masculine. He possessed the material and symbolic interest which invested his political status with power.

Hester Eisenstein, in her analysis of contemporary feminist thought, traces the dilemmas created by the connection between the parallel growth of feminism and liberalism because the roots of both lie in the emergence of individualism as a general theory of social life. Both feminism and liberalism have conceived in some way of individuals as free and equal beings, emancipated from the ascribed, hierarchical bonds of traditional society. Feminism in the late nineteenth and early twentieth centuries was, Eisenstein argued, merely making claims for an extension of these liberal principles to women. In attempting to universalize liberalism across gender, it inevitably challenged it because of the essential separation between public and private spheres in liberalism, which excluded women from public roles and which perceived of the family as a natural given. The contradiction which emerged centred on the issue of participation and equality when feminists were to claim equal rights to participate in the public sphere in terms of the vote (Eisenstein, 1985, p.xv).

Feminists turned to more radical and socialist demands for equal economic rights in the workplace — equal opportunity in access to education and occupation and equal rewards in terms of pay — on realizing the 'hollowness of political liberalism without the economic means' to achieve its promises (Eisenstein, 1985, p.xvi). But the failure of Marxists to explicate the alliances of interests which have acted to maintain the masculinist ideological hegemony continues to, and in fact has exacerbated, the sexual division of labour and existing power structures in capitalist societies (Stacey and Price, 1981). As with liberal feminism, socialist feminism has tended to perpetuate the private/public dichotomy, and thus fails to produce an adequate theory of social change which can lead to radical social action. Both theories look to universal categories of 'individual', 'worker' and are

> sexually particular, constructed on the basis of male attributes, capacities and modes of activity. . . . The 'individual' is masculine, but because he appears to be universal and because the categories of liberalism and socialism appear to hold out a universal promise, it seems either (for liberals) that the task of feminism is to make good this promise and incorporate women into existing institutions as equals, or (for socialists) to carry out the class revolution which will bring true universalism into being. (Pateman, 1986, p.7)

Liberal political theory has thus reified the notion of the abstract individual, freely making choices, autonomous and motivated by external rewards. At the same time liberal capitalism has spawned another form of organizational life — the bureaucracy.

Ferguson traces the links between liberalism, the bureaucratization of social life and the 'feminization' of the lower ranks of educational bureaucracies since the late nineteenth century (Ferguson, 1984; Hansot and Tyack, 1981). The significance of the bureaucratization of education for women in education lies in the embeddedness of the hierarchical relationships, the division of labour premised upon expertise and notions of bureaucratic rationality. It is best exemplified in the gendered and hierarchical distinction between administration and teaching as categories of work based on expertise, for example, rather than as inextricably dependent and within the same field of practice (Blackmore, 1987). Such hierarchies reinforce existing power relations and the ways in which feminity and masculinity are socially constructed and reproduced in schools. The emphasis on authority as being legitimately and rationally imparted through neutral organizational or bureaucratic means renders the gender relationships which co-exist in bureaucratic life non-problematic. Thus

> bureaucratic control . . . operates through denial that there is discrimination. It is asserted that gender is irrelevant, that women can make it the same as men, that all will be rationally and fairly evaluated according to the same criteria. This ignores . . . the way the world is structured around men's norms. (Game and Pringle, 1983)

Mary O'Brien considers the epistemological and political implications of this unsteady co-existence of liberalism and the bureaucratization of social life.

> Liberal statism has spawned an administrative mode — bureaucracy — in which crass indifference to the much vaunted rights of individuals is passed off as 'objectivity and efficiency'. Objectivity too is the myth on which liberal theory and research thrive, forming the intellectual — or preferably scientific — basis of liberal perceptions of knowledge. As liberal statism has grown and flourished to the point of bloat, the attenuated epistemology of liberalism and the notion of state organization and control of knowledge and/or ideology have been central to liberal strategy for the maintenance of political power. Further, the major strategic achievement for liberalism — the vitiation of democracy by the political party system — ensures the limitations of women's political power . . . liberal aspirations to epistemological sophistication and the development of scientific, empiricist and structuralist research models probably owe more to the capitalist political economy than to the development of liberal philosophy. (O'Brien, 1986, p.96)

The irony remains that the expansion of bureaucracies which increasingly regulate all aspects of social life has been accompanied by modern political theory centring on individual freedom and autonomy (Ferguson, 1984, p.31). 'Educational institutions generate and reflect both the course of bureaucracy and the roles and events that recruit individuals into bureaucracies' in that the bureaucratic discourse seeks to promote individual merit and bureaucratic rationality (Ferguson, 1984, p.42). In this sense leadership is 'earned' by those with merit. Meanwhile, corporate capitalism leads to the fragmentation of work and the productive process, which has meant 'the withdrawal of aspirations from the workplace into private goals, the disruption of indigenous networks of support and mutual aid' (quoted in Ferguson, 1984, p.48). Individual happiness has come to be identified with success in organizational life. 'Hence parents seek upward mobility for their chidren increasingly looking to education, not simply to provide access to a better job at a higher salary, but to supply an institutional linkage to an established occupational hierarchy' (Ferguson, 1984, p.45). Bourgeois individualism so promoted this bureaucratic means of organization to the extent that children have come to appreciate and understand the workings of hierarchical organizations at an early age. They do not distinguish hierarchy as characteristic merely of organizational life but of social relationships generally (Ferguson, 1984, p.46).

Thus the tenet of liberal, bourgeois individuality has done little to alter the gendered division of labour in work, school or at home. Instead, liberalism has advocated equality for women as articulated through the notion of individual merit and success, the autonomous, universal individual making rational decisions. The upward mobility of individual, generally middle-class, women through affirmative action and the institutionalization of equality as conceptualized in the liberal state have been illusory in that the rhetoric is not matched by the reality of what is occurring in the organization and structuring of education (particularly state education). Walkerdine indicates how class and gender within the liberal paradigm have continued to be the main structuring factors:

> Females may cross over on to the side of masculinity in so far as they are permitted to enter into these practices. Similarly, given it is bourgeois individuality, possessed of rationality, which is taken as the key to normality, the working class can in principle become 'bourgeois individuals' by dint of those liberal practices which provide that possibility. However such an individuality and autonomy is produced at a price. Playful rationality is made possible through work, the hidden work of servicing, manual labour and nurturance. Here the ultimate irony is to be found in the position of the middle-class male, whose powerful position is guaranteed by the trap of reasoned argument. (Walkerdine, 1985, p.235)

The unfortunate consequence of the adoption of the liberal tenets of individualism is that feminist values are incorporated, appropriated and submerged. There is little opportunity to question the fundamental nature of organizations, to challenge relationships premised on hierarchy or individualistic competitiveness or the privileging of scientific knowledge upon which it is premised.

Positivism and the Rationalization of Administrative Work

Nineteenth century liberalism was imbued with a worldview well suited to capitalist economic structures and work ethic. By the mid-twentieth century positivistic social science offered predictability, universality and certainty to the policy-makers of the developing liberal bureaucratic state. Thus many tenets of liberalism, individual merit and expertise, for example, found justification in positivistic epistemology. Positivistic theories of knowledge hold that all genuine human knowledge is contained in the boundaries of science, that is, the systematic study of observable phenomena that can be explained by scientific laws. Social science, in emulating the physical sciences, also made claims of prediction and control, thus giving privilege to its knowledge claims of objectivity and universality over other forms of 'subjective', non-observable, particularistic or experiential knowledge. The implications for women have already been addressed in the discussion of how positivistic social science constructed a masculinist model of leadership.

Educational scholars and practitioners alike, by claiming status for educational administration as a science in a period when both progressivist and conservative educational traditions valued social efficiency, sought to gain both professional and public legitimation in the first decades of the twentieth century (Hansot and Tyack, 1981). Since the 1950s the theory movement in educational administration has taken as its own the industrial metaphor central to administrative theory, and applied the industrial model to schooling (Griffiths, 1979). Implicit in the functionalist view of education was the epistemological assumption that scientific knowledge, gleaned through observation and empirical studies, was objective; that knowledge derived through scientific method could be generalized across situations, time and gender. In this way positivism and liberalism shared like views about the abstraction of the individual in order to universalize experience.

In this framework organizations such as schools were considered to be value-free contexts, in which organizational objectives could be stated and adhered to; in which individuals were treated as autonomous beings whose interests and objectives could be moulded through the gentle direction of their leaders to those of the organization or school; in which consensus was the norm and conflict regarded as aberrant behaviour by those in authority; in which power was not confused with notions of authority and control. Organizational control was legitimately invested in formal institutional roles. Power was ignored as having connotations of being manipulative, political and devious. Administration in schools thus came to be conceived as a neutral practice carried out by experts in a scientific and rational manner. Decision-making was seen as a rational and a linear procedure, not a matter of values or subjective opinion. Means were separated from ends, fact from value. Valerie Walderkine comments:

> The investment of reason in the sexed-body, as the foundation of modern western scientific rationality, not only locates self-control in rational argument, but also places it at the centre of an omnipotent fantasy of control over the workings of the universe.

Mastery and control of the 'real' are centrally located in claims to truth and therefore to possess knowledge. In this sense mastery, control and bourgeois masculinity are conjoined in that uncertain pursuit of truth. (Walkerdine, 1985, p.235)

What are the consequences of this privileging of positivism in educational administrative theory? External factors (family, relationships, politics, etc.) have come to be seen as merely disruptive to productive organizational relationships (Stewart, 1978; Shakeshaft and Hanson, 1986). When women's subjective experience does not fit this 'reality' of scientific management, it is treated as an aberration, non-relevant and deviant. Jan Grant suggests that women's incorporation into masculine domains in organizations has been at a cost. It often requires women publicly to reject and submerge their definition of self as women (Grant, 1985). Such co-option is because women's subjugated knowledge or subjective experience is not valued as a resource or valid alternative worldview. Conversely, it means that radical action or opposition by women in organizations such as teachers (predominantly female) to employers has been interpreted by sociologists and political scientists primarily as a male search for professional status rather than a female rejection of the values implicit in a systematic and dehumanizing control by men of women. Women's activities are thus cast more as 'submission' than 'subversion', but in neither case legitimate (Markus, 1987, p.98). This is not to suggest that male teachers do not value other than occupational success, or are not motivated by humane values, or that women do not aspire to occupational mobility or status, but rather that dominant explanations for particular attitudes and activities are framed by narrow and limiting masculinist perceptions and experience of what is problematic. Likewise, the dominant definition of educational leadership has been historically constructed in a manner which ignores, reinterprets or denigrates feminine values and experience.

The positivistic epistemology underlying conventional organizational and administrative theory has undergone an attack from within its ranks since the early 1970s for its naive scienticism which separates fact from value, and assertion that administration is a value-free science (Hodgkinson, 1981; Greenfield, 1986; Codd, 1988; Bates, 1986). This 'intellectual turmoil' in educational administration has not ruffled the calm of masculine domination in education at either the theoretical or practitioner level. The inability to incorporate a theoretical explanation for continued masculine domination, despite increased sensitivity to gender issues, has been excused on the grounds that 'organisational theories have been based on the perspective of executives', the emphasis being on the disempowerment resulting from the emphasis on social control, hierarchy and bureaucracy rather than recognition of the reproduction of gendered dominance as a set of power relations as a significant phenomenon of educational organizations (Griffiths, 1979, pp.43-65). The interpretivist perspective of educational administration which has emerged maintains as its essence the individualism of liberal political theory and the fact/value distinction of positivistic epistemology (see Greenfield, 1984, 1986). That there may be some shared experience of particular social groups who have a different way of seeing from their position of non-control at the base of *male* dominated, hierarchical organizations is only implied. Perhaps women share certain common organizational experiences through their patterned subordination and powerlessness as women, and not merely in their commonality as subordinates. The issue is one of control, but by whom, over whom, and on what basis?

Both the positivistic and interpretivistic traditions which have dominated approaches to educational administration have come under attack from the perspective of critical theory for their common epistemological assumption of the distinction between fact and value, which effectively excludes moral commitment and ignores the historical, political and personal nature of organizational relationships (Codd, 1988). Such critiques tend to presume that discussions of domination and subordination, of power relations and the significance of ideology, necessarily include women as objects of subjugation. But there has been little attempt overtly to connect this powerlessness to matters of the social construction and reproduction of gendered power relations in educational organizations (see Fraser, 1987). Depending upon whose interpretation of the Frankfurt school is taken to portray their position best, there would appear to be some convergence of feminist approaches and that of the critical theorists. Salleh discards the view that critical theory is 'drenched in a Freudian inspired nostalgia for patriarchy, an obsession with the "ideal bougeois" family, a static and cynical brand of individualism' (Salleh, 1981, p.5). What is evident, she argues, is the shared concern for the merging of theory and practice, the moral commitment to social change, the ongoing critique of all ideologies (including that of critical theory itself), and an historically materialistic analysis which displays a sensitivity to subjectivity without neglecting structural constraints, a dimension ignored or exaggerated in positivistic and interpretivist approaches respectively to educational administration. Salleh suggests that critical theory in fact contributes to the radical feminist problematic in that its analysis rests upon a 'more profound materialism than that of the "mode of production"', that perceives that social change must have a biological and psycho-social basis and which has an epistemology which does not split consciousness from the act of knowing (Salleh, 1981, p. 12).

Lather and Fraser share similar optimism when considering how critical theory, and the work of Jürgen Habermas in particular, can contribute to feminist theory. Lather suggests that critical theorists and feminists share the desire to transform the production and dissemination of knowledge, a commitment to more democratic forms of governance which empower disadvantaged groups, a view that looks to the sociality rather than the autonomy of individuals as the guiding force of practice (Lather, 1984). Whilst Fraser is happy to extrapolate from Habermas what she perceives as the gender sub-text, she is still conscious that Habermas fails to theorize 'the norm mediated character of late capitalist official-economic administrative systems . . . the systemic, money and power-mediated character of male dominance in the domestic sphere . . . nor the gender-based separation of the state-regulated economy of sex-segmented paid work and social welfare. Ultimately, he also seeks to universalise experience' (Fraser, 1987, p. 55). Yet critical theory and feminist theory would appear to share common concerns. The extent of this commonality needs to be explored further.

So far I have elaborated upon the ways in which gender-biased educational structures, organization and practice have been justified as necessary and rational. The gendered and hierarchical division of labour in educational administration, for example, has rested at various times upon notions of natural, psychological and social difference. It is further legitimated by theories of knowledge which are supportive of notions of rational and hierarchical forms of administration as givens or technical necessities. Leadership has thus been portrayed within liberal political theory and positivistic theories of knowledge as an individualistic enterprise essential to the given hierarchical arrangements and premised upon notions of technical expertise.

Individualism, Rationality and Morality

A feminist critique of educational organizations and the ways in which educational leadership has been conceptualized would therefore involve a reconsideration of the concepts of the universal individual, abstract morality and bureaucratic rationality central to liberalism and positivism.

Carol Gould sees the starting point of liberalism as the assumption that 'human individuals are essentially solitary, with needs and interests that are separate from, if not in opposition to, those of other individuals' (Gould, 1983, p.24). It has already been illustrated how social contract theory, upon which liberal polemics is based, specifies the interests of the individual as protection of life, civil liberties and property as exemplified in the autonomous, abstract individual. The emphasis on the individual's interests in liberal political and positivistic organizational theory has many consequences. In particular it denies the individual's need for collective action and sociality. Elshtain argues:

> The problem with a politics that begins and ends with mobilizing resources, achieving maximum impacts, calculating prudentially, articulating interest group claims, engaging in reward distribution functions and so on is not only its utter lack of imagination but its inability to engage the reflective allegiance and committed loyalty of citizens. Oversimply, no substantive sense of civic virtue, no vision of the political community that might serve as the groundwork of a life in common is possible within a political life dominated by self interested, predatory individualism. (Elshtain, 1982, p.141)

Liberal theory also produces an instrumental interpretation of rationality which assumes that the individual has a set of interests and preferences which are known and constant, and that individuals are motivated purely out of a desire to maximize these preferences. The state merely facilitates this process and protect the individual's preferences. Rational behaviour is therefore depicted as when individuals (as organizations) act to maximize their own interests. Gould refutes this assumption, arguing that humans must live in social groups, and that 'human interdependence is thus necessitated by human biology and the assumption of individual self-sufficiency is plausible only if one ignores human biology' (Gould, 1983, p.24). At the same time she is not advocating biological determinism, but rather recognition that 'interests' (whether self-interests or altruistic interests) must take into account the material situation of people and their relationships with others — that is, community. A rational person in Gould's perspective values her abilities to empathize and connect with particular others by recognition not ignorance of social interdependence. It is a notion which is both materialist and non-deterministic. This requires turning liberal theory upon its head. Instead of community and cooperation being problematic in liberal theory, the existence of egoism, competitiveness and conflict, which liberalism sees as endemic and natural, would be the puzzle.

Thus feminists argue that the notion of the abstract individual so implicit in liberalism ignores the essential interdependency of human beings. Sandra Harding suggests that notions of abstract rationality expressed by Kohlberg, Kant and Rawls exemplify a modern liberal ideal not only of the individual as a citizen but also an abstract, transcendental view of morality which is ahistorical (Harding, 1983, pp.40-50). In their view the resolution of moral problems in a 'rational' manner requires abstract judgments arrived at through abstract principles. Harding points out that such a view of moral reasoning does not take into account the contextual and inductive thinking characteristic of taking the role of the particular other. In so doing it creates an opposition between reason and affectivity. Furthermore, the hallmark of this moral reason is impartiality.

> Impartiality names a point of view of reason that stands apart from interests and desires. Not to be partial means being able to see the whole, how all the particular perspectives and interests in a given moral situation relate to one another in a way that, because of its partiality, each perspective cannot see itself. The impartial moral reasoner thus stands outside and above the situation about which he or she reasons, with no stake in it. . . . (Young, 1987, p.60)

This causes a problem which Adorno has called 'the logic of identity' in that it looks to order and describe particulars of experience, to create unity, to eliminate uncertainty and unpredictability. It requires the reasoner to treat all situations alike according to a set of rules, in effect to universalize.

> as a consequence of the opposition between reason and desire, moral decisions grounded in considerations of sympathy, caring, and an assessment of differentiated need are defined as not rational, not 'objective', merely sentimental. To the extent that women exemplify or are identified with such styles of moral decision making, then women are excluded from moral rationality. (Young, 1987, p.63)

This dichotomy between reason and desire, we have shown, appears in political theory as the distinction between the public realm of the civic and the state and the private realm of needs and desires (Young, 1987, p.63).

What are the implications of such a stance for leadership? Such a view does not require the impartial reasoner to acknowledge other subjects' perspectives, since they are incomplete. Thus impartiality often results in authoritarianism, in that one claims authority to decide. Furthermore, it is argued that the impartial reasoner has a holistic view, able to abstract himself or herself from self-interests in the interests of the unity (organization). Chris Hodgkinson in his books, *A Philosophy of Leadership* and *A Theory of Educational Administration,* exemplifies such an approach. Hodgkinson calls for a new form of moral leadership in which he posits a hierarchy of values giving priority to cognitive reason over emotive preferences. Thus conflict and self-interest are seen as a debasement of human activity. Throughout his analysis he assumes Plato's view of a leader as a philosopher-king, a rational individual able to abstract *himself* from value judgments embedded in specific situations but based upon universal principles (Hodgkinson, 1981). Such a position assumes a notion of transcendental morality which is ahistorical and ignores the sociality of humans. Such a view invests this capability for superior moral reasoning in the occupants of formal institutional positions, and would divest all others of the moral potential to take decisions which are rational. Hodgkinson does not tell us how to learn or acquire such superior moral powers or how they are recognized. In effect, the consequence would be to reassert the hierarchical relationships premised upon a concept of moral rationality and impose them upon organizational reality in a manner which is detrimental to certain types of valuing and reasoning which are other centred, affective and caring.

Thirdly, in educational administration, as in organizational theory, the dominance of a science of administration has legitimated power relations in schools and maintained a myth of bureaucratic rationality and individualism. Administration is value-free, hierarchy is technically rational and domination legitimate. Urban talks of this bureaucratic rationality 'as a mode of thought, which can be understood as an expression of power relations in the social world, on the one hand, and a mystification of those relations on the other'. Furthermore, 'the defining element of relations inside a bureaucracy is hierarchy, itself another word for domination. Given the worldview of technical rationality, however, bureaucracy does not appear as a structure of domination; on the contrary, the bureaucratic hierarchy manifests itself as a technical necessity (to co-ordinate the subdivided tasks), as a rational organisational arrangement for the accomplishment of collective ends' (Urban, 1982, pp.23-4). The hierarchical arrangements in organizations such as schools are thus premised upon such notions of individualism and rationality. Rizvi has elsewhere developed the ways in which this notion of bureaucratic rationality has particular political implications. He suggests that the traditional notion of administrative leadership reifies the role of the principal as a leader. Principals are seen to be effective only when they are 'in charge' or 'in control'. This encourages manipulation and control of subordinates by principals, generally not conducive to mutual benefit (Rizvi, 1986). He suggests that if schools are seen in terms of individuals and their position in hierarchies, then 'leaders will always be set apart from followers', 'relationships will be one-sided' and mediated through bureaucratic definitions of role (Rizvi, 1986, p.39).

Ferguson criticizes this bureaucratic mind set in which the 'interaction with others is debased and the self is created as a rationalised commodity' (Ferguson, 1984, p.20). In her view bureaucracy rests on assumptions of scientific rationality, the generalized other which is apolitical and ideologically invisible (Ferguson, 1984, p.16). Women are thereby a marginalized group who possess 'subjugated knowledges' located low down the hierarchy. At the same time women are both active creators and passive victims because their experience is more continuous with than in opposition to others. That is, women are neither purely self-interested nor purely altruistic and self-sacrificing. Rather, self and other can be seen to be attached and continuous, making human sociality a fundamental component of the individual. Because women tend to assume responsibility for taking care of others as defined by traditional roles, they tend to pass judgments that are based on contextual rather than abstract criteria, focus more on process than outcome. In management terms this has been recognized as women's tendency (and failure) to be task- rather than organizationally oriented (Ferguson, 1984, p.25). This is not to deny that men live in families and women work, but the traditional public-private dichotomy means that the members of each gender carry the worldview of their own domain with them into the other realm, and must consciously put it aside to succeed in the other world on its own terms (Ferguson, 1984, p.27).

The masculine image of leadership in education is therefore historically constructed and maintained by its ideological underpinnings of dominant theories of a value-free science and liberal political theory. Leadership is justified on the grounds of rational necessity, individual behaviours and opportunities, and technically necessary hierarchical social arrangements. Founded upon a positivistic epistemology which separates the body from the mind, which extracts feeling and emotion from the material, leadership is defined to be a rational, cognitive process. Because expressive behaviours are denigrated as irrational, it is possible to argue that gender relations are unproblematic and are not a substantive issue in the culture and structure of organizations. The lack of women in higher positions can be excused within such a theoretical framework as a consequence of women's irrationality, subjectivity and emotionality. They choose not to aspire for such positions, or are excused on the grounds of their moral inadequacy in not being able to make the 'hard' decisions in the interests of the organization. The question remains, how then can feminist theory not only deconstruct these dominant epistemological and political perspectives but also reconstruct an alternative which opens up different ways of seeing educational leadership. What then would constitute a feminist perspective of leadership?

The Elements of a Feminist Reconstruction of Leadership

Feminist theory does not ask merely to include women as objects in the patriarchal discourse, in which sameness is emphasized rather than difference. It rapidly becomes evident that it is impossible to incorporate or 'add on' a feminist perspective. Rather, a feminist critique ultimately leads to the need to reformulate the methodologies, criteria of validity and merit and ultimately the political and epistemological commitments underlying the dominant notions or discourse. Feminists demand not just equality, but that they become the subjects and objects of an alternative, autonomous discourse which chooses its own measures and criteria. It is necessary not only to explain the pervasiveness and persistence of gender divergence and gender subordination (which are not the same thing) but also to provide an explanation that avoids a rigid universalism and provides a way of understanding cultural and historical difference. It is also essential that theory provides the basis for a politics directed towards changing this subordination, a politics of change (Thornton 1982, p.53).

A feminist alternative to the view of leadership criticized in this chapter would consist of a number of elements including the central concepts already discussed, concepts which are common to most feminist perspectives. Such a view would focus on the relationship between the individual and a more egalitarian notion of community and civic participation which does not adhere to abstract principles of rational judgment or morality outside specific contexts. Harding, for example, calls for a more practical, contextualized notion of rationality. Perhaps a more politically universal conception of human rationality would refer to normative conditions as personhood and human good in a relational morality which emphasizes attachments and responsibilities to others as well as to self. This suggests that 'interest' should not be regarded as either total self-interest or altruism. A relational view of morality and judgment recognizes the interdependence of people, and sees moral judgment as not being predicated upon some abstract universal morality or individual rights, but upon concern and responsibility consequent upon the relationships of self to others within specific contexts. In this sense administration as moral judgment would need to be aware of the context of the judgment and the responsibilities of the actors. In effect, it is arguing that the relational bias in women's thinking, which has been seen to compromise their moral judgment in the past and impede their moral development, in fact has significant moral value for all. Gilligan has argued that this relational morality should not be regarded as the deficit model, but that it merely reflects a different social and moral understanding — a different set of interests (Gilligan, 1977, pp.481-2).

I do not take the stance that women's worldview or perspective is either biologically determined or premised on an essentialism which perceives female morality, interests or behaviours as being superior to those of males. Rather, I adhere to the view that at a specific historical moment, traditional patterns of behaviours prescribe certain roles to which individuals, males and females, partially conform to differing degrees. For example, women's centrality to the family and as principal child rearer is not greatly challenged in practice, and is therefore a dominant part of women's identity, value systems and needs. That is, women's 'interests' are associated with caring and commitment to others. Carol Gould argues that 'a dialectical conception of human biology sees human nature and the forms of human social organisation as determined not by biology alone but rather a complex interplay between our biological constitution, our physical environment and our forms of social organisation, including our level of technological development' (Gould, 1984, p.22). Within this framework feminism would not expect that everyone be treated exactly the same, since responsibility and relationships have specific temporal and historical contexts.

Such a perspective would mean a reconstitution of the public sphere in what Markus calls 'the more or less fluid self-organisation of a public committed to principles of equality, plurality and democratic forms' (Markus, 1986, p.9). This is not to return to the Enlightenment ideal of civic public

> which excludes the bodily and affective particularity as well as the concrete histories of individuals that make groups unable to understand one another. Emancipatory politics should foster a concept of public which in principle excludes no person, aspects of persons' lives or topic of discussion and which encourages aesthetic as well as discursive expression. In such a public, consensus and sharing may not always be the goal, but the recognition and appreciation of difference, in the context of confrontation with power. (Young, 1987, p.76)

It is also time to consider why it is that women's accounts of power differ so systematically from those of men. Men see in power domination, whilst Hartsock argues that women take a more emancipatory perception in that they see 'power as a capacity of the community as a whole'. Women tend to characterize power over others as domination and illegitimate, without questioning why there are systematic relations in which some have more power over others. Individual power (or leadership) is often treated with scepticism. This comes largely from Arendt's formulation, when she treats individual actions outside community with contempt, as non-political. Hartsock warns that in so doing power is described in terms

> that emphasise the submersion of the identity of the individual in the community, thereby falling into a form of female pathology of loss of self, a fluidity that may submerge individual identity. . . . It is better to have an understanding of power for the individual which stresses both its dimensions of competence, ability and creativity and does not lose sight of the import-ance of effective action . . . in part defined by its sensuality and its variety of connections and relations with others in the community. (Hartsock, 1983, pp.253, 256)

Rather than condemn the notion of leadership as anathema to democratic community, it is essential to reconceptualize a different type of leadership in a caring community, to recognize that at particular instances individuals can and do act in a powerful manner but with good intention for the community, whilst laying themselves open to communal scrutiny (Noddings, 1985).

An adequate theory of power, according to Hartsock, would give an account of how social institutions have come to be controlled by only one gender; it would locate where and how the points of conflict between men and women are generated; and it would make clear the specific relations between individual intentional actions and structural con-straints (p.254). Such an approach would necessarily subvert the hierarchical structures of social institutions such as bureaucracies. Ferguson argues that women already offer an alternative construct to the dominant bureaucratic discourse in which 'women's lives constitute a submerged voice'. She continues:

> The traditional experiences of women in our society shed light on bureaucracy in two ways — by revealing persistent patterns of dominance and subordinance in bureaucracy that parallel power relations between men and women, and by suggesting a different way of conceiving the individual and the collective that reflects

the caretaking and nurturant experiences embedded in women's role. (Ferguson, 1984, p.x)

She suggests that a feminist discourse in organizations would therefore encourage the caring and reciprocity central to a relational worldview which gives prior concern to others, which would recognize both familial and friendship connectedness and acknowledge the civic as well as the personal importance of friendship. It would also be committed to participatory democracy, whilst being aware that the sharing of power, language and knowledge critical to participation can assume gendered formations which must be constantly analyzed.

Given the attack on abstract individualism and organizational hierarchy implicit in feminism, an alternative conception of leadership emerges. It is suggested here that leadership can take other forms than having *power over* others and that leadership 'skills' can be used in a different way. Rather than privileging the individual who is often already in a position of status and power because of the possession of specialist knowledge, capacities, skills or role allocation, expertise can, in a cooperative environment, empower the individual *and* the group. Leadership, and the power which accompanies it, would be redefined as the ability to *act with* others to do things that could not be done by an individual alone. Leadership, therefore, would be a form of empowerment and not of dominance or control (Ferguson, 1984, p.206; see also Burbules, 1986). Hartsock takes up this point when she claims that 'to lead is to be at the centre of the group rather than in front of the others' (Hartsock, 1983, p.8). Authority based on skill and knowledge (both of which are imbued with power) would be, according to Hartsock, 'compelled persistently to demonstrate its force to those concerned in terms which they can grasp and, by dint of being so compelled, be made in some real measure responsible to them' (Hartsock, 1983, p.10).

It is suggested that women have been alienated by the masculinist portrayal of leadership and organizational life which emphasizes control, individualism and hierarchy. The false dichotomy between fact and value, ends and means, derived from the positivistic assumptions of the traditional 'science of educational administration' has political repercussions in the sense that it is exclusive of women's experience by rejecting all that is affective or experientially-based. It casts particular groups as 'others', and privileges certain types of knowledge, experience and expertise over others. Furthermore, organizational theory has assumed and maintained the dualisms derived from social and political theory which have portrayed women's experiential and knowledge claims to be in opposition, and thus peripheral or insubstantial. This has been exacerbated in practice by the historical and social construction of the gendered division of labour in schools and educational administration.

What does this mean in practical terms and policy in educational administration? Educational leadership as portrayed in the conventional literature may have little to attract women. That is, the perception of what constitutes leadership is problematic, not women. If administration is no longer treated as separate from teaching, if leadership is not merely equated to formal roles and responsibilities, if what is worthwhile knowledge and experience is not restricted to formal qualifications or institutional experience, then it calls upon a new set of informed judgments which must be brought to bear on the valuing of people's activities in educational organizations. What counts as *administrative* and *leadership* experience and skills or potential could therefore include community activities, teaching, curriculum development and child rearing, which recognizes what difference can bring to education. This would go some way towards recognizing women's experience in the 'private' sphere, and imbuing it with equal status to male experience in the public sphere. It may challenge what Jan Grant describes as the way in which organizations reproduce themselves in the masculine view via 'homosocial reproduction' (Grant, 1985).

It would also require a shift to be made from the individual to a collective focus in terms of what is meant by leadership. This would require going against the renewed push towards more masculinist notions of leadership embedded in corporate managerialism, the impetus for current restructuring of secondary and tertiary education, which equates efficiency and effectiveness with organizational rationality and hierarchy (Blackmore and Kenway, 1988). While administration and leadership are premised upon conventional theories which reify hierarchy, rationality and individualism, which are perceived to be masculinist attributes or behaviours, women's experiences and values will continue to be displaced. To conclude, Hartsock suggests that '. . . it would raise for the first time the possibility of a fully human community, a community structured by its variety of direct relations among people, rather than their separation and opposition' (Hartsock, 1983, p.262).

References

Acker, J. and Van Houten, D. (1974) 'Differential recruitment and control: The sex structuring of organisations,' *Administrative Science Quarterly*, 19,2, pp.152-63.

Adkinson, J. (1981) 'Women in school administration: A review of the research,' *Review of Educational Research,* 51,3, pp.311-43.

Antill, J.K. and Cunningham, J.D. (1979) 'Self esteem as a function of masculinity in both sexes,' *Journal of Consulting and Clinical Psychology,* 47,4, pp.783-5

Apple, M. (1985) 'Teaching and "women's work": A comparative historical and ideological analysis,' *Teacher's College Record,* 86,3, pp.455-73.

Ball, S. (1987) *The Micropolitics of the School: Towards a Theory of School Organisation,* London, Methuen.

Bates, R. (1986) *The Management of Knowledge and Culture,* Geelong, Deakin University Press.

Bayes, M. and Newton, P.M. (1978) 'Women in authority: A psychosocial analysis,' *Journal of Applied Behavioural Science,* 14,1, pp.7-20.

Benhabib, S. and Cornell, D. (1986) *Feminism as Critique: Essays on the Politics of Gender in Late-Capitalist Societies,* London, Polity Press.

Biklen, S. and Brannigan, M. (Eds) (1980) *Women and Educational Leadership,* Lexington, Mass., Lexington Books.

Blackmore, J. (1987a) 'Tensions to be resolved in participation and school based decision making,' *Educational Administration Review,* 4,1, pp.29-47.

Blackmore, J. (1987b) 'Contradiction and contestation: Theory and ideology in teacher's work,' Paper presented to the British Educational Research Association Conference, Manchester, September.

Blackmore, J. and Kenway, J. (1988) 'Rationalisation, instrumentalism and corporate managerialism: The implications for women of the Green Paper in Higher Education,' *Australian Universities Review,* 31, 1.

Bormann, E., Pratt, J. and Putnam, L.L. (1978) 'Power, authority and sex: Male response to female leadership,' *Communication Monographs,* 45, pp.119-55.

Brown, L.K. (1979) 'Women and business management,' *Signs,* 5,2, pp.266-8.

Brown, S. (1979) 'Male versus female leaders: A comparison of empirical studies,' *Sex Roles,* 5,5, pp.596-611.

Burbules, N. (1986) 'Theory of power in education,' *Educational Theory,* 36,2, pp.95-114.

Burns, J.M. (1978) *Leadership,* New York, Anchor Books.

Burton, C. (1985) *Subordination: Feminism and Social Theory,* Sydney, George Allen and Unwin.

Burton, C. (1987) 'Merit and gender: Organisations and the mobilisation of masculine bias,' *Australian Journal of Social Issues,* 23,2, pp.424-35.

Carlson, R. (1972) 'Understanding women: Implications for personality theory and research,' *Journal of Social Issues,* 28,2, pp.17-32.

Chapman, J. (1985) 'Women principals in Australia,' Paper presented to the joint conference of the Australian College of Education and the ACT Schools Authority, Women in Management in Primary and Secondary Education, Canberra, August.

Chapman, J. (1986) 'Decentralisation, devolution and the teacher: Participation by teachers in the decision making of schools,' Paper, Monash University.

Chapman, J. and Luthans, F. (1975) 'The female leadership dilemma,' *Public Personnel Management*, 4, pp.173-9.

Cockburn, C. (1983) *Brothers: Male Dominance and Technological Change*, London, Pluto Press.

Codd, J. (1988) *Knowledge and Control in Evaluation in Educational Organisations*, Geelong, Deakin University Press.

Cohen, G. (1979) 'Symbiotic relations: Male decisionmakers-female support groups in Britain and the United States,' *Women's Studies International Quarterly*, 2, pp.391-406.

Condry, J. and Dyer, S. (1976) 'Fear of success: Attribution of cause to the victim,' *Journal of Social Issues*, 32,3, pp.68-83.

Connell, R. (1987) *Gender and Power: Society, the Person and Sexual Politics*, Sydney, Allen and Unwin.

Deaux, K. and Emswiller, T. (1974) 'Explanations of successful performance on sex-linked tasks: What is skill for a male is luck for a female,' *Journal of Personality and Social Psychology*, 29,1, pp.80-5.

Eisenstein, H. (1985) *Contemporary Feminist Thought*, Sydney, George Allen and Unwin.

Ellis, G. (1983) 'Women primary teachers' aspirations to administrative positions,' MEd. project, Monash University.

Elshtain, J. (1982) 'Feminist discourse and its discontents: Language, power and meaning,' in N. Keohane, M. Rosaldo and B. Gelpi, *Feminist Theory: A Critique of Ideology*, Chicago, Ill., University of Chicago Press.

Fargani, S. (1986) *Social Reconstruction of the Feminine Character*, Totowa, N.J., Rowman and Littlefield.

Ferguson, K. (1984) *The Feminist Case against Bureaucracy*, Philadelphia, Pa., Temple University Press.

Fiedler, F.E. (1978) 'Recent developments in research on the contingency model,' in L. Berkowitz, (Ed.) *Group Processes*, New York, Academic Press.

Fildes, S. (1983) 'The inevitability of theory,' *Feminist Review*, 14,2.

Foster, W. (1986) *The Reconstruction of Leadership*, Geelong, Deakin University Press.

Fraser, N. (1987) 'What's critical about critical theory: The case of Habermas and gender,' in S. Benhabib and D. Cornell, *Feminism as Critique*, London, Polity Press.

Frasher, J. and Frasher, R. (1979) 'Educational administration: A feminine profession,' *Educational Administration Quarterly*, 15,2, pp.1-13.

Game, A. and Pringle, R. (1983) *Gender at Work*, Sydney, George Allen and Unwin.

Gatens, M. (1986) 'Feminism, philosophy and riddles without answers,' in C. Pateman and E. Gross (Eds), *Feminist Challenges, Social and Political Theory*, Sydney, Allen and Unwin.

Gilligan, C. (1977) 'In a different voice,' *Harvard Educational Review*, 47,4, pp.481-517.

Gould, C. (Ed.) (1983) *Beyond Domination: New Perspectives on Women and Philosophy*, Totowa, N.J., Roman and Allenheld.

Grant, J. (1985) 'Women: What can they offer organizations?' Paper presented at Joint Conference of the Australian Psychological Society and the New Zealand Psychological Society, Christchurch, New Zealand, August.

Greenfield, S., Greiner, L. and Wood, M. (1980) 'The "feminine mystique" in male dominated jobs: A comparison of attitudes and background factors of women in male-dominated versus female-dominated jobs,' *Journal of Vocational Behaviour,* 17, pp.291-309.

Greenfield, T. (1984) 'Leaders and schools: Wilfulness and nonnatural order in organisations,' in T. Sergiovanni and J. Corbally (Eds), *Leadership and Organisational Culture,* Urbana, Ill., University of Illinois.

Greenfield, T. (1986) 'The decline and fall of science in educational administration,' *Interchange,* 17,2, pp.57-80.

Griffiths, D. (1979) 'Intellectual turmoil in educational administration,' *Educational Administration Quarterly,* 15,3, pp.43-65.

Gross, Elizabeth (1986) 'What is feminist theory?' in C. Pateman and E. Gross (Eds), *Feminist Challenges,* Sydney, George Allen and Unwin.

Hamilton, R. and Barrett, M. (Eds) (1986) *The Politics of Diversity: Feminism, Marxism and Nationalism,* London, Verso.

Hansot, E. and Tyack, D. (1981) 'The dream deferred: A golden age for women school administrators,' Policy Paper, 81-C2, Stanford, Calif., Institute of Research on Educational Finance and Governance.

Harding, S. (1983) 'Is gender a variable in conceptions of rationality? A survey of issues,' in Gould (1983).

Hartsock, N. (1979) 'Feminist theory and revolutionary strategy,' in Z. Eisenstein (Ed.), *Capitalist Hierarchy and the Case for Socialist Feminism,* New York, Monthly Review Press.

Hartsock, N. (1983) *Money, Sex and Power: Towards a Feminist Historical Materialism,* New York, Longman.

Hearn, J. (1987) *The Gender of Oppression: Men, Masculinity and the Critique of Marxism,* Brighton, Wheatsheaf books.

Hearn, J. and Parkin, W. (1983) 'Gender and organisations,' *Organisation Studies,* 4,3, pp.219-42.

Hennig, M. and Jardim, A. (1977) *The Managerial Woman,* Garden City, N.Y., Anchor Press.

Hodgkinson, C. (1981) *The Philosophy of Leadership,* London, Basil Blackwell.

Horner, M. (1972) 'Towards an understanding of achievement-related conflicts in women,' *Journal of Social Issues,* 28,2, pp.157-75.

Hoy, W.K. and Miskel, C.G. (1978) *Educational Administration: Theory, Research and Practice,* New York, Random House.

Jenkins. L. and Kramer, S. (1978) 'Small group process: Learning from women,' *Women's Studies International Quarterly,* 1, pp.67-84.

Johnson, B. (1981) Translator's Introduction, in J. Derrida, *Dissemination,* trans by B. Johnson, Chicago, Ill., University of Chicago Press.

Johnson, M. (1980) 'How real is the fear of success?' in Biklen and Brannigan (1980).

Kanter, R. (1975) 'Women and the structure of organisations,' in M. Millman and R. Kanter (Eds), *Another Voice,* New York, Anchor Press.

Kellerman, B. (Ed.) (1984) *Leadership: Multidisciplinary Perspectives,* Englewood Cliffs, N.J., Prentice Hall.

Kenway, J. and Willis, S. (1988) *Hearts and Minds: Girls, Schooling and Self Esteem,* forthcoming.

Lather, P. (1984) 'Critical theory, curricular transformation and feminist mainstreaming,' *Journal of Education,* 166,1, pp.49-62.

McNeil, M. (Ed.) (1987) *Gender and Expertise,* London, Free Association Books.

Markus, M. (1987) 'Women, success and civil society,' in Benhabib and Cornell (1986).

Marshall, C. (1979) 'Career socialisation of women in school administration,' Paper presented to AERA, San Francisco.

Marshall, C. (1985) 'The stigmatised woman: The woman in a male sex-typed career,' *Journal of Educational Administration,* 13,2, pp.131-52.

Martin, J.R. (1984) 'Bringing women into educational thought,' *Educational Theory,* 34,4, pp.341-53.

Ministry of Education, Victoria (1986) *Ministry Structures Project Team Report: The Report in Outline,* Melbourne, Ministry of Education.

Moore, L. and Rickel, A. (1980) 'Characteristics of women in traditional and non-traditional managerial roles,' *Personnel Psychology,* 33, pp.317-33.

Morris, M. and Paton, P. (Eds) (1979) *Michel Foucault: Power, Truth and Strategy,* Sydney, Feral Publications.

Nails, D., O'Loughlin, M. and Walker, J. (1983) Women and Morality, Special Issue, *Social Research,* 50,3.

Noddings, N. (1985) 'In search of the feminine,' *Teachers College Record,* 87,2, pp.195-204.

O'Brien, M. (1986) 'Feminism and the politics of education,' *Interchange,* 17,2, pp.91-105.

O'Donnell, C. and Hall, P. (1988) *Getting Equal, Labour Market Regulation and Women's Work,* Sydney, Allen and Unwin.

Pateman, C. (1970) *Participation and Democratic Theory,* Cambridge, Cambridge University Press.

Pateman, C. (1986) 'The theoretical subversiveness of feminism,' in C. Pateman and E. Gross (Eds), *Feminist Challenges: Social and Political Theory,* Sydney, Allen and Unwin.

Putnam, L. and Heinen, J.S. (1976) 'Women in management: The fallacy of the trait theory approach,' *MSU Business Topics,* 24, pp.47-53.

Rizvi, F. (1986) *Administrative Leadership and the Democratic Community as Social Ideal,* Geelong, Deakin University Press.

Salleh, K. (1981) 'Of Portnoy's complaint and feminist problematics: A reconciliation with critical theory,' *Australian and New Zealand Journal of Sociology,* 17,1, pp.4-13.

Sampson, S. (1983) 'Women and men in the teaching service,' *The Secondary Administrator,* pp.51-2.

Sampson, S. (1987) 'Equal Opportunity, alone, is not enough or why there are more male principals in schools these days,' *Australian Journal of Education,* 31,1, pp.27-42.

Sassen, G. (1980) 'Success anxiety in women: A constructivist interpretation of its source and significance,' *Harvard Educational Review,* 50,1, pp.13-24.

Sayers, J. (1986) *Sexual Contradictions: Psychology, Psychoanalysis and Feminism,* London, Tavistock.

Schein, V. (1975) 'Relationships between sex role stereotypes and requisite management characteristics among female managers,' *Journal of Applied Psychology,* 60, pp.340-4.

Schmuck, P., Charters, W.W. and Carlson, R. (Eds) (1982) *Educational Policy and Management: Sex Differentials,* New York, Academic Press.

Sergiovanni, T.J. and Carver, F. (1980) *The New School Executive: A Theory of Administration,* New York, Harper and Row.

Shakeshaft, C. (1986) 'A gender at risk,' *Phi Delta Kappan,* March.

Shakeshaft, C. and Hanson, M. (1986) 'Androcentric bias in the *Educational Administration Quarterly,*' *Educational Administration Quarterly,* 22,1, pp.68-92.

Sherif, C. (1979) 'Bias in psychology,' in J. Sherman and E. Beck (Eds), *The Prism of Sex,* Madison, Wisc., University of Wisconsin Press.

Stacey, M. and Price, M. (1981) *Women, Power and Politics,* London, Tavistock.

State Board (1986) *School Council Involvement in the Selection of Principals of Post-Primary Schools: The Status of Women,* Melbourne, State Board, July.

Stewart, J. (1978) 'Understanding women in organisations,' *Administrative Science Quarterly,* 15,3, pp.336-50.

Thiele, B. (1986) 'Vanishing acts in social and political thought: Tricks of the trade', in C. Pateman and E. Gross (Eds), *Feminist Challenges: Social and Political Theory,* Sydney, Allen and Unwin.

Thornton, Merle (1982) 'Psychoanalysis and feminist social theory of gender,' *Politics,* 17,2, pp.52-64.

Urban, M.E. (1982) *The Ideology of Administration: American and Soviet Cases,* Albany, N.Y., State University of New York Press.

Walker, H. and Fennell, M. (1986) 'Gender differences in role differentiation and organisational task performance,' *American Review of Sociology,* 12, pp.255-75.

Walkerdine, Valerie (1985) 'On the regulation of speaking and silence,' in C. Steedman, C. Urwin and V. Walkerdine (Eds), *Language, Gender and Childhood,* London, Routledge and Kegan Paul.

Watkins, P. (1986) *A Critical Review of Leadership Concepts and Research: The Implications for Educational Administration,* Geelong, Deakin University Press.

Yeakey, C., Johnston, G. and Adkinson, J. (1986) 'In pursuit of equity: A review of the literature of research on minorities and women in education,' *Educational Administration Quarterly,* 22,3, pp.110-49.

Young, I. (1987) 'Impartiality and the civic public,' in Benhabib and Cornell (1986).

Chapter 5

Leadership and the Rationalization of Society

Richard Bates

The Problems of Leadership

Leadership seems to be a problem. There appears to be widespread agreement on its necessity, but little agreement on its substance. This difficulty is graphically illustrated in the recent *Report of the National Commission on Excellence in Educational Administration* (NCEEA, 1987) which claims at one and the same time that 'A revolution in education requires competent, skilled, visionary leadership' and that there is 'a lack of definition of good educational leadership' (p.xvi). Leaders in educational administration seem to be acknowledging the importance of an activity they cannot define.

This curious approach continues through the authors' discussion of what educational leaders must do: for example, they must symbolize education; they must recognize excellence; they must resolve conflicts; they must manage competently (NCEEA, p.7). Here the same hiatus exists. The importance of the activity is emphasized while the substance is denied. Actions which take place within concrete situations are abstracted to appear, like Platonic shadows, dimly and distantly grappling with each other on the walls of our (increasingly shaky) educational cave. 'Between the idea and the reality . . . falls the shadow' (Eliot, 1974). How can such a situation arise? What are its effects? How can they be overcome? These are the questions that this chapter addresses.

Educational administration as a field of study has for a long time been misinformed by two fundamental errors. The first error is to believe that the processes of abstraction and reification constitute an appropriate path toward powerful theory. The second error is the belief that the language of technique is an appropriate substitute for the discourse of ethics. Each of these mistakes is apparent in the traditions of educational administration and in the vacuous nature of its contemporary advice to those who see the necessity of renewal in education.

The Process of Reification

One of the fundamental assumptions of positivistic science is that under similar conditions similar events will occur with similar results. Thus, all other things being equal, water will always boil at the same temperature, (at 100°C at sea level, for instance). Moreover, because these relationships are so consistent and because variation in one aspect is systematically related to variation in others (such that water boils at a lower temperature if barometric pressure is reduced) we can calculate precisely the amount of heat needed to produce the required transformation and therefore bring about the phenomenon when and where we wish with precise economy.

A particular characteristic of such a theory is that the abstractions used to define relationships between variables are defined reciprocally in terms of those variables and their interaction. Thus 100°C *defines* the point at which water boils at sea level just as 0°C defines the point at which ice melts. The abstraction *temperature* is given precision by such definitions.

In positivist social science similar attempts at the definition of precise reciprocal relationships between phenomena have largely failed. This has not prevented the frequent adoption of the *form* of theory typical in natural science. Its effect, however, has been dramatically different, for instead of producing a practical tool (such as a sort of behavioural thermometer) with application in many actual situations, what has resulted is a *reification* of certain ideas which constitute a symbolic world through which the concrete characteristics of an actual situation can be *mis*interpreted. What such theory has produced is not 'scientifically managed social control, but a skilful dramatic imitation of such control' (MacIntyre, 1981, p.102). The result is a theory built upon histrionics rather than subtance. The theory of leadership is such a theory.

Treating leadership as if it were a notion similar in kind to that of temperature has some rather bizarre consequences. For instance, while one can easily demonstrate (and thus accept the axiomatic structure of the consequent theory) that the application of a certain quantum of heat to a certain quantity of water at sea level raises the temperature of the water to 100°C at which point the water boils, the construction of a theory of leadership on an equivalent basis looks very peculiar indeed.

Taking for instance the four components of leadership identified by the National Commission on Excellence in Educational Administration as the key variables involved in the exercise of leadershp, such a 'theory' might suggest that the application of a certain quantum of 'symbolization' to a known quantity of 'recognition of excellence' under controlled 'conditions of conflict', while raising the level of managerial competence to 90 per cent, would consistently produce results whereby incompetent, unskilled, visionless leadership changed states and became 'competent, skilled, visionary leadership'. Moreover, having demonstrated through observation and experiment the consistent relationships between these variables in many apparently otherwise disparate situations, an axiomatic theory could be deduced which would allow us to reproduce particular conditions at will, transforming incompetent into competent leadership wherever and whenever we so desired.

The patent absurdity of a research agenda based upon such a thoughtless parody of natural science has not prevented behavioural scientists from pursuing such agendas. In the case of leadership the results of several decades of research have been, as one might expect, either trivial or equivocal or both. For instance, in what might be regarded as the state of the art review of leadership in educational administration Immegart (1988), in a review of reviews on 'Leadership and Leader Behaviour', reaches several less than startling conclusions, among them that:

1 'The weight of evidence to date, then, does indicate what most people seem to feel, if only experientially: Leadership and leader behaviour can make a difference' (p.261). (The equivalent here is presumably that 'most people feel — if only experientially — that heating water makes a difference'.)

2 'The traits of *intelligence, dominance, self-confidence,* and *high energy/activity level* are most often mentioned and are commonly agreed on across reviewers' (p.261). Nevertheless, 'that others possess such traits but are not leaders does not refute the evidence in this regard, anymore than does the fact that some leaders in some situations do not possess such characteristics' (pp.261-2). (The parallel here is presumably that 'researchers commonly agree that water boils when heated to 100°C but the fact that it sometimes boils without the application of heat and sometimes doesn't boil when heated past 100°C even when all other variables are held constant does not refute the evidence'.)

3 'Amid much conflicting evidence and drawing from most lines of inquiry using pure or continuous categorizations of style . . . it has become apparent that most effective or successful leaders

demonstrate style variability: that is, they score high on both or all dimensions employed in studies' (p.262). (The parallel here might be that 'it has become apparent that water boils whatever the situation is, but it boils differently in different situations'.)

4   'Style is, from enquiry to date, highly situational, and it has been found to be related to leadership success and effectiveness in a highly [sic] situational or contextual sense' (p.262). (The equivalent here is presumably that 'the boiling of water is a highly situational affair: a little bit more or a little bit less of a situation makes quite a difference'.)

In summary, '. . . the behavioural study of leadership has strongly affirmed the situational nature of the phenomenon . . . and has revealed the reciprocal effect between leader behavior and other organizational or situational variables' (p.264). The precise nature of these 'reciprocal' effects between leader behaviour and particular situational variables is not spelled out. Nothing remotely equivalent to the proposition that 'all other things being equal water boils at 100°C at sea level but variations in barometric pressure systematically alter the boiling point' is suggested.

The reason for such failure in four decades of research is sought in 'the aconceptual and atheoretical nature of all too many studies' (p.273), and the conclusion is drawn that 'perhaps the real problem with respect to leadership theory and conceptualization has been the lack of attention to *theoretical* development' (p.273).

Nonetheless, Immegart, putting the best possible gloss on his review, subsequently decides that 'leadership study has moved ahead over the past few decades despite . . . problems that are both inherent in the territory and in research more generally'; that 'optimism . . . about leadership research remains justified'; and that the '. . . continued advancement of the understanding of leadership is, in any case, contingent on sound *empirical* activity' (p.275, emphasis added).

What Immegart shows in his review of the literature is precisely what might be anticipated: a confusion of situationally specific non-replicable results showing little consistency and offering (despite his claim to the contrary) no possibility of an axiomatic theory which specifies the reciprocal and systematic variations produced in one phenomenon through alteration in another. There is no calculus of leadership in the offing.

Nonetheless, we are assured by the National Commission, despite the fact that behavioural science does not know what leadership is nor how it works, that we desperately need more of it in education. Such a position is not necessarily absurd. It is only made so by the processes of abstraction and reification encouraged by the application of a myopic behavioural science to the practice of educational administration.

Leadership and the Science of Administration

This abstraction of 'leadership' and the reification of a (yet to be constructed) calculus of 'leadership behaviour' is informed by similar logic to that which Greenfield criticizes in the wider field of organizational and administrative science. Greenfield has dicussed the failure of administrative science in considerable detail (Greenfield, 1975, 1978, 1979/80, 1980, 1983, 1984, 1985, 1986), but has recently summarized his argument in four main points (Greenfield, 1986).

The first concerns the main criteria by which administrative science asks to be judged — its efficacy in facilitating the control of organizations. Here Greenfield points out that

. . . administrative science does not work as a science; it has not brought us increased understanding and control of organizations. Yet this outcome is what both early and contemporary proponents of the science of administration claim to be its whole justification. Administrative science was to provide useful and powerful knowledge. This was the very criterion by which the fledgling science of administration rejected all previous knowledge in the field.(1986, p.71)

Greenfield's second point turns on an assertion similar to that made above in regard to leadership: that the reification of the abstraction deflects attention from the substantive concerns that must be dealt with on a day-to-day basis. Thus '. . . administrative science has ignored power relationships and has been content to deal with administrative problems that ignore substantive problems in education' (1986, p.71).

Thirdly, Greenfield suggests that the reification of the organization has created a theoretical blindness to the actual behaviour of those who wield power and make decisions.

. . . administrative science has focussed its efforts not upon the phenomenological realities of administration — upon the experience of wielding power and making decisions — but upon the organization. It has been content to regard organizations rather than people as the real actors in society. (1986, p.71)

Finally, Greenfield argues, the claim of administrative science to be value-free and interested only in rational explanation of behaviour (to separate facts from values and deal only with facts) has both diminished awareness of the importance of the study of values in human behaviour and focused on a limited definition of rationality. While making such claims, it has surreptitiously placed particular instrumental values at the heart of 'objective' administrative science. Thus

> . . . administrative science has devalued the study of human choice and rationality. It has insisted that decision making be dealt with *as though it were* fully explainable in rational and logical terms. This has allowed administrative science to deal with values surreptitiously, behind a mask of objectivity and impartiality, while denying it is doing so. (1986, p.71)

But what is to replace this inefficacious administrative science? Greenfield suggests that an alternative set of assumptions needs to be embraced. The first suggests that we stop treating organizations as though they are part of the natural order:

> Organizations are not things. They have no ontological reality, and there is no use studying them as though they did. They are an invented social reality of human creation. It is people who are responsible for organizations and people who change them. Organizations have reality only through human action, and it is that action (and the human will driving it) that we must come to understand. (1986, p.71)

Such an assumption makes a considerable difference to the notion of leadership that is possible, for, in contrast to the leader whose mastery of administrative science supposedly brings about an effective application of a technology of control, Greenfield's leader must be preoccupied with maintaining an organizational illusion. 'Organizations are a nexus of freedom and compulsion. As invented social realities, they can not only be created but also manipulated. The creation and maintenance of this illusion is the root of what the world understands as leadership . . .' (1986, p.72).

As a result of this redefinition the focus of study in the analysis of organizations and of those who lead through their creation and maintenance of the organizational illusion must also shift. 'The world of will, intention, experience and value is the world of organizations and administration. The building of a new science of administration will depend upon our ability to understand these realities' (1986, p.72).

Inevitably, envisaging the world of organization in this way suggests a rather different model than that of the homeostasis and equilibrium of conventional organizational theory. Quite the opposite may need to be considered:

> Conflict is endemic in organizations. It arises when different individuals or groups hold opposing values or when they must choose between accepted but incompatible values. . . . Administrative science must come to understand these complexities if it is to speak meaningfully to the world of practice. (1986, p.72)

The consequence is that leaders can be defined as those who articulate particular values within organizations and who negotiate those values into the organizational illusion that shapes, sustains and justifies behaviour. This is essentially a moral task. 'To help us begin to think of leaders in moral terms we should recognise that they are representatives of values: indeed, they are both creators of values and entrepreneurs for them' (1986, p.73).

However, as there is a plurality of values within society, leaders will embody differing values and the differing interests of differing groups.

> What we are left with, therefore, is contention among values or, more accurately, among those who espouse different values. In this view we are all leaders in some degree. We all have legitimacy in the degree to which we act out our own values and can involve others in them. (Greenfield, 1984, p.165)

The world Greenfield leaves us with is a world of illusion where leaders embody the values of particular groups and grapple with each other through symbols and moral preferences.

What are we to make of such an alternative to the behavioural science of traditional administration? Clearly Greenfield is right concerning the human construction of organizations and the presumption that as organizations are constructed they can therefore be reconstructed. He is also correct regarding the moral basis of organizational order. He is well justified in arguing the symbolic nature of leadership — even the theorists of corporate management concede this point (see Bates, 1987). But having accepted the major portion of Greenfield's argument, are we justified in accepting his conclusion that the only alternative to behavioural science is the path of existentialism, mysticism or anarchy? While we may concede that

> there is, therefore no ultimate reality in the understanding of organizations and those who would apply science to gain such understanding so that we may 'control' organizations in the same way that physical science enables us in some circumstances to

control nature are moving on a path that leads either to disappointment and defeat or else to self delusion. (1984, p.151)

do we necessarily have to agree that therefore '. . . understanding leads not to technique and technique to control; understanding leads only to greater understanding and (if we follow the insights of Eastern religions) to escape through insight, art, suspension of the will, and ultimately to oblivion (Greenfield, 1984, p.151)?

Does the rejection of behavioural science (for the quite proper reasons that Greenfield provides) *necessarily* entail the adoption of the existentialism, moral relativism, mysticism and organizational voluntarism that Greenfield seems to advocate? Does the critique of positivism lead us into the adoption of a subjectivist position (which Rizvi, 1986, and Lakomski, 1985, criticize in Greenfield's work) or to Hodgkinson's (1978) transcendental position to which Greenfield sometimes appeals (and which has been criticized by Evers, 1985, and Rizvi, 1986)? Or are there other, and perhaps more satisfactory, options?

The work of several contemporary theorists suggests that Greenfield's insights might well be extended in a somewhat different direction with quite encouraging results. In particular, the work of Giddens, Foucault and Habermas addresses a number of issues that lie at the heart of Greenfield's critique. The most important of these are:

1   the relation of individual to organization or, in Giddens' terms, between agency and structure;
2   the relation of power to knowledge and the historical processes of the institutionalization of power such as those discussed by Foucault;
3   the progressive rationalization of social, political and economic structures and of ethical and cultural concerns that forms the core of Habermas' work.

There are major differences and some strong disagreements between these three theorists and a fully worked out analysis would, of course, have to deal with these. The purpose of this chapter is not to present such a fully articulated theory, but simply to sketch areas of relevance and possible theoretical development that might serve to extend the current debate over leadership in new and more fruitful directions.

Agency and Structure

In his protest against the reification of organizations Greenfield declares that 'organizations are not things. . . . They are an invented social reality of human creation. It is people who are responsible for organizations and people who change them' (1986, p.71). So far, so good. Greenfield's protest against the granting of ontological status to organizations can be upheld. However, what is necessary in order to develop his criticism into a more defensible theoretical position is, first, some explanation of the processes of creation and re-creation of the 'invented social reality' of organizations, and secondly, some explanation of the status of the resulting organization and its effects on the creativity and re-creativity of individuals.

The starting point for an analysis of this issue must surely be Marx's familiar insight that while '. . . men make their history . . . they do not make it just as they please; they do not make it under circumstances chosen by themselves, but under circumstances directly encountered, given and transmitted from the past' (1951, p.225). Giddens takes up this insight and develops it into a theory of *structuration* which accounts for the reciprocal effects of agency and structure and which emphasizes

> . . . the essential recursiveness of social life, as constituted in social practices: [where] structure is both medium and outcome of the reproduction of practices. Structure enters simultaneously into the constitution of the agent and social practices, and 'exists' in the generating moments of this constitution. (1979, p.5)

Or, to adapt Marx's insight, '. . . all human action is carried out by knowledgable agents who both construct the social world through their action, but yet whose action is also constrained by the very world of their creation' (Giddens, 1981, p.54). The relationship of agency to structure is presented, therefore, as one in which neither organization (as in behavioural science) nor individual (as in Greenfield's critique) has primacy. Rather, they not only exist but are recursively defined and redefined in terms of each other; that is, *dialectically*.

As far as agency is concerned, Giddens argues that a theory of the acting subject must be constructed; one which situates and explains individual behaviour in terms of action located in time and space. That is, agency can only be understood if the continuity and location of experience are taken into account.

> An adequate account of human agency must, first, be connected to a theory of the acting subject; and, second, must situate action in *time and space* as a continuous flow of conduct, rather than treating purposes, reasons, etc., as somehow aggregated together. (1979, p.2)

At the same time social structures are sedimented into the consciousness (or if Gramsci's point is to be taken, into the *unconsciousness*) of individuals, and are both facilitating and constraining in terms of human agency. They are not, therefore, 'to be conceptualised as a barrier to action, but as essentially involved in its production' (1979, pp.69–70). Once again the dialectical relationship of agency with structure is argued.

Such a position sustains Greenfield's attack on the reification of organizations implicit in administrative science, but extends his argument to show not only how the 'invented social reality' of social practice is constituted and reconstituted by individuals but also how such social practice simultaneously *plays a part in the constitution and reconstitution of individuals*.

Giddens also argues that such dialectical processes must be understood historically. Both administrative science and Greenfield's critique are notable for their historical amnesia, and any adequate theory of agency and structure on which an appropriate theory of leadership can be built must recover a historical memory and situate its explanations in place and time if only because 'the sedimentation of institutional forms in long term processes of social development is an inescapable feature of all types of society. . . . Only by grasping this conceptually, rather than repudiating it, can we in fact approach the study of social change at all' (1979, p.7). Thus an understanding of human agency can only be gained through a focus on action as a 'continuous flow of conduct', while social change can only be understood through a historical analysis of the recursive paths of social and individual life.

Knowledge and Power in the Constitution of Social Life

If a dialectical approach to agency and structure offers an appropriate development of Greenfield's questions regarding the effects of the individual in the invention and reinvention of organization as a form of social reality, then attention may be turned to the second of Greenfield's concerns: the exercise of power in social life, especially in organizations.

Greenfield places the issues of power at the centre of his discussion by asserting that 'organizations are a nexus of freedom and compulsion' which constitute 'an order that is arbitrary, nonnatural, and often backed by enormous power, even by violence' (1986, p.72). Here Greenfield is drawing attention to a fundamental issue, one which Foucault has addressed across a number of historical contexts and within a number of important institutional structures. Foucault begins work from the following observation:

> Mechanisms of power in general have never been much studied
> by history. History has studied those who held power. . . . But
> power in all its strategies, at once general and detailed, and in its
> mechanisms, has never been studied. What has been studied even
> less is the relation between power and knowledge, the articula-
> tion of each on the other. (1980, p.51)

It is this relationship between power and knowledge and the constitution
of both by individuals through institutional development in time and
space which is at the heart of Foucault's work. Knowledge and power are
not only related but they are indeed *constitutive* of each other.

> The exercise of power constantly creates knowledge and,
> conversely, knowledge constantly induces effects of power. . . .
> Knowledge and power are integrated with one another. . . . It is
> not possible for power to be exercised without knowledge, it is
> impossible for knowledge not to engender power. (1980, p.52)

Much of Foucault's work has focused on the development of a particular
form of power in the eighteenth and nineteenth centuries, a form that he
calls 'panoptism'. It is a form of power that relies on the production of
quite specific forms of knowledge through surveillance. Panoptism,
claims Foucault, 'was a technological invention in the order of power,
comparable with the steam engine in the order of production' (1980,
p.71). It depended upon the collection and collation of certain kinds of
knowledge at local levels:

> This invention had the peculiarity of being utilised first of all on
> a local level, in schools, barracks and hospitals. This was where
> the experiment of integral surveillance was carried out. People
> learned how to establish dossiers, systems of marking and
> classifying, the integrated accountancy of individual records.
> . . . And, at a certain moment in time, these methods began to
> become generalised. (1980, p.71)

But they were not methods invented by the state, for instance, or by
large organizations. Panoptism was a local invention applied locally and
concerned with local control.

> In consequence one cannot confine oneself to analysing the State
> apparatus alone if one wants to grasp the mechanisms of power in
> their detail and complexity. . . . In reality, power . . . passes
> through much finer channels, and is much more ambiguous,

since each individual has at his [sic] disposal a certain power, and
for that very reason can also act as the vehicle for transmitting a
wider power. (1980, p.72)

Here is a point of contact with both Giddens' notion of the reciprocal
relations of agency and structure and with Greenfield's assertion of the
importance of individual subjectivity in the maintenance of the 'social
reality' of organization. Foucault addresses both these points directly.

Power must be analysed as something which circulates, or rather
as something which only functions in the form of a chain. It is
never localised here or there, never in anybody's hands, never
appropriated as a commodity or a piece of wealth. Power is
employed and exercised through a net-like organisation. And not
only do individuals circulate between its threads; they are always
in the position of simultaneously undergoing and exercising this
power. They are not only its inert or consenting target; they are
always also the elements of its articulation. In other words,
individuals are the vehicles of power, not its points of
articulation. . . . The individual which power has constituted is
at the same time its vehicle. (1980, p.98)

The production and exercise of such power is achieved through the
production of various discourses. As Foucault suggests:

. . . in a society such as ours, but basically in any society, there
are manifold relations of power which permeate, characterise and
constitute the social body, and these relations of power cannot
themselves be established, consolidated nor implemented without the production, accumulation and functioning of discourse.
There can be no possible exercise of power without a certain
economy of discourses of truth which operates through and on the
basis of this association. We are subjected to the production of
truth through power and we cannot exercise power except
through the production of truth. (1980, p.93)

Foucault concentrates his analyses of the production of various forms of
discourse and the coincidental production and exercise of various forms of
power on a number of pivotal institutions, medicine, psychoanalysis,
criminology, sexuality, mental health and *en passant* education. He shows
how the development of particular forms of discourse and the exercise of
particular kinds of power were interdependent and related to an overall
imperative: social production.

In the seventeenth and eighteenth centuries a form of power

comes into being that begins to exercise itself through social production and social service. It becomes a matter of obtaining productive service from individuals in their concrete lives. And in consequence, a real and effective 'incorporation' of power was necessary, in the sense that power had to gain access to the bodies of individuals, to their acts, attitudes and modes of everyday behaviour. Hence the significance of methods like school discipline, which succeeded in making children's bodies the objects of highly complex systems of manipulation and con-ditioning. But at the same time, these new techniques of power needed to grapple with the phenomena of population, in short to undertake the administration, control and direction of the accumulation of men . . . hence there arise the problems of demography, public health, hygiene, housing conditions, longevity and fertility. (1980, p.125)

Such problems were addressed through the development of a particular form of discourse which articulated, served the needs of and was dependent on a particular exercise of power. The result was a specific 'political economy' of truth.

In societies like ours, the 'political economy' of truth is characterised by five important traits. 'Truth' is centred on the form of scientific discourse and the institutions which produce it; it is subject to constant economic and political incitement . . .; it is the object, under diverse forms, of immense diffusion and consumption . . .; it is produced and transmitted under the control, dominant if not exclusive, of a few great political and economic apparatuses . . .; lastly, it is the issue of a whole political debate and social confrontation. (1980, p.132)

However, as Foucault points out, such official discourse and the exercise of powers it encourages is always open to subversion. Indeed, the more generalized and abstract the discourse becomes, the more generalized the form of power exercised, the more likely it is that at the local level alternative forms of discourse and alternative forms of power will develop. This phenomenon Foucault labels the *insurrection of subjugated knowledges* (1980, p.81). By this he indicates the resurgence of personal, local and specific knowledges which have been marginalized or disenfranchized by the operation of scientific discourse and centralized power. Here the parallel with Greenfield is strong, as one of the objects of Greenfield's critique is to assert the primacy of personal subjectivity in the face of organizational science.

Foucault claims that it is these subjugated knowledges which form the basis of criticism of the dominant discourse/power. The tactics of attempts to reactivate such local discursivities Foucault calls a genealogy of power.

> By comparison, then, and in contrast to the various projects which aim to inscribe knowledges in the hierarchical order of power associated with science, a genealogy should be seen as a kind of attempt to emancipate historical knowledges from subjection, to render them, that is, capable of opposition and of struggle against the coercion of a theoretical, unitary, formal and scientific discourse. It is based on the reactivation of local knowledges . . . in opposition to the scientific hierarchisation of knowledges and the effects intrinsic to their power. . . . (1980, p.85)

Here Foucault's analysis is in sympathy with Greenfield's contention that conflict is endemic to organizations. That is, if organization is concerned with power, and power is organized through the production, articulation and imposition of particular forms of discourse, then the emergence of 'subjugated knowledges' within organizations (the emergence of Greenfield's critique within the organization of administrative science in education, for instance) presents not simply a challenge to the official discourse (or truth telling) but also a challenge to the exercise of power.

As a result of such a view, Foucault suggests that it would be possible to develop an analysis of the 'geopolitics' of discourse/power, thus linking the production of subjectivity through the exercise of truth and power with historical and spatial descriptions of 'territories' both occupied and disputed. His studies of the discourse/power which produced the clinic, the hospital, the asylum, the prison and the school give some indication of how such a geopolitics could be constructed. This endeavour would catch up, extend and concretize some of Greenfield's concerns as well as satisfy Giddens' admonition to locate such analyses of the relation between agency and structure in space and time:

> . . . the formation of discourses and the genealogy of knowledge need to be analysed, not in terms of types of consciousness, modes of perception and forms of ideology, but in terms of tactics and strategies of power. Tactics and strategies deployed through implantations, distributions, demarcations, control of territories and organisation of domains. . . . (1980, p.77)

Such a geopolitics of knowledge/power would be simultaneously a study of the administration of knowledge/power.

Once knowledge can be analysed in terms of region, domain, implantation, displacement, transposition, one is able to capture the process by which knowledge functions as a form of power and disseminates the effects of power. There is an administration of knowledge, a politics of knowledge, relations of power which pass via knowledge and which, if one tries to transcribe them, lead on to consider forms of domination designed by such notions as field, region, territory. And the politico-strategic term is an indication of how the military and the administration come to inscribe themselves both on a material soil and within forms of discourse. (1980, p.69)

In focusing on inscription of knowledge/power on the terrain of local and specific institutions, Foucault provides graphic descriptions of the formation and effects of knowledge/power on everyday life and of the embodiment of that knowledge/power in the physical subjectivities of individuals. He is surely correct to point out that '. . . one cannot confine oneself to analysing the State apparatus alone if one wants to grasp the mechanisms of power in their detail and complexity. . . . In reality, power in its exercise goes much further, passes through much finer channels and is much more ambiguous . . .' (1980, p.72).

On the other hand, Foucault does not accept the Nietzschian idea (one echoed by Greenfield) that power is the outcome of individual will: '. . . power is not built up out of "wills" (individual or collective), nor is it derivable from interests. Power is constructed and functions on the basis of particular powers, myriad issues, myriad effects of power' (1980, p.188). Or in a parallel with Marx's insight into the nature of class, Foucault suggests that 'in reality power means *relations*, a more or less organised, hierarchical, co-ordinated cluster of *relations*' (1980, p.198, italics added).

The new relations of power that Foucault sees as arising in the eighteenth and nineteenth centuries were driven by the reorganization of another, symbiotic, set of relations: those of production. Indeed, Foucault argues that the engine of this change derived from the concern with 'obtaining productive service from individuals in their concrete lives' (1980, p.125). Thus, for instance, the reconceptualization and reconstruction of poverty are analyzed, beginning with a functional discrimination between the 'wilfully idle' and the 'involuntary unemployed'. 'This analysis has as its practical objective at best to make poverty useful by fixing it to the apparatus of production. . . . The problem is to set the "able-bodied" poor to work and transform them into a useful labour force . . .' (1980, p.169). What Foucault suggests, then, is that the emergence of panoptism was essentially provoked by the idea of making order out of disorderly lives; the new order of power and the new order of knowledge were driven by a new order of production and demanded a particular rationalization of consciousness and behaviour.

At this point the emerging argument can be seen to have addressed the issue of subjectivity and objectivity raised by Greenfield; the issues of temporal and spatial location of the dialectic of agency and structure raised by Giddens; and to have incorporated Foucault's account of the interpenetration of the production and execution of power and knowledge within the context of a transformation of various mechanisms of social and economic production.

What still has to be addressed before we can provide some respectable theoretical substance for the empty notion of leadership presented in the literature is the problem of order. Do we live in a world where all that is possible is existential choice, moral and cultural relativism and the ultimate ennui of religious oblivion, or is order possible? Can we construct, though within limits not of our choosing, a history that is both productive and moral? Weber, whose sociology (along with that of Marx) has dominated the twentieth century, thought not.

Disenchantment and the Iron Cage of Reason

Weber believed on the basis of his historical research that the ideas of Protestantism broke down the religious enchantment of the Middle Ages by transforming the world of superstition and custom into a world of rational examination and a 'methodological organization of conduct'. While the impetus of this transformation was in itself religious, the major focus of the methodological organization of conduct was that of productive, entrepreneurial action.

According to Weber, Protestantism was differentiated from all other religions by several quite specific characteristics.

> It demanded of the believer not celibacy, as in the case of the monk, but the elimination of all erotic pleasure or desire; not poverty, but the elimination of all enjoyment of unearned wealth and income, and the avoidance of all feudalistic, life-loving ostentation of wealth; not the ascetic death-in-life of the cloister, but an *alert, rationally controlled conduct of life* and the avoidance of all surrender to the beauty of the world, to art, or to one's own moods and emotions. The clear and uniform goal of this

asceticism was *the disciplining and methodological organisation of conduct*. Its typical representative was the 'man of vocation' and its specific result was the *rational, functional organization of social relations*. (Weber, in Pusey, 1987, pp.49-50)

In part, at least, such developments were a result of the increasing size of traditional societies where the differentiation of various pursuits led to a differentiation of knowledge and control.

> As these pre-modern traditional societies of Europe grow larger and more complex there is an increasing 'specialization' and differentiation of those spheres of activity that Weber identifies as political activity, art, religion, intellectual development, economic activity and even the pursuit of erotic pleasure. Weber emphasizes that in the course of this differentiation each of these spheres becomes 'autonomous' and that this simply means that, gradually, each sphere is regulated by axioms and norms that are increasingly incommensurate with those of the others. (Pusey, 1987, pp.50-1)

But the driving force that emerged from this transformation was not religious but *productive*: that of capitalist entrepreneurialism. The result, according to Weber, was the transformation of a moral order into a mechanical order.

> For when asceticism was carried out of monastic cells into everyday life, and began to dominate worldly morality, it did its part in building the tremendous cosmos of the modern economic order. This order is *now bound to the technical and economic conditions of machine production which to-day determine the lives of all the individuals who are born into this mechanism*, not only those directly concerned with economic acquisition, *with irresistable force*. (Weber, in Pusey, 1987, p.52)

The logic of the machine, constructed through a new organization of power and knowledge, in Weber's view, becomes the dominating logic of social organization. It creates an iron cage by means of bureaucracy: 'Bureaucracy is *the* way of translating social action into rationally organized action' (Weber, 1968, p.987). There was, however, a problem. The process of bureaucratization '. . . develops the more perfectly, the more it is dehumanised, the more completely it succeeds in eliminating from official business, love, hatred, and all personal, irrational and emotional elements which escape calculation' (Weber, 1968, p.975). The result is an inevitable progression towards a terminal world whose inhumanity produces a final 'mechanised petrification, embellished with a sort of convulsive self-importance' (1968, p.182).

Weber saw the 'evolution' of society as benefiting humanity (at least initially) through the processes of disenchantment and rationalization; processes that eventually (and paradoxically) destroyed human values.

Weber was essentially pessimistic about the course of human history. The source of this pessimism lies, as MacIntyre (1981) suggests, in a fundamental mistake over the nature of values, for Weber is essentially committed to an *emotivist* theory of values.

> Emotivism is the doctrine that all evaluative judgements and more specifically all moral judgements are *nothing but* expressions of preference, expressions of attitude or feeling, insofar as they are moral or evaluative in character. . . . [Thus] moral judgements, being expressions of attitude or feeling are neither true nor false; and agreement is not to be secured by any rational method, for there are none. (MacIntyre, 1981, pp.11-12)

The adoption of such a theory of value (under the influence of Nietzsche) created a difficult paradox for Weber. In the first place the increasing rationalization of society is a triumph for reason and social order. But the whole edifice lacks any other justification than its own instrumental effectiveness, for if values are simply a matter of individual preference, there can be no rational agreement over ends, and therefore no agreed justification for the purposes to which the enormously effective machines of bureaucracy can be put.

This paradox is amply displayed in Weber's account of the realm of politics, to which he allocated questions of purpose and value. Politics, suggested Weber, was the province of power seekers who pursued not only 'objective goals' but also 'the patronage of office' (Weber, 1970, p.147). It is a world where even apparently objective goals are chosen on an essentially irrational basis 'because the various value spheres of the world stand in irreconcilable conflict with each other' (1970, p.147). Ultimately it is a world in which '*Weltanschauungen* clash, world views among which in the end one has to make a choice' (1970, p.117). But there is, according to Weber's emotivist position, no *rational* way of making such choices; they are simply a matter of preference. The inevitable conclusion of such an argument is that what passes for judgment and value in political life (as in the sphere of values) is simply the result of superior power, for 'the decisive means of politics is *violence*' (1970, p.121).

Such violence is not necessarily physical. Indeed, Weber saw politics as a matter, largely, of symbolic violence, of *charisma* where the force of will (echoes of Greenfield) on the part of 'great men' provides justification for particular purposes and forms of social organization. The result is, however, the same. From the emotivist position there can be no justification for the moral choices of great men other than their success in imposing those choices on others.

But there is surely something inconsistent in this view, for Weber argues elsewhere that the process of rationalization takes place in *each* of the increasingly autonomous spheres of activity as the disenchantment of the world of tradition and superstition proceeds. Thus, for instance, religion, ethics, art and law develop their own relatively separate forms of argument and debate, which produce increasingly formal and increasingly *rational* statements of principle and norm. The whole point of such rationalization is to produce agreed and defensible accounts of such principles and norms. Moreover, the process of criticism and debate fundamental to the progressive rationalization of such spheres is continuous and communal.

Here, suggests MacIntyre, is the key to Weber's problem, for despite Nietzsche and the tradition of the Enlightenment which promoted the emotivist theory of values (along with a notion of liberal individualism), the only ground on which values can be constructed and reconstructed is that of a *shared* tradition of practice. Thus

> . . . if the conception of the good has to be expounded in terms of such actions as those of a practice, of the narrative unity of a human life and of a moral tradition, then goods, and with them the only grounds for the authority of laws and virtues, can only be discovered by entering into those relationships which constitute communities whose central bond is a shared vision and understanding of goods. (MacIntyre, 1981, p.240)

This is not to say that the traditions and beliefs of such communities are to be accepted without question, for that would be simply to return to the processes of enchantment from which reason has allowed us to escape. Rather, MacIntyre suggests, the processes of argument and conflict that take place within such communities help to clarify and redefine tradition in the sphere of values *as in other spheres of human activity*. Thus '. . . if my account of the nature of moral tradition is correct, a tradition is sustained and advanced by its own internal arguments and conflicts' (1981, p.242). Such an argument would seem very close to the original argument proposed by Weber as fundamental to the process of rationalization. Moreover, it supports Weber's original contention that such processes occur within each of the increasingly autonomous spheres of human action, including those concerned with values: art, religion, political activity, erotic pleasure. How, then, could Weber end up succumbing to the irrationality of the emotivist theory of values or to the existential despair of his description of the paradox of the iron cage?

Weber Reconstructed: A Dialectic of Values and Interests

Weber couched his early analysis of the rationalization of society brought about by Protestantism in terms of the cultural and psychological processes involved. As Pusey puts it, 'For Weber . . . the reconciliation of subjective experience with the objective world was a solitary personal struggle with fate' (1987, p.50). The result of this struggle was a transformation of ethics and culture and the rationalization of personal conduct on a methodical basis. However, as Habermas points out so clearly, Weber's later discussion of the processes of rationalization is located solely in the social, political and economic organizations characteristic of the modern state. The result is the substitution of a rationalized world of coercion for the liberated world of individual action.

> The rationalization process is no longer primarily a cultural and 'psychological' process: we are no longer tracing a process that unfolds, as it did before, in the dimensions of *culture* and *personality*. The perspective has changed, and it is now the functional imperatives of the state and the economy that together drive the rationalization process in a gloomy path that leads ultimately to spiritual, intellectual, and moral extinction. (Pusey, 1987, p.53)

Along with this shift in the focus of Weber's work Habermas suggests there has also been a *narrowing* of focus so that Weber now dwells exclusively on the development of instrumental (rational purposive) action. His earlier focus on the development of ethical and cultural (value rational) action simply disappears. Habermas suggests that this is a fundamental mistake, for what Weber implies is that rational purposive action *displaces* value rational action as the process of modernization proceeds.

Habermas argues that Weber erred in regarding the modernization of society as taking place along a single continuum, where concerns with ethics and culture are inevitably displaced by concerns with the social, economic and political structures of power. Rather, Habermas suggests, the rationalization of society takes place through a *dialectic between two parallel processes* of rationalization, one concerning ethics and culture and one concerning structures of power. As a result of his failure to recognize this, 'Weber's account of the rationalization process is incomplete, discontinuous, and inconsistent' (Pusey, 1987, p.54). Pusey presents this argument schematically (see Figure 1).

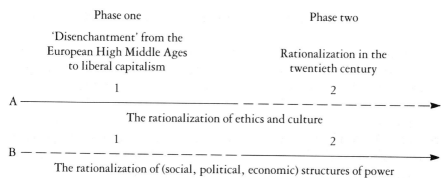

Figure 1. *The reconstruction of the process of rationalization*

As Pusey suggests,

> . . . Weber's focus moves along the two (solid) lines A1 and B2. Weber's analysis of the first (phase one) of the rationalization process is cast in terms of an unfolding logic of development in the realm of culture and ethics (along line A1). The mistake and the inconsistency arise in the discontinuity of the explanatory framework as Weber 'switches tracks' in the shift from the first to a second phase that he thereafter 'one-sidedly' explains in terms of the social and structural institutionalization of power in the economy and the state (line B2). (1987, p.54)

What Habermas is suggesting is that in order to 'correct' Weber the rationalization of culture and ethics (line A2) must be understood as progressing *independently* of the rationalization of the structures of power. Moreover, the development of this process of rationalization leads from the early challenge presented by Protestantism to tradition-bound ethics through a 'legislative ethic' and an 'ethic of conviction' towards an 'ethics of responsibility' which points towards an eventual 'universalistic ethics of brotherhood' (Pusey, 1987, pp.56-7). Such ethics has a dialectical relationship with the structures of power (potentially, at least), calling them to account and promoting 'the institutionalization of an increasing measure of justice, truth and freedom' (Pusey, 1987, p.57).

What both MacIntyre and Habermas suggest is that the moral relativism engendered by the emotivist theory of values is mistaken, indeed, that notions of value can only be validated with respect to a *public* tradition. This tradition is open to scrutiny and debate which, far from inhibiting or destroying the tradition, serves continuously to strengthen and rationalize the tradition towards a more inclusive account of justice, truth and freedom. The world of ethics is not, therefore, simply a matter of arbitrary choice, nor is the world of values simply a matter of subjection to the will of the powerful; rather, it is a world where reasons may be given and considered and argument provided, which lead to the progressive articulation of formal principles and rational action. Moreover, rather than being dependent on, or resulting from, the world of functional imperatives associated with the increasing rationalization of interests (through social, economic and political power), they have a life of their own. As Pusey suggests, 'Habermas wants to press the . . . view that the "normative structures" of culture, morality and collective identity do not simply follow economic or system imperatives and that they *evolve according to their own logic*' (1987, p.40).

If this is so, then a dialectic between values on the one hand and interests on the other becomes possible. Under such conditions Weber's existential despair at the dominance of the iron cage can be rejected, for the recovery and recognition of a public tradition of ethical discourse provides a basis *other than mere personal preference* for the interrogation of the ethical and cultural effects of such a rationalization of interests. Truth, justice, freedom and progress towards a 'universalistic ethics of brotherhood' become counterweights to the efficient use of power in the rationalization of cultural as well as productive life.

Rationalization and the Laws of Leadership

We are now in a better position from which to consider the issues raised by Greenfield in his analysis of leadership and of the 'science of administration'. We have considered the relationship between individual and social organization through the ideas of agency and structure. We have spoken of the necessary spatial and temporal location of any analysis of action. We have discussed the relationship between power and knowledge. We have examined the 'geopolitics' of discourse. We have reconstructed Weber's analysis of the rationalization of society. We have rejected the emotivist theory of values. We have outlined a dialectical view of relationships between the rationalization of values and the rationalization of interests. What remains is to sketch the relationship between this reconstruction of social theory and the reconstruction of the notion of leadership. The key to such a reconstruction is the idea of the law.

Those committed to administrative science of the traditional kind were, as we initially suggested, committed also to the discovery of 'laws' of administration akin to those that were presumed to exist in the field of natural science. We have seen some of the absurdities towards which such an idea leads. Almost without exception the search for such laws has led to conclusions that are either trivial or so surrounded by contingencies of one kind or another as to be surrounded by caveats. Such results should have told us something about our construction of the problem of administration. Even after Greenfield's warning that we had a confused notion of our objectives, most advocates of administrative science simply redoubled their efforts. There simply *had* to be laws that would allow us to increase our control of organizations: that would allow leaders to lead more effectively.

What Greenfield showed us was that the search for such laws was problematic. The focus on structure denied the obvious power of agency (indeed, the very notion of leadership demanded a notion of agency that theories of structure denied). The attempt to abstract and to generalize 'laws' of organization reified 'organization', detaching the idea from the reality of place and time. The separation of form from substance produced a social and historical amnesia regarding cultural (including educational) concerns. In addition to these problems the previous discussion has suggested that the adoption by both administrative scientists and Greenfield of an emotivist theory of values leads to the denial of the importance of public tradition and debate over values and a fundamentally inadequate theory of individualism. Each of these difficulties suggests that the notion of laws of administrative life (and hence of leadership) that previously informed the debate is inadequate.

Once again Habermas attempts a reformulation of an idea of central importance in the progressive rationalization of society. Rather than speak of a codified body of laws, Habermas speaks of the public tradition of the law. Following Weber's notion of the progressive differentiation of various institutions, Habermas argues that the law occupies a strategic location in the rationalization of society. Many commentators have suggested that the law is invariably an instrument of the exercise of power. Habermas' view is more complex than this, as Pusey suggests:

> The blade of Habermas's argument is aimed at positivist and functionalist interpretations that try always to depict the law merely as a completely malleable instrument of power and interest. It does, of course, serve power interests and it is indeed used as a cruel instrument of repression, but Habermas's point is that the *form* of 'post-traditional' law, from about the sixteenth

century, embodies a logic of cultural and ethical development
that *sets ever more coherent limits to what it can and cannot legitimate.*
(1987, p.55)

Thus, in Habermas' view, the law is not a one-way street through
which the instrumental interests of the powerful are imposed upon the
powerless. Rather, the progressive rationalization of cultural and ethical
principles demands that the law impose restrictions on the untrammeled
deployment of power.

> Through the law, power is therefore constrained by cultural and
> ethical 'principles' that lie beyond its reach, and, for an
> understanding of *society* this is of equal importance to other faces
> of the law as a medium through which culture and ethics are
> neutralized and appropriated in the service of power. In the
> course of history, as now, legal structures mediate between ideas
> and interests in *both* directions. (Pusey, 1987, p.55)

The law as a practice is, then, one of the mediators of the dialectic
between agency and structure, and between cultural and ethical
developments on the one hand and organizational developments on the
other.

If this is so, then the notion of the leader which is implicit in
administrative science — that of one who discovers and applies the laws
of organizational control — requires revision. So does the notion of the
great man of iron will who imposes his moral vision upon his followers by
force of presence. Neither is an adequate account of the idea of
leadership.

What the perspective sketched here suggests is that leaders might
better be thought of as located in space and time within particular
discourses of power and knowledge, within particular definitions of
agency and structure, and within particular discourses which address
issues involved in the rationalization of culture and ethics on the one
hand and power and organization on the other, a well as within the
dialectic between them. A model based upon such assumptions might
well allow us to develop a theory of leadership which is somewhat akin to
Foucault's notion of power: that it is something that inheres not in
people nor in positions but in relationships, relationships which are
constantly open to definition and redefinition. Such a notion would allow
us to study the constitution and reconstitution of 'networks' of
leadership, and to produce a 'geopolitics' of leadership which took into
account the specific nature of the spatial and temporal location of
leadership as well as the nature of the discourse by which leadership was

defined. We might also think of leadership in the same way as Habermas encourages us to think of the law: as a process of mediation between interests and values. Moreover, we might be able to reintroduce substantive issues into the discussion of leadership as the dialectic between interests and values is seldom negotiated solely at the level of principle: it invariably has an empirical content which is contested.

Such a notion of leadership needs further elaboration, further justification, further substantiation than can be provided in this brief paper. However, it seems possible that some of the considerations that have been prompted by Greenfield's analysis of educational leadership and administration and by particular developments in social theory could lend themselves to a radical reconceptualization of notions of both educational administration and educational leadership.

Such an alterntive theory might also allow the apparent absurdity of the National Commission's call for more leadership of a kind it cannot name to be resolved. For the conundrum with which the Commission is faced is that produced by a vestigial awareness of the need for cultural and ethical leadership in a field where leadership is defined in terms of technique — of the mastery of instrumental rationality in the service of social, economic and political power. A theory that allowed a tradition of ethical and cultural discourse to re-enter debate over leadership in education might be rather more helpful than the prolongation of the search for the administrative laws of educational life and for their imposition by leaders of iron will.

References

Eliot, T.S. (1974) *Collected Poems 1909-1962,* London, Faber.

Evers, C. (1985) 'Hodgkinson on ethics and the philosophy of educational administration,' *Educational Administration Quarterly,* 22,4, pp.27-50.

Foucault, Michel (1980) *Power/Knowledge: Selected Interviews and Other Writings 1971-1977,* New York, Pantheon.

Giddens, A. (1979) *Central Problems of Social Theory,* London, Macmillan.

Giddens, A. (1981) *A Contemporary Critique of Historical Materialism,* London, Macmillan.

Greenfield, T.B. (1975) 'Theory about organization: A new perspective and its implications for schools,' in M. Hughes (Ed.), *Administering Education: International Challenge,* London, Athlone, pp.71-99.

Greenfield, T.B. (1978) 'Reflections on organizational theory and the truths of irreconcilable realities,' *Educational Administration Quarterly,* 14,2, pp.1-23.

Greenfield, T.B. (1979/80) 'Research in educational administration in the United States and Canada: An overview and critique,' *Educational Administration,* 8,1, pp.207-45.

Greenfield, T.B. (1980) 'The man who comes back through the door in the wall,' *Educational Administration Quarterly,* 16,3, pp.26-59.

Greenfield, T.B. (1983) 'Against group mind: An anarchistic theory of organisation,' in L. Rattray-Wood (Ed.), *Reflective Readings in Educational Administration,* Geelong, Deakin University Press, pp.293-301.

Greenfield, T.B. (1984) 'Leaders and schools: Wilfullness and nonnatural order in organizations,' in T.J. Sergiovanni and J.E. Corbally (Eds), *Leadership and Organizational Culture,* Urbana, Ill., University of Illinois, pp.142-69.

Greenfield, T.B. (1985) 'Theories of educational organization: A critical perspective,' in T. Husen and N. Postlethwaite (Eds), *International Encyclopedia of Education,* Oxford, Pergamon, pp.5240-51.

Greenfield, T.B. (1986) 'The decline and fall of science in educational administration,' *Interchange,* 17,2, pp.57-80.

Hodgkinson, C. (1978) *Towards a Philosophy of Administration,* Oxford, Basil Blackwell.

Immegart, Glen L. (1988) 'Leadership and leader behaviour,' in Norman J. Boyan (Ed.), *Handbook of Research on Educational Administration,* New York, Longman, pp.259-78.

Lakomski, G. (1985) 'Theory, value and relevance in educational administration,' in F. Rizvi (Ed.), *Working Papers in Ethics and Educational Administration: 1985,* Geelong, School of Education, Deakin University, pp.35-64.

MacIntyre, A. (1981) *After Virtue: A Study in Moral Theory,* London, Duckworth.

Marx, K. (1951) 'The eighteenth brumaire of Louis Bonaparte,' in *Marx and Engels, Selected Works,* London, Lawrence and Wishart.

NCEEA (National Commission on Excellence in Educational Administration) (1987) *Leaders for America's Schools,* Tempe, Ariz., University Council for Educational Administration.

Pusey, Michael (1987) *Jurgen Habermas,* London, Tavistock.

Rizvi, Fazal (1986) 'Re-establishing values in organisation and administrative theory: Comments on papers by Greenfield, Holmes and Hodgkinson,' Paper presented at the annual conference of the American Educational Research Association, San Francisco.

Weber, Max (1968) *Economy and Society: An Outline of Interpretive Sociology,* 3 vols, Eds R. Gunter and C. Wittich, trans E. Fischoff, New York, Bedminster Press.

Weber, Max (1970) *From Max Weber,* Trans H. Gerth and C. Mills, London, Routledge and Kegan Paul.

Chapter 6

Educational Leadership as Reflective Action

John Codd

The notion that leaders should be philosophers is not new. Indeed, it can be found as far back as Plato but it has never been widely accepted. As social institutions have become more bureaucratic and have acquired more specific functions, leadership has come to be identified either with managerial or interpersonal skills, or with charismatic personality. The idea that leadership could be the natural manifestation of a philosophical disposition has been rejected as being both impractical and elitist. It is an idea that has seemed to be incompatible with the industrial imperatives of modern society. As these imperatives have embraced more and more areas of institutional life, including the institutions of education, leadership has been defined increasingly in terms of management, efficiency and productivity. But this is a view of leadership which does not value critical reflection, personal autonomy or collective deliberation. It is, therefore, a view of leadership that is particularly inappropriate to educational institutions because it negates the *educational* purposes of those institutions.

This chapter argues that the practice of *educational* leadership is a form of philosophy in action, that it is an area of philosophical practice. On first consideration this may seem paradoxical, for while it is self-evident that leadership is a practical activity, it is often assumed that philosophy is a form of intellectual contemplation somewhat removed from the everyday world of decision-making and action. Action is thus divorced from reflection and leadership is seen to be inspired not by philosophical conjecture but by intuition and common sense. In the discussion that follows it will be suggested that these assumptions reflect both a narrow conception of philosophy and a fundamental misconstrual of the relationship between human thought and action. More positively, it will be argued not only that educational leadership can and should be both reflective and active, but also that philosophy can and should be more than merely passive speculation. Before these arguments can be developed, however, it is necessary to distinguish the *educational* aspects of educational leadership from the managerial aspects.

Rethinking Educational Leadership

The trend towards a 'management' approach to educational leadership is part of a much broader process in which economic and political concepts initially employed to describe and define particular forms of interaction within industrial contexts have been gradually transported into the cultural sphere as part of an ideology of control (Callahan, 1960). That there has been apparently little resistance to this trend amongst educators themselves is in part due to the pervasiveness of the ideological forces involved, but it is also a reflection of the failure of traditional theories guiding educational administration to recognize and promote the distinctively *educational* features of those institutions where educational administration takes place (Griffiths, 1985). Thus administrative theory has become separated from educational theory with the effect of distorting and narrowing the way educational administrators interpret their roles. If the concept of educational leadership is to include significantly more than is implied by educational management, then it is necessary to consider what education means and how this can be related to the goals of schooling.

In thinking about education, it is sometimes useful to make a distinction between its *formal* and *informal* aspects. In formal education, to use Langford's (1973) definition, two parties may be distinguished, one of whom, the teacher, accepts responsibility for what the other, the pupil, learns. When learning occurs without this condition being met, the term *informal education* may be used. This distinction has acquired greater significance in recent years as it has been recognized that schools and other educational institutions have many socializing effects, producing learning that is not necessarily related to the purposive, self-conscious practical activities associated with teaching. These effects have been referred to as a 'hidden' or 'unstated' curriculum that can be contrasted with the 'formal' or 'planned' curriculum of schools. Indeed, it is frequently argued that the socializing effects of the hidden curriculum are miseducative to such a degree that formal education becomes thwarted by the institutions in which it is carried out, namely schools (Jackson, 1968; Illich, 1971).

But formal education is not *necessarily* a process of socialization or schooling in this narrow sense, and as educators become more concerned with increasing educational opportunity and less concerned with preserving the institution of schooling we may begin to see substantial reforms in both the structure and functioning of schools. Such reforms, however, are not possible within a management ethos because the relationship of managerial activities and long-term educational outcomes remains unclear. Managerial strategies are basically supportive of the status quo. They rest on the assumption that what is learned in schools should be determined, either directly or indirectly, by social and cultural factors that impinge on the classroom from the wider community outside the school gates.

Thus when managerial effectiveness usurps more important educational aims, we are more likely to have schools in which the needs of society are given priority over the development of rational autonomy and independent thought. Under these conditions, political forces are better able to ensure that the school remains an instrument for social control. But this is a function that perhaps should be called into question because implicit in such a view is a strong commitment to the harmonious continuity of prevailing values and the perpetuation of the existing social order.

In order to place the role and responsibilities of educational administrators into a wider perspective, we need to consider some of the central criteria of the concept of education itself, as distinct from the process of schooling. When we do this, we begin to see that specifying a set of 'social functions', which a particular administrative arrangement can be said to serve, is not the same as specifying its educational justification. Likewise, to invoke as a rationale for administrative practice its particular managerial consequences may have very little to do with whether it is valuable or worthwhile, or ought to belong in an educational context or situation. The fact that schools may function more smoothly under some administrative arrangements rather than others provides no sure measure of their educational value.

The industrial management model, with its emphasis on efficiency, treats teachers as workers rather than professionals and thereby diminishes their commitment to the values and principles which define the field of educational practice. Specification of objectives, close supervision and other management techniques may encourage teachers to behave in ways that are antithetical to certain fundamental educational values such as intellectual independence and imagination. Conformity to institutional norms may ensure that minimal levels of performance are maintained and managerial competence can improve efficiency, but educational excellence derives from personal initiative and professional autonomy. The educational administrator is more than a facilitator of learning or an agent of socialization; he or she is a person who embodies fundamental educational values.

Particular managerial skills may be useful, but for the educational administrator, 'a fully professional commitment is always to a set of values and principles for practice rather than to a particular institution in which the individual happens currently to hold an appointment' (Taylor, 1976, p.44). This commitment will spring from a knowledge that formal education should be a purposeful and responsible activity — that it should be a practical activity, not completely determined by the institution of schooling, but arising out of the personal decisions of administrators, teachers and pupils and carried out within the specified social context of the school.

Professional educators, whether they be policy-makers, administrators or teachers, are inevitably involved in the business of judging and deciding what ought to be done. Whether they are determining ends or means, they cannot escape the commitment to values; neither can they ignore the careful appraisal of facts — psychological, sociological or historical — pertinent to each decision. It is the bringing together of these two components that produces the *responsibility* criterion which is so important in formal education, and which can distinguish it from socialization or schooling in the narrow sense. As a practical activity, therefore, educational administration should entail responsible deliberation and decision-making, enabling teachers within the school to have an active role in producing an educated community of individuals who will have the capacity to promote dynamic, democratic social order. Unless the administrator is committed to basic educational principles, it is likely that the social functions of the school will assume priority over its educational goals. This is a major consideration in that area of educational administration concerned with curriculum planning.

From the outset it should be recognized that specifying 'social functions' with respect to the curriculum has similar effects to specifying them for any other administrative arrangement. Indeed, as with other practices, to invoke as a rationale for some specific curriculum content its 'social functions' may have very little to do with whether it has educational value and therefore ought to be taught to students in the school. For example, the fact that achievement-motivation and competition are essential to a capitalist economy is no argument for their educational value. Indeed, the very point of social education, if it is to be morally defensible, is that existing social practices be subjected to critical evaluation and rational scrutiny aimed at finding out whether such practices are worth perpetuating and whether they are capable of being defended with respect to the educational goals of autonomy, emancipation and human well-being (Giroux, 1983).

To accept existing social practice as the basis for curriculum planning is to confuse education with socialization, and this is a confusion to which many educational administrators are susceptible. Although it is part of the purpose of education to transmit the prevailing norms and ways of behaving that characterize some of the groups in society to which the individual will ultimately belong, it is not enough in a democratic society to achieve this using procedures that lead to lack of awareness of or tolerance towards various alternatives, or to bring it about in any way which denies the individual the capacity for rational and independent judgment.

A curriculum for education then would differ from a curriculum for socialization in at least four ways.

1 Whereas education would be aiming at the development of rationally autonomous individuals, socialization would be concerned with developing people who could function smoothly within their society.

2 Whereas education would endeavour to provide the concepts, capacities and knowledge required for testing truth claims and justifying beliefs, socialization would provide those skills, beliefs, attitudes and intelligence required to bring the individual into a harmonious relationship with society.

3 Whereas education would emphasize the importance of producing evidence and rational arguments in support of one's actions and beliefs, in socialization belief and action would be sanctioned either by heritage and tradition or by the power of the majority.

4 Whereas in the educational process the ends of actions, policies and institutions are matters for open inquiry, in the socialization process ends are largely presupposed and unquestioned.

The central point of the above discussion has been to expand the notion of educational leadership so that it cannot be reducible to management strategies or narrow proficiency in particular skills. It has been argued that educational leadership entails commitment to a set of educational values and principles for practice which should be embodied in the curriculum itself. These values and principles do not constitute a body of doctrine or a particular set of beliefs, but rather a disposition towards rational reflection and deliberative action which is fundamentally philosophical in nature.

Rationality and Values in Administrative Action

If we are to understand the philosophical nature of leadership, we need first to clear up some common misapprehensions concerning the place of theory in social life. Foremost among these misapprehensions is the belief that social theories are discovered in a context that is quite separate from their application. On this view, administrators are thought to be necessarily engaged in political practice, whereas social scientists are not; conversely, social scientists are thought to be necessarily engaged in constructing theories, whereas administrators are not. It is assumed, in other words, that the task of social scientists is to produce a body of knowledge encompassing various administrative theories and domains of policy science which administrators may then either ignore or take up and convert into social action. Thus the social theorist is taken to be the technical handmaiden of the administrator, giving rise to what Fay (1975) calls 'the technological view of politics'.

Behind this technological view is the assumption that policy science makes available to administrators a theoretical basis upon which to decide the 'best means' of achieving certain predetermined goals. Thus policy science and administrative theory are relegated to a totally instrumental function, succinctly described by Fay in the following terms:

> A policy science is supposed to be a device for organising political thought in a rational way, merely a method for clarifying empirical relationships among alternative actions and for sorting out their likely consequences, and a procedure for making 'correct' decisions; as such, it is supposed to be employable by anyone, regardless of his political views, for any end whatsoever, and its results are supposed to be impartial in the sense of not being dependent upon the particular evaluations of the policy scientist for their truth. (Fay, 1975, p.57)

Such a position, when examined closely, is seen to be founded upon two dichotomies, neither of which holds up under critical scrutiny. The first is a dichotomy between 'facts' and 'values', and the second is a dichotomy between 'observation' and 'interpretation'. Each is an example of what the sociologist George Homans called a 'false dichotomy'. 'To the classic peril of being impaled on the horns of a dilemma, we moderns should add a new one, being split by a false dichotomy' (Merton, quoting Homans in Homans, 1951, p.xxiii). But if we are to understand the place of theory in administrative action, each of these dichotomies should be challenged. It is not possible to arrive at a critical view of educational leadership while entertaining the technological view of politics in which administrators are thought to be independent arbiters of scientific theory, using it to determine objectively the best course of action to take. The executive and the contemplative dimensions of social theory should not be forced apart in such an artificial or simplistic manner.

There is an important sense in which administrators are not like social scientists. They are more concerned with using knowledge than with seeking it, with application than with abstraction, and with problem-solving than with problem-finding. But this points to a difference of focus or emphasis rather than a substantive difference of kind. Both administrators and social scientists are necessarily engaged in arriving at judgments based upon interpretations of social reality.

We can elaborate on this point by returning to the first of the two dichotomies mentioned above, namely, the separation of 'facts' from 'values'. It is often assumed that administrators can derive their values from one source and ascertain the facts of the situation from another completely independent source, in particular the organizational theorist or the behavioural scientist. This implies that the goals (of a school, for example) are politically determined and institutionally located in one context, while in another context the social scientist can be considered competent only to recommend the 'best means' or the most economical/effective/functional procedures which are instrumental in attaining those already posited goals. Thus we have the simplistic identification of decisions concerning means with the factual side of the fact-value dichotomy. But it is an identification which cannot be sustained logically because it overlooks completely the assumed values in terms of which the 'best' means are to be ascertained. This produces a contradiction, as Fay points out, implicit in the claim that social science can be value-free.

> So it is that a policy science that attempts to provide a structure in terms of which political questions could be settled 'rationally' must involve reference to just those considerations that the idea of policy science was designed to eliminate, namely, notions of significance and worth. As a result, debates between policy scientists about the most efficient means would still be inherently 'political' in the sense that the choice of standards of what is to count as evidence and proof of some social policy being the 'best' (in this case, the meaning of the criterion of efficiency) would necessarily reflect the values of the disputants. (Fay, 1975, p.51)

The significance of this dilemma for the administrator is profound. For not only are there institutional values to be articulated and defended through administrative practice, but there are also values that are inherent within the very process of policy formation itself. As Fay makes clear,

> all political decisions, even those which are seen as means to an end, are social policies, and as such they embody a notion of what people ought to be required or permitted to do to others. No social policy's worth can be solely instrumental because any such policy will require that people interact with one another in certain definite ways, and for this reason it must have a moral value *in itself*. . . . All political proposals, no matter how instrumental, will alter and shape the personal relations of at least some of the members of a society, and will affect the relative welfare of various classes of people; as such they embody moral notions as to what is permissable, just, or right in human affairs. They are a species of moral statement. (Fay, 1975, p.52)

Thus it is clear that administrative action is necessarily a form of moral action and, as such, it must always come to rest upon fundamental cultural or ideological assumptions, hypotheses or beliefs about the nature of social reality. This brings us back to the second of the false dichotomies referred to above, that is, the separation of 'observation' from 'interpretation'. Here the mistake is to assume that any kind of observable data is completely independent initially from the theoretical interpretations that can be placed upon it. That it is a mistake can be shown only by arguing for the proposition that all observation is theory-laden. But what can be said, briefly, in defence of this very important philosophical claim?

Forming Cognitive Appraisals

It is a truism that human activity is very complex — so complex that it can never be completely encompassed by any description of it, by any explanation or by any theory concerning what it means. Any attempt to understand even a small facet of human conduct requires a cognitive appraisal, a culturally appropriate interpretation of what is occurring. How a social situation is defined will depend almost entirely upon the cultural or ideological viewpoint through which it is perceived. Hence, to say that all administrative action necessarily entails theoretical interpretations, which in turn necessarily entail a cultural context, is to draw attention to the special kind of cognitive appraisals upon which practical decision-making depends. The nature of these cognitive appraisals can best be understood by analogy with the notion of 'seeing as'.

Figure 1

The philosopher Wittgenstein illustrates the notion of 'seeing as' by taking the well-known duck-rabbit figure (Figure 1). This figure can be seen *as* either a 'duck' or 'rabbit'. The beak of the 'duck' becomes the ears of the 'rabbit'. The eye is common to both. The indentation to the right becomes the 'rabbit's' mouth and is irrelevant on the 'duck'. In each case the figure remains the same, but we see it under a different aspect. The particular aspect under which someone sees it may be revealed in the way it is described. Wittgenstein comments on this as follows: 'If I heard someone talking about the duck-rabbit, and *now* he spoke in a certain way about the special expression of the rabbit's face I should say, now he's seeing the picture as a rabbit' (Wittgenstein, 1953, p.206e). Now ask yourself the following questions:

1 Can you see the picture as both a duck and a rabbit simultaneously?
2 Could you see it as either if you did not have the appropriate concepts?

How the picture is seen depends upon the concepts that can be brought to it. Thus our concepts and theories influence our picture of the world. Just as seeing is more than a visual sensation because it includes the whole cognitive process by which visual experience is interpreted, so observation is more than merely 'seeing what is there' because it includes the theoretical framework in which we interpret what we see. Therefore, what we observe, and what we decide to do on the basis of what we observe, will be illuminated by what we know, by the concepts we already have. Hanson (1958) points this out with a number of examples:

> Would Sir Lawrence Bragg and an Eskimo baby see the same thing when looking at an X-ray tube? Yes, and no. Yes, — they are visually aware of the same object. No, — the *ways* in which they are visually aware are profoundly different. Seeing is not only the having of a visual experience; it is also the way in which the visual experience is had.
>
> At school the physicist had gazed at this glass-and-metal instrument. Returning now, after years in University and research, his eye lights upon the same object once again. Does he see the same thing now as he did then? Now he sees the instrument in terms of electrical circuit theory, thermodynamic theory, the theories of metal and glass structure, thermionic emission, optical transmission, refraction, diffraction, atomic theory, quantum theory and special relativity.
>
> Contrast the freshman's view of college with that of his ancient tutor. Compare a man's first glance at the motor of his car with a similar glance ten exasperating years later. (Hanson, 1958, pp.15-16)

Even an object that is common or universal to all mankind, such as the sun, may be 'seen as' something entirely different by people who hold different beliefs and theories about it. Compare the ways in which the sun might be seen by (1) a member of a culture who worships the sun as a god, and (2) a present-day scientist. For the Aztec the sun had a central significance in a whole interlocking network of religious and moral codes, social practices, rituals, artistic traditions and language. To a scientist, on the other hand, for whom it is nothing but a mass of burning gas, 'the sun' cannot be regarded as having the same meaning. Indeed, there is an important sense in which an Aztec and a twentieth century scientist, both looking at the sun (albeit at different times) could not be said to be seeing the same thing since the theoretical frameworks under which they see it would be so different.

Such examples show that knowledge, theories and concepts make a substantial difference to what is seen; so that, as Hanson suggests, 'there is a sense, then, in which seeing is a 'theory-laden' undertaking. Observation of X is shaped by prior knowledge of X' (Hanson, 1958, p.19). This means that all seeing and all perceiving involve forming hypotheses and using observational categories. Indeed, language itself functions as a classificatory system for that which is perceived. Hence, we must conclude that the presumed dichotomy between observation and interpretation is indeed false, and that we have a strong case for the position that all practice is theory-laden.

The Separation of Theory and Practice

What does this philosophical analysis of perception contribute to our understanding of educational leadership? The point is simply to show that educational administrators, like any other practitioners, must interpret their social world, and to this extent at least they cannot avoid holding theories about the nature of that world. What concerns us here is the justification for those theories, their origin, the way in which they are held, and the extent to which they can be changed or modified to meet the demands of practice. In all these respects we are taking educational leadership to be a form of reflective action, but this requires a reconceptualization of the relationship between theory and practice.

A considerable amount of academic discussion within the field of educational administration revolves around the problem of theory and practice. But this problem is generally presented as though it existed within the field in which educational administration is *studied* rather than a problem within the field in which it is *practised*. Thus it is recognized that the cumulative body of extant theory *about* educational administration is so diverse and unwieldy that it is more often found to be confusing rather than constructive in its influence upon practice. This body of theory has been accumulated within the main tradition of social scientific inquiry and largely reflects the changing orientations and paradigm shifts that have occurred within that tradition. It is not surprising, therefore, that administrative theory contains alternative views of social science, alternative methodological assumptions and alternative ideological bases. The understanding and explanation of organizations, for example, can be sought within a structuralist-functionalist orientation or within a voluntarist-phenomenological orientation. The problem for the practitioner appears to be one of choice but this is to presuppose a dichotomy between the contemplative and executive *uses* of theory. To talk of 'making choices' among alternative theoretical positions is to assume that the domain of theory is removed from the domain of practice, and that it is a field of *study* rather than a field of *action*.

Basically there are three distinct ways in which educational administrators come to hold theories which will shape and determine their practice. The first is by taking up the conceptual orientations contained within an extant body of 'theory' derived from the endeavours of those who make a scientific study of educational administration. The second is by following the promptings of habit, convention and intuition derived from personal experience and contained within the domain of common sense. The third is by a philosophical critique of practice in which deliberative action is derived from a combination of empirical and interpretive modes of inquiry that have been brought to bear upon both the public domain of extant theory and the private domain of common sense. In what follows a strong case is argued for the third of these alternatives because it is the only one in which theory and practice can be fully integrated.

What is required is a major reconceptualization of the theory-practice problem. Perhaps the best way of achieving this is to explore the problem in slightly different terms. Since we have suggested that educational leadership is a philosophical activity, and since philosophy is often taken to be a form of reflective thinking removed from the practical realities of common sense, we can approach the theory-practice problem by examining the relationship between philosophy and common sense.

Philosophy and Common Sense

For many analytical philosophers common sense is the raw material upon which philosophical reasoning 'does its work'. In this view common sense and philosophy are worlds apart. For instance, Richard Pring (1976, p.86) defines common sense as 'that range of beliefs which people share and hold in an unquestioning sort of way, and which provide a basic view of the world, of their position within the world, and of how they ought to act.' When these beliefs are called into question, the task of philosophy gets under way. Its goal is not to replace such commonsense beliefs with others that may be closer to the truth, but rather to produce what Russell called the experience of 'liberating doubt'. In this analytical view the philosophical task is confined to addressing the Socratic questions, 'what do you mean?' and 'how do you know?'

Analytical philosophy casts philosophers into a spectatorial role (Harris, 1980) so that philosophical thought takes on a 'second-order' character in which 'first-order' ideas are examined against criteria of clarity, and 'first-order' arguments are examined against criteria of validity. Not being experts in moral sensitivity, practical wisdom or political judgment, analytical philosophers can only try to clarify our ways of thinking *about* domains of human activity such as education, illuminating the concepts we employ, the inferences we make and the choices we express. They can only render explicit, for example, the criteria of judgment we already use in reaching educational decisions. They can only analyze the major positions taken on issues of educational policy by questioning their premises, consequences and alternatives (O'Conner, 1957; Scheffler, 1958; Hirst, 1963; Peters, 1965, 1966).

According to Russell (1912):

The value of philosophy is, in fact, to be sought largely in its very uncertainty. The man who has no tincture of philosophy goes through life imprisoned in the prejudices derived from common sense, from the habitual beliefs of his age or his nation, and from convictions which have grown up in his mind without the co-operation or consent of his deliberate reason. . . . Philosophy, though unable to tell us with certainty what is the true answer to the doubts which it raises, is able to suggest many possibilities which enlarge our thoughts and free them from the tyranny of custom. (Russell, 1912, pp.242-3)

In this view philosophy either shakes us out of the complacency of common sense and into a more sceptical, and presumably more desirable, frame of mind, or it enables us to exercise our 'deliberate reason' so as to purge us of prejudices or release us from the bondage of muddled thinking.

From the analytic point of view, 'common sense' is implicitly equated with 'muddled thinking' and the 'tyranny of custom', a confusion which it is the task of philosophy to correct. From another *liberal* point of view, however, commonsense knowledge may be defended against such philosophical criticism on the grounds that it is closer to the domain of action and experience than are specialized forms of knowledge. Perry, for instance, writing about the importance of commonsense thought, knowledge and judgment for education, argues that common sense provides the essential awareness of what kinds of specialized knowledge it is necessary to apply to particular problems or situations. Commonsense thinking, according to Perry,

may legitimately object to being superseded when specialized thinking makes an unjustified claim to deal more effectively with a subject: unjustified, because specialized verdicts have to be modified, as a rule, to be useful in the general field of experience, and it is the task of common sense to do this, and to judge what weight to assign to the various kinds of relevant specialized knowledge. Because common sense thought is concerned with experience lying outside the specialized area, it is justified not only in modifying but even on occasion overruling expert knowledge. Thus the politician overrules the general, the businessman the architect, or the teacher the psychologist. (Perry, 1965, p.128)

Such a view seems to overlook completely the possibility that commonsense appraisals of a situation may be distorted by contextual and situational factors, rendering them less justifiable than the specialized judgments that pertain to the same situation. Which appraisal wins out may depend ultimately on who has the power to act or who controls the situation, rather than on which appraisal is more valid. When the politician overrules the general, it is a social political action that is being made, not a logical deduction.

This example points to the fundamental epistemological assumption behind each of these constructions of the relationship between philosophy and common sense. They all rest upon a dualistic separation of thought and action, or theory and practice. Whether we take Russell's suggestion that the function of philosophy is to 'enlarge our thoughts', or Pring's point that common sense provides a framework of unquestioned beliefs, or Perry's argument that common sense is the final court of appeal in arriving at justifiable judgments, we have the basic assumption underlying all these positions that philosophy and common sense are distinct, though related, ways of *thinking* rather than *acting*. It is assumed that problems of philosophy must be distinguished from problems of practice such that — although any particular action we make upon the world may arise either from common sense or from philosophical thought, or from elements of both — it is not the action itself that makes the difference, it is the way we think about it. What we have then, as a result of such arguments, is a gap between theory and practice.

Philosophy as Reflective Action

For both the analytical philosopher and the liberal theorist, the ideal pursuit of theory is essentially removed from practical and public affairs, and the role of the philosopher is staunchly to maintain an uncommitted view towards different and competing ways of life. Thus, in the words of Richard Bernstein: 'Thinkers who are at variance on almost every other issue take the defence of this ideal as virtually synonymous with a defence of free, self-corrective, open inquiry which is subject only to the critical norms of intersubjective discourse' (Bernstein, 1976, p.173). Indeed, from the time of Plato and Aristotle, the gap between theory and practice has had a powerful effect on the nature of social and political life, influencing not only the structure of social knowledge itself, but also determining the social transformation that could be considered possible.

This ideal image of the detached theorist has become the hallmark of both analytical and liberal philosophy, implying as it does that theoretical knowledge is independent of its practical application and that factual accounts of the social world can, and should, be independent of the particular interests and values of those who construct them. That these distinctions have been vigorously debated, even among analytical and liberal philosophers, has not diminished the persuasiveness and potency of the image. However, this very image is now under attack from another source, from one that takes the critical relationship between theory and practice as its essential and initial point of departure. According to Bernstein:

> It is an orientation that has its roots in Hegel, and in Marx's use and understanding of *critique*; that has been given a classical formulation by the central figures of the Frankfurt School; and that has been refined and developed by Jurgen Habermas. . . . What I take to be most central in this tradition is the way it attempts to at once recover and defend the critical moment or impulse required for any adequate social and political theorizing. As I read the contemporary scene, it is this critical impulse that is breaking out among thinkers trained in radically different traditions. There is a dialectical movement from the advocacy of empirical theory to the realisation of the necessity for interpretation and understanding of social and political reality. And finally, there is growing recognition of the need for the type of critique that has a practical interest in the fate and quality of social and political life. The search for empirical correlations, the task of interpreting social and political reality, and the critique of this 'reality', are not three distinct types of inquiry. They are three internal moments of theorizing about social and political life. (Bernstein, 1976, p.174)

Within such a tradition of critical theorizing about social and political life, the relationship between philosophy and common sense can be reconstructed. Indeed, this very task was first undertaken by the Italian Marxist, Antonio Gramsci (1971) in his *Prison Notebooks*.

To appreciate the significance of Gramsci's critique of common sense, it is necessary to examine several other elements in his unique contribution to Marxist social theory and political strategy. Recognizing the limitations within the traditional Marxist theory of the state, Gramsci set out to explain how culture and ideology become productive forces within advanced capitalist societies. The traditional view had emphasized the material mode of production and the economic base as the main buttresses which kept the state in place, protected by physical coercion (or the threat of it) and other direct forms of social control carried out through the state apparatus. But this mechanistic explanation could not account for the failure of the working class to develop revolutionary consciousness, even with changes to the economic base. Gramsci concluded that there must be forces deep within the popular psyche itself which induced the oppressed to accept or 'consent' to their own exploitation and daily misery. He advanced the concept of ideological hegemony to explain how the ruling class maintains its dominance by achieving a popular consensus mediated through the various institutions of civil society, including the schools, the mass media, the law, religion and popular culture. This form of ideological domination evades resistance by permeating consciousness itself, becoming embedded in popular beliefs, values, folklore and common sense.

Thus commonsense knowledge structures mass consciousness in ways which mask and mystify the existing power relations and social arrangements. Cases of how this functions through such institutions as schooling are not difficult to find. Many working-class parents, for example, subscribe to the commonsense view that schools provide equal opportunities for all to succeed on the basis of merit. They believe that examinations and other forms of pupil assessment are objective and impartial devices for the distribution of educational rewards and that these rewards are allocated to individuals on the basis of ability and effort. Thus the rhetoric of equality of educational opportunity coheres with commonsense knowledge about schooling.

Although common sense, in Gramsci's view, lacks intellectual order and logical coherence, it is nevertheless a product of history and a part of the historical process. Its origins lie within a coherent and comprehensive worldview, a philosophy that has been widely shared in the past. It therefore contains within it a residue of intuitions about life and the world which Gramsci calls 'good sense'.

The task of philosophy is to articulate and render this 'good sense' into a coherent and systematic worldview, free from hegemonic ideological distortion. In this view philosophy is both critical and logically coherent, grounded in everyday experience, while at the same time articulated through strategic political action. Only in this way can philosophy have cultural significance. The cultural contribution of philosophy is not to be found in its discovery of truths but in 'the diffusion in a critical form of truths already discovered'. Gramsci asserts that: 'For a mass of people to be led to think coherently and in the same coherent fashion about the real present world, is a "philosophical" event far more important and "original" than the discovery by some philosophical "genius" of a truth which remains the property of small groups of intellectuals' (Gramsci, 1971, p.325). When this is achieved, and clearly it is an educational achievement, philosophy supersedes common sense — indeed it coincides with 'good' as opposed to 'common' sense. Philosophy should not be removed from everyday life to occupy some remote or esoteric realm of abstract ideas; it should be an essential dimension of everyday human experience and the criticism and reformulation of common sense. For Gramsci the majority of mankind are already philosophers insofar as they engage in practical activity for, in their practical activity, 'there is implicitly contained a conception of the world, a philosophy' (Gramsci, 1971, p.344). Thus to realize each person's philosophical capacity is 'not a question of introducing from scratch a scientific form of thought into everyone's individual life, but of renovating and making "critical" an already existing activity' (Gramsci, 1971, pp.330-1).

Gramsci's reconstruction of the relationship between philosophy and common sense provides a dialectical dimension to the notion of philosophy as reflective action. It renders the critique of practice a philosophical task no less significant than the analysis of theory. In Gramsci's terms the dialectic of philosophy is that it is simultaneously both active and reflective. On one hand, philosophy cannot be divorced from politics because the choice and the criticism of a conception of the world are always a political matter. But, on the other hand, philosophy is also 'the invitation to people to reflect and to realise fully that whatever happens is basically rational and must be confronted as such, and that one should apply one's power of rational concentration and not let oneself be carried away by instinctive and violent impulses' (Gramsci, 1971, p.328). Gramsci does not suggest a specious unity of theory and practice but regards them as interdependent and dialectically related. To collapse theory into practice would be to ignore the creative and critical functions of theory; to make practice into something theoretic would be to diminish its social and historical dimensions.

Leadership: Action and Reflection

The foregoing discussion has attempted to set out some of the epistemological conditions implied by a dialectical (or critical) conception of thought and action. Such a conception, it is argued, places philosophy at the centre of social action and enables the philosopher to be an educational leader rather than a detached spectator.

Gramsci's view of educational leadership can be found within his notion of the 'organic' intellectual (Gramsci, 1971, pp.5-23). Such intellectuals are capable of both leading and representing groups of people who are dominated by social structures. In accordance with his conviction that ordinary people are philosophers insofar as they participate in a particular conception of the world, Gramsci argues that 'organic' intellectuals are those who participate fully in the everyday life of a community, while at the same time manifesting political and moral leadership. Unlike 'traditional' intellectuals, these new 'organic' intellectuals refuse to join the privileged elite, and their influence goes much deeper than the level of facile persuasion and empty rhetoric. 'The mode of being of the new intellectual can no longer consist in eloquence, which is an exterior and momentary mover of feelings and passions, but in active participation in practical life, as constructor, organizer, "permanent persuader", and not just a simple orator . . .' (Gramsci 1971, p.10).

This notion of intellectual leadership has much in common with the radical pedagogy of Paulo Freire (1970, 1976, 1978). Freire argues that human beings constitute their own reality through cultural action, which may be directed towards liberation or oppression. Only the former, however, is humanity's true ontological and historical vocation, while the latter is a distortion of this vocation.

> Within history, in concrete, objective contexts, both humanization and dehumanization are possibilities for man as an uncompleted being conscious of his incompletion.
>
> But while both humanization and dehumanization are real alternatives, only the first is man's vocation. This vocation is constantly negated, yet it is affirmed by that very negation. It is thwarted by injustice, exploitation, oppression, and the violence of the oppressors; it is affirmed by the yearning of the oppressed for freedom and justice, and by their struggle to recover their lost humanity. (Freire, 1970, p.28)

The distortion of humanity's ontological vocation is produced by a form of cultural action that constructs an oppressive reality, a cultural hegemony that absorbs those within it and functions to submerge their consciousness. This produces a domination that can be overcome only by cultural struggle, even revolution, in which education plays a crucial role.

Freire takes education to be a form of cultural action that also has the potential to be either oppressive or liberating. Oppressive education treats people as adaptable, manageable beings. It is antidialogical cultural action, which is characterized by the 'banking' concept because the teacher 'makes deposits' of knowledge, or information, and the scope of action allowed to the students 'extends only as far as receiving, filing, and storing the deposits' (Freire, 1970, p.58).

In contrast, liberating education is problem-posing and results in acts of cognition rather than transferrals of information. It is a form of cultural action that is dialogical and capable of transforming human consciousness from a condition of alienation to a condition of 'freedom'. Such freedom results from a process of *conscientization,* which enables people to become fully human and to possess 'critical consciousness'. This can be achieved only by taking knowledge beyond the level of mere opinion or belief *(doxa)* to the level of *historical commitment.*

> It implies that men take the role of agents, makers and remakers of the world; it demands that men create their existence with the elements that life offers them. This is the reason why the more they are concientized the more they exist, not just live. Man, as a historical being, a maker of history, will be more subject of the historical process the more he discovers himself as the object of it. (Freire, 1976, pp.224-5)

But 'conscientization' is more than just the realization of oppression, it must also be 'a permanent critical approach to reality in order to discover it and discover the myths that deceive us and help to maintain the oppressing dehumanizing structures' (Freire, 1976, p.225).

In similar vein to Gramsci, Freire argues that critical awareness is never sufficient in itself because it achieves only liberation of the mind. Such awareness must combine with action (praxis) to achieve real social change. In this notion of praxis moreover, both reflection and action are unified so that neither can be sacrificed without rendering true human dialogue impossible. Reflection without action is verbalism; action without reflection is activism (Freire, 1970).

> Concientizing education — for liberation — instead of being an act of transferring knowledge is an act of knowing. It therefore implies, in its process, that educators and learners all become learners assuming the same attitude as cognitive subjects discovering knowledge through one another and through the objects they try to know. It is not a situation where one knows and others do not; it is rather the search, by all, at the same time to discover something by the act of knowing which cannot exhaust all the possibilities in the relation between object and subject. In other words, education for liberation tries to make history — not just receiving or reading history. (Freire, 1976, p.225)

There are strong similarities here between Freire's notion of praxis embodied in dialogue and Gramsci's reconstruction of the relationship between philosophy and common sense. Each has given us a dialectical view of educational leadership in which reflection and action are unified.

Conclusion

This chapter has attempted to develop the notion of educational leadership as reflective action by reconstructing the relationship between thought and action. It began by questioning the educational value of managerial techniques, and suggested that such techniques can be miseducative insofar as they serve to facilitate the social function of schooling as an agency of social control. However, because schools are not factories, and because the administration of education is not reducible to management strategies, it was argued that professional administrators should be distinguished by their overall commitment to a set of educational values and principles for practice, rather than their competence in particular management skills.

Thus the view taken in this chapter is that the only concept of 'leadership' that can be properly wedded to the concept of 'education' is one which preserves democratic administrative practices. If schools are to educate for democracy, they must embody within their own structures such central moral principles as justice, freedom and respect for persons, combined with an overriding concern for truth. It is only with the vigorous defence of these principles that schools can move beyond the narrow functions of socialization to provide settings in which individuals can become rational autonomous beings. The central aim of education is not passive social conformity but active and properly informed social critique.

This view of education requires that educational administration combine both an executive and a critical-reflective dimension. This means rejecting the technological or instrumental view and recognizing that such a view arises from a number of false conceptual dichotomies. The assumed dichotomies between fact and value, observation and interpretation, practice and theory cannot be sustained.

It has been argued that educational leadership is a form of moral action which can be meaningful only within a given cultural context. It is a form of cultural expression and negotiation deriving its meaning from the way in which social situations are cognitively appraised. Each decision made by an administrator is based upon a cognitive appraisal of the social and political context in which she or he is located. In this sense, therefore, all administrative practice is theory-laden.

In attempting to locate leadership within the domain of philo- sophical practice it has been necessary to reject the philosopher's spectatorial role, imbued as it is with idealist assumptions, and to reconstruct the relationship between philosophical epistemology and social action. By taking Gramsci's conception of philosophy as being a counter-hegemonic critique of common sense, the traditional dichotomy between reflection and action is shown to be untenable. Indeed, when it is construed in this way, philosophy ceases to be mere armchair speculation and becomes capable of freeing agents from a kind of coercion that is at least partly self-imposed. Philosophy can free agents from the self-frustration of commonsense beliefs that have the effect of preventing those agents from determining what their true interests are and hence acting in accordance with those interests. This is the goal of Freire's 'education for liberation'. It can be achieved only by leadership that is based on dialogue and historical commitment. The praxis for such leadership is reflective action.

References

Bernstein, R.J. (1976) *The Restructuring of Social and Political Theory,* Oxford, Blackwell.

Callahan, R. (1960) *Education and the Cult of Efficiency,* Chicago, Ill., Chicago University Press.

Fay, B. (1975) *Social Theory and Political Practice,* London, Allen and Unwin.

Freire, P. (1970) *Pedagogy of the Oppressed,* Trans M.B. Ramos, Continuum, New York, Seabury Press.

Freire, P. (1976) 'A few notions about the word "concientization",' in R. Dale, G. Esland and M. MacDonald (Eds), *Schooling and Capitalism: A Sociological Reader,* London and Henley, Routledge and Kegan Paul in association with The Open University Press.

Freire, P. (1978) *Pedagogy in Process: The Letters to Guinea-Bissau,* Trans C. St John Hunter, New York, Seabury Press.

Giroux, H.A. (1983) *Theory and Resistance in Education,* South Hadley, Mass., Bergin and Garvey.

Gramsci, A. (1971) *Selections from the Prison Notebooks,* Ed. and trans Q. Hoare and G. Nowell Smith, London, Lawrence and Wishart.

Griffiths, D.E. (1985) *Administrative Theory in Transition,* Geelong, Deakin University Press.

Hanson, N.R. (1958) *Patterns of Discovery,* Cambridge, Cambridge University Press.

Harris, K. (1980) 'Philosophers of education: Detached spectators or political practitioners?,' *Educational Philosophy and Theory,* 12,1, pp.19-35.

Hirst, P.H. (1963) 'Philosophy and educational theory,' *British Journal of Educational Studies,* 12,1, pp.51-64.

Homans, G. (1951) *The Human Group,* London, Routledge and Kegan Paul, Introduction by Robert Merton, p.xxiii.

Illich, I.D. (1971) *Deschooling Society,* London, Calder and Boyars.

Jackson, P. (1968) *Life in Classrooms,* New York, Holt, Rinehart and Winston.

Langford, G. (1973) 'The concept of education,' in G. Langford and D.J. O'Connor (Eds), *New Essays in the Philosophy of Education,* London, Routledge and Kegan Paul.

O'Connor, D.J. (1957) *An Introduction to the Philosophy of Education,* London, Routledge and Kegan Paul.

Perry, L.R. (1965) 'Commonsense thought, knowledge and judgement, and their importance for education,' *British Journal of Educational Studies,* 13,2, pp.125-30.

Peters, R.S. (1965) 'The philosophy of education,' in J.W. Tibble (Ed.), *The Study of Education,* London, Routledge and Kegan Paul.

Peters, R.S. (1966) *Ethics and Education,* London, Allen and Unwin.

Pring, R. (1976) *Knowledge and Schooling,* London, Open Books.

Russell, B. (1912) *The Problems of Philosophy,* London, Williams and Norgate.

Scheffler, I. (Ed.) (1958) *Philosophy and Education,* Boston, Mass., Allyn and Bacon.

Taylor, W. (1976) 'The head as manager: Some criticisms,' in R.S. Peters (Ed.), *The Role of the Head,* London, Routledge and Kegan Paul.

Wittgenstein, L. (1953) *Philosophical Investigations,* Trans G.E.M Anscombe, Oxford, Blackwell.

Chapter 7

A 'Pedagogical' and 'Educative' View of Leadership

John Smyth

One of the problems with a construct like leadership is that although it may have some meaning in the management sciences, it is difficult to transport it into schools in a way that makes much sense. The notion of one group (the leaders) who exercise hegemony and domination over another (the followers) is, in a sense, an anti-educational one. If schools are to be the inquiring kinds of places we would want them to be, then the values espoused and the activities pursued will be as a consequence of dialogue about the nature of schooling and what is considered important in the development of children, and not as a result of bureaucratic or autocratic decree. This chapter takes the notion of what has been described as the 'educative', contained in the work of social theorist Brian Fay (1975, 1977, 1987), and explores how those ideas might inform an alternative, more inclusive and less privileged view of leadership in schools.

The ideas presented in this chapter do not, therefore, conform with those generally addressed when matters of educational leadership are canvassed. For one thing there is no consideration of the styles of educational leaders, nor are there any prescriptive indicators on how people in leadership positions should think or act in particular circumstances. What is presented instead is an argument about a way people in school settings might actively assist one another in uncovering meaning in what they do, while investing in them the capacity to change, improve and transform those practices.

The first part of the chapter explores some of the ideas of the social philosopher Brian Fay (1977) as they relate to his notion of the 'educative'. For him ideas are a function of social conditions, but they also create and sustain particular social structures. To an extent, therefore, notions of leadership in schools are closely related to ways of assisting people in schools to see the 'embeddness of self-

(mis)understandings in concrete social structures' (p.205), and how to work in ways that amount to confronting and contesting the very nature and existence of those social structures. Having briefly sketched out some alternative theoretical terrain, the second part of the chapter looks at some arguments that have been falsely mounted as to why teachers are not generally regarded as fitting traditional leadership moulds. The passivity and subservience implicit in this essentially hierarchical view of leadership are questioned, and the counter-argument presented that in the interests of democratic schooling teachers must reclaim their rightful leadership role by continually raising critical questions about the social, cultural, political and moral nature of their work. The third and final section looks to the conditions that might enable thought and action about leadership in schools to progress away from managerialist views to ones in which teachers can become 'militant observers' (Reed, 1974, p.8) in their own schools and classrooms, rather than continue to be silenced and treated in invisible ways in the debates about schooling. A number of specific possibilities are suggested as a way of starting this rethinking process.

The claim is that by starting with the 'practical' as teachers are prone to do, and proceeding in ways that permit and encourage 'deliberative exchanges', teachers are able to develop an increasingly powerful language for examining and speaking about the circumstances of their working lives. Useful though this may be, it is still only part of a much wider 'critical' process of uncovering the contradictions and dilemmas in teaching and schooling. When the ends of teaching and the part schooling plays in reproducing and mediating inequality and injustice are regarded problematically, then teaching becomes less a technical process of imparting knowledge and more a process of social change.

The danger in this, of course, is that what starts out as a genuine process of acquiring 'self-knowledge' for liberatory and emancipatory purposes, through a disclosure of how power is inequitably distributed throughout our social structures, can wind up with a mind of its own as a revolutionary process in which one form of oppression comes to replace another. As Fay (1987) indicates, when this happens, we have a situation of 'enslavement' (p.209). This is not to suggest that we should abort the search for forms of domination that currently deny certain groups involvement in shaping the way they lead their lives. Rather, it is a warning to us that in moving away from dominant forms of leadership to more collective forms of self-determination we should be mindful of a number of caveats that will prevent a replaying of the degenerative scenario. We will come to those shortly.

To diverge slightly for a moment, and against this backdrop, from a definitional point of view educative leadership is something of a misnomer. By definition, if not through common usage, the notion of leadership has come to be associated with a functional and hierarchical division of labour in which one group (the leaders or the 'visionaries') exercise power over another group (the followers). Within this scheme there are those who hold clear visions about the way the world of schooling ought to be, and others who lack this perspicacity and who are expected to acquiesce in and implement the dictates of visionary leaders. There is a ring of authenticity about this that seems to fit the hierarchical, corporatist and undemocratic nature of society in which there are those who have power, and others who do not.

It is interesting to speculate on Pondy's (1978) question about what the field of leadership, as it relates to schools in particular, might look like if we move away from the view of leadership as involving manipulating (or influencing) others towards goal-setting and achievement. According to Pondy, leadership encompasses the process of making activity meaningful for others. Providing others with a sense of understanding where they have come from, what they are doing, and where they are headed, amounts to construing action so that people can extract meaning from it and communicate about those meanings. Generating knowledge in a social context, such as this, enables meanings to be viewed as social artefacts capable of being exchanged, talked about, modified and amplified. As Pondy (1978) noted:

> The real power of Martin Luther King was not only that he had a dream, but that he could describe it, that it became public and therefore accessible to millions of people. This dual capacity . . . to make sense of things *and* to put them into language meaningful to large numbers of people gives the person who has it enormous leverage. (p.95)

In speaking about school settings (and teachers in particular), Berlak and Berlak (1981) put it this way: 'It is necessary for anyone who presumes to influence teachers, to seek teachers' knowledge and perspectives, work with them closely in ways that foster respect for one anothers' experiences, acknowledging one anothers' areas of partial and gross ignorance' (p.236).

The Notion of the 'Educative'

The American social philosopher Brian Fay (1977, 1987) is especially important in the way he presents an altered conceptualization of the relationship between theory and practice, that serves as a corrective to present dominant (instrumentalist) views. The implication of Fay's argument is that rather than one group or class being subservient to or beholden to another because of trait or status, relationships prevail instead such that all members are able to arrive at new self-understandings that empower them to 'reduce their suffering by creating another way of life that is more fulfilling' (p.204). For some this may seem to be bordering upon the 'subversive' in that action is 'directed against those who are benefitting from social arrangements that cause others to suffer' (p.233). Yet it is not simply that Fay (1977, 1987) is proposing what amounts to an anti-leadership view of leadership (Greenfield, 1981, p.27); there is more to it than that. What he proposes is a well articulated agenda (not without its limitations) of how those who are exploited can arrive at new levels of collective self-understanding as a basis for action. To that extent the argument is about the abolition of privileged and elitist forms of leadership in schools and their replacement by a form that stimulates dialogue about teaching and learning in schools — to that extent it is a discourse about the pedagogic as contrasted to the managerial within schools.

The notion of leadership pursued here is, therefore, fundamentally an enabling one that has to do with school people acquiring an understanding of how the social and institutional circumstances of their school lives cause them frustration, and how the anxiety which that generates detracts from the self-fulfilment of what they do. Expressed in these terms, leadership becomes a form of enablement through which people 'can change their lives so that, having arrived at a new self-understanding, they may reduce their suffering by creating another way of life that is more fulfilling' (Fay, 1977, p.204). This educative (or 'transformative') perspective rests on the assumption that, through assisting people to understand themselves and their world, it becomes possible for them to engage in the radical changes necessary for them to overcome the oppressive conditions that characterize work patterns and social relationships. Rather than knowledge being a means by which those in dominant positions acquire power and exert control over others, it becomes a means through which people are able to arrive at self-understanding and self-awareness of the conditions that disable them. Knowledge becomes the means by which people come to identify their social and institutional constraints, and work at changing them. To the extent that ideas and knowledge emerge from and help to sustain certain social conditions, they take on a dialectical relationship that contributes towards changing the social structure that spawned them.

Without going into detail at this stage, the view of leadership endorsed here is one that involves aiding or helping others, who have hitherto been denied the opportunity, to comprehend complexity and to make sense of contradiction and ambiguity. This process of making activity meaningful is also reflexive in nature. As Grob (1984) reminds us:

> . . . leadership, *more than any other kind of human activity,* must demand of its practitioners a willingness to open themselves to critique . . . leadership must be born — and perpetually sustained — in the movement to turn back upon itself and establish its own credentials . . . in so far as leadership is the work of humans who are moral agents — it must root itself in . . . humility. . . . (p.269)

Grob's (1984) claim is that to be authentically human is 'to see our conduct as problematic' (p.269).

More inclusive forms of leadership, therefore, involve school participants in coming to see how, through their own actions, they are 'unwitting accomplices' (Fay, 1977, p.205) in perpetuating 'self destructive patterns of interactions that characterise their social relationships' (p.204). All social practices, including those within schools, are created and sustained by certain interests, and when participants unknowingly collude with those who hold power, they succeed in frustrating even their own interests. If leaders in school settings have any legitimacy at all, then it must be in reducing the way in which school people are systematically unclear about what it is they do, and how and why it is that they continue to have unfulfilled ambitions and aspirations in working with students. Assisting students, teachers and members of the wider community to unveil or unmask those self-understandings that conceal the way in which people unwittingly collude or 'participate in their own misfortune' (p.205) is what leaders in schools should be primarily about. In Fay's (1977) terms, a leader is one who 'sparks . . . people into changing the way they live and react to others' (p.206).

What is noticeable by its absence from this construal of leadership is any mention of the imperative to define schools and what they do in terms of attaining and maintaining 'standards', or pursuing ill-defined system or nation-wide goals. Calls for instrumental leadership of this kind are nothing more than a thinly disguised attempt to manipulate schools to satisfy narrow sectional economic interests. Under prevailing corporatist models of school leadership, we have a concerted 'attempt to evacuate politics from the agenda' (Hextall, 1984, p.254) by having school participants believe that the running of schools should be left in the trusted hands of a disinterested civil servant class who operate according to value-free managerialist principles of accountability, efficiency and effectiveness. Such procedures are, of course, nothing of the kind. Their undisclosed and conservative politics is that of maintaining existing power relationships within the status quo.

We need to be careful, however, that an educative view of leadership in schools does more than merely 'involve' those who have previously been uninvolved in school matters. To have involvement or participation as the agenda is to miss the fundamental way in which school structures themselves are systematically distorted, sustained and textured by the misunderstandings school people hold. As Fay (1977) argues, structures and beliefs are dialectically related in that: '. . . ideas are a function of social conditions, but . . . they [in turn] . . . play a causal role in creating and sustaining particular social structures. [The educative model] tries to see the relation of conditions and ideas as a dialectical one' (p.205).

Put more straightforwardly, this amounts to school participants being able to see not only the nature and extent of their misunderstanding and that their ignorance was not accidental, but that it has its roots deep in the layered, stratified and supposedly objectified social order of which they are a part. Once school participants can begin to see the interpenetration of structures and beliefs, it becomes possible for them to challenge and question the constructed and taken-for-granted way schools are portrayed. This is to adopt an essentially optimistic and empowering approach, as distinct from a moribund and pessimistic one. It is also to elevate school people, and to see them as having the capacity to understand how their schools as institutions came to be the way they are. Fay (1977) put this succinctly, when he said of the educative model that it takes seriously the need to change '. . . people's basic understanding of themselves and their world [as] a first step in their radically altering the self-destructive patterns of interaction that characterise their social relations' (p.204).

The basis of such change within an educative model of leadership necessitates teachers, as well as students and parents, being given an opportunity to decide for themselves 'on the basis of lucid, critical self-awareness, the manner in which [they] wish to live' (Fay, 1977, p.207). In Kant's terms this amounts to an emergence from a state of immaturity which involves accepting someone else's authority, to a situation that calls for the use of reason. It implies a view of autonomy in which the rational thinking of the participants becomes the major source of what happens inside schools, rather than the dictates of those who operate at a distance from schools. Instead of leaders enslaving or duping their followers into accepting 'the correct path' (Fay, 1977, p.226) to be followed, participants acquire their freedom through 'reasoned argument and rational persuasion' (Fay, 1977, p.226).

In all of this the point of departure for the educative approach lies in the different view it espouses of school people. Rather than regarding them as untrustworthy and needing to be controlled by tight bureaucratic structures, an educative view of leadership starts from the presumption that people in schools are 'conscious of themselves as active deciding beings, bearing responsibility for their choices and able to explain them by referring to their own purposes, ideals and beliefs' (Fay, 1977, p.229).

It is this reclaiming of control through reflection based upon rationally informed discourse that represents the major point of departure between the educative and corporatist models of leadership. Acting rationally, according to Fay (1977), amounts to groups and individuals changing their self-understandings on the strength of 'the force of the argument and not [because] some extraneous factor . . . leads [them] to adopt a new viewpoint' (p.229). Within this scheme 'persuasion, argumentation, debate, criticism [and] analysis . . . are [at] the heart of the educative model' (p.229). To that extent it does not involve the replacement of one form of dogma with another. Rather, change is rejected on the basis of reason, rather than having to be followed because of administrative fiat.

Leadership of the alternative kind being spoken about here is, therefore, primarily concerned with the notion of power, and how informed self-knowledge can enable people to see how the conditions that constrain them are created and sustained by leadership elites. This is not to suggest, however, that knowledge made possible through the educative mode of leadership will per se lift people out of situations that caused them to be constrained in the first place. Rather, the intent is to develop a capacity for critical self-reflection that reveals to those who have been relegated to the subservient role of 'followers' how it is that they have come to be deprived of the power of self-determination. Put another way, people who had previously been 'objects' in the world are transformed into active self-determining 'subjects'.

Reclaiming the Pedagogical and the Critical

There is an extensive history (albeit desultory) in the educational literature, backed up by educational research, on the issue of leadership in schools — what it means, who should provide it, how it might occur, and who wears the responsibility for its non-occurrence. A major problem with this largely uninspiring literature has been the form that discussion has tended to take. There has been a widespread and largely unquestioned acceptance that discussions should occur against the backdrop of the formally legitimated structure of the school. What is interesting about this largely uninformed discussion of leadership in schools is that it has been untouched by the intense and acrimonious debate that has raged over the past decade about the nature of theory in the social sciences, and in educational administration in particular, and its relationship to research and practice. Without canvassing the debate in all its detail, it is sufficient to say here that as long as schools as organizations are portrayed as if they were 'real' with a separate existence from the individuals who comprise them, then it is likely that notions of leadership will continue to reflect this reified view. The level of consciousness necessary for teachers, and those who work with them, to understand and dramatically alter the nature of their practice may occur through a consideration of 'the practical'. For Schwab (1983, p.239) this consists of 'a deliberative exchange and consideration among several persons or differing selves about concrete alternatives in relation to particular times and places.'

By theorizing about the social, political and cultural nature of their work, teachers can develop a language about teaching, and an understanding that to change teaching requires altering the constraints that impose limits upon it. Through developing a more coherent understanding of what it means to be a teacher in the broadest sense, it becomes possible to encourage and foster those circumstances that permit teachers to transform their work. Clearly, therefore, leadership in schools is not something that is exercised in a vacuum; it exists in the context and culture of the school and is grounded in instruction and pedagogy.

It is here that we encounter a problem of major proportions, for, as Bernstein (1986) argues, in all societies 'there are at least two basic classes of knowledge, the esoteric and the mundane . . .' (p.208). Educational researchers and scholars have been less than charitable in the credit given to teachers for creating worthwhile knowledge about their teaching. Indeed, there is a good deal of negativism reflecting upon the alleged lack of rigour, and the absence of disciplined thinking by teachers in what they do. Berlak and Berlak (1981, p.235) claim that 'authorities' such as Lortie (1975) and Jackson (1968) 'assume that the experts in teaching are not the teachers but scientifically trained administrators, or educational scholars who study schooling scientifically.'

According to Jackson (1968), 'teachers have a tendency to rely on spontaneous expressions of interest in their students rather than on scientific or objective measures', and their actions are characterized as exhibiting 'conceptual simplicity', an 'uncomplicated view of causality', an 'intuitive rather than a rational approach to classroom events', and an 'unquestioning acceptance of classroom miracles' (cited in Berlak and Berlak, 1981, p.235). These critics do little to advance the cause of teachers by proposing that as well as being unable to construe knowledge about teaching, teachers are also unable to share knowledge among themselves because of a lack of a 'technical vocabulary.' As Jackson put it:

> One of the most notable features of teacher talk is the absence of a technical vocabulary. Unlike professional encounters between doctors, lawyers, garage mechanics and astrophysicists, when teachers talk together almost any reasonably intelligent adult can listen in and comprehend what is being said. (Jackson, 1968, p.143)

The difficulty with interpretations like these that purport to address the limitations of teachers as an occupational group, is that they are unhelpful and only partial accounts. Given these comments, it is interesting to speculate on how it may be possible to redirect thinking away from a despondent view of teachers and their capabilities, towards more productive possibilities.

One possibility lies in reconstruing the way those 'outside' schools are prepared to view the work of teachers. Elbaz (1981, p.45), for one, claims that in official circles at least a relatively low value is placed on experiential knowledge which is such an important part of teachers' knowledge. The consequence is that teachers are not only unaware of the status and value of their own knowledge, but they receive little in the way of encouragement to view themselves as originators of knowledge both culturally and socially. According to Elbaz (1981):

> The view of teachers as lacking in knowledge is, I believe, mistaken and misleading, and has maintained credibility partly because of conceptions of . . . teaching through which teachers have been viewed. Once these conceptions are suspended, a very different picture of teachers' knowledge comes to the fore. (p.45)

Available evidence suggests that teachers do in fact have stable bodies of ideas about how and what to teach (Reid, 1979), and that their ways of thinking and dialoguing about the issues are rational, at least *in their terms*. Lampert (1984) found that although teachers may not have had an analytic language for reflecting on the contradictory themes that emerged from their teaching, they did have concrete ways of talking about their work (p.13). This fits with Floden and Feiman's (1981) conclusion that:

> Although teachers do not engage in conscious and systematic deliberation, they still have good ways of thinking about what they are doing, even if those ways do not closely approximate the a priori models. Teachers develop heuristic strategies for dealing with the fast-moving complexity of the classroom; some of these short-cuts are better than others. Teachers are rational in their actions, not as defined by a priori models of action, but as defined by choosing appropriate means to reach their goals. (p.275)

To follow this line of reasoning is to suggest (Smyth, 1987a) that perhaps what is required is that those outside schools cease concerning themselves with teachers' apparent lack of a technical language which is said to prevent them from being able to 'tap a pre-existing body of practical knowledge' (Lortie, 1975, p.231), but instead enact forms of leadership that amount to allowing teachers to work together on their own terms. Such a 'deliberative' view (Schwab, 1983) of teachers and their work would at least elevate teachers to the level of active creators and users of practical knowledge about their own teaching. It is seductive too because of the way in which it reconstrues the nature of the relationship between theory and practice. Where teaching is conceived as a static process of transmitting accepted bodies of knowledge, and where the 'ends' of teaching are artificially divorced from the 'means', there are continual problems about how to translate somebody else's theory into practice. By using concrete and practical experience with all its frustrations and contradictions as the basis upon which to theorize, teachers become agents in the creation of their own structures of knowledge in regard to a range of matters, including subject matter and curricular content, classroom organization, strengths and weaknesses in their teaching, along with the interests and needs of students. Schwab (1983) argues that problems in teaching cannot be resolved in any final sense procedurally, but only through strategic action involving an interactive consideration of means and ends. He describes as 'personal practical knowing' the situation in which

> . . . teachers *must* be involved in debate, deliberation, and decision about what and how to teach. Such involvement constitutes the only language in which knowledge adequate to an art can arise. Without such a language, teachers not only feel decisions as impositions, they find that intelligence cannot traverse the gap between the generalities of merely expounding instructions and the practicalities of teaching moment. (p.245)

Commentators like those cited above, who concentrate on the

practical worth of what teachers do, give all the appearances of heading in the right direction. It is, after all, only as a consequence of carefully examining practice, and constructing accounts that portray those practices, that theorizing can occur. The problem, however, with accounts of this kind is in their limited conceptualization of what it means to be involved in pedagogical acts. Notions of power, resistance, agency and structure developed elsewhere in detail in this volume are largely ignored in these one-dimensional representations. The extensive work of Giroux (1983) stands out as an example of a way of portraying schools that stresses the breaks, discontinuities and tensions in the history of schooling. He claims that we need to penetrate the ways in which schools are publicly portrayed as politically opaque institutions, and concentrate instead on schools as constructed and contested terrains in which greater attention is paid to the hidden curriculum and the contradictory lived experiences of teachers and students. In arguing for a critical pedagogy of schooling, Giroux (1983) lays claims to the particular importance of the construction and analysis of meaning in everyday experience. As Fay expressed it, the purpose of examining practice must be to:

> free people from causal mechanisms that had heretofore deter-mined their existence in some important way, by revealing both the existence and precise nature of these mechanisms . . . (in other words, to) . . . aid people who are objects in the world in transforming themselves into active subjects who are self-determining. (Fay, 1977, p.210)

It is not so much that teachers refuse to view their teaching in social, cultural and political terms, but rather that they have tended to be preoccupied with teaching in practical (albeit insular) ways and have had little cause to portray it in extended ways. They have become submerged in situations they only partially understand and which they feel powerless to change. It is the internalization of beliefs, values and even world views that prevents people distancing themselves from the press of events and actions that constrain what they do. Speaking of Freire's (1972) work, Fay says that people who are oppressed '. . . do not perceive that they have the potential power to intervene in the social world and to transform it, making it other than it is. They are passive, fatalistic, dependent, adaptive to whatever occurs' (Fay, 1977, p.220).

Carr (1984) expressed the dilemma confronting teachers in these words:

It is one thing to acquire a stock of sophisticated teaching techniques and master the intricacies of modern technological aids; it is quite another to have the educational character of teaching as an ultimate professional concern. Within contemporary society, this kind of concern is often treated as a major weakness and to actually practice the educational philosophies that schools so often *say* are desirable, is to risk being thought a crank, a fool or, at best, somebody who has no interest in climbing up the ladder of his chosen profession. (p.4)

The problem of leadership is one of enabling teachers to move from a situation of dependence and non-reflectivity to one of becoming active inquirers into their own and each other's practices by acquiring new lenses for critically assessing their circumstances and their role in determining them.

Shifting Away from a Managerialist View of Leadership

Articulating a form of leadership that is more empowering of followers means moving considerably beyond the traits, characteristics and situations in which standard views of leadership are contingent. It entails a preparedness to incorporate all school participants in an active and inclusive process of questioning, challenging and theorizing about the social, political and cultural nature of the work of schools. As Grob (1984) put it, such a view of leadership requires a 'critical spirit' of continual contestation and reformulation of goals, rather than accepting them the way they are. Those who lay claim to be the visionary thinkers in schools must be prepared to analyze their own intentions, lest they become manipulative. Grob (1984) notes:

> . . . without that willingness to examine one's life, alleged leaders . . . must, of necessity, become identified with their purposes which inevitably congeal into fixed doctrines or dogma. In short, potential leaders *without this ground* find themselves in the service of fixed ideas or causes, and thus agents of the use of power in their behalf. *No longer nourished by a wellspring of critical process at its center, leadership 'dries up' and becomes, finally the mere wielding of power on behalf of static ideals.* (p.270; emphases in original)

Leadership in schools, therefore, requires an enabling capacity that incorporates (or empowers) those in schools to frame problems, and to discuss and work individually and collectively to understand and to change the situations that caused these problems. As Fried (1980) expressed it, empowerment as used in this sense means 'helping people to take charge of their lives, people who have been restrained, by social or political forces, from assuming such control' (p.8). This view of leadership is understandably at odds with the conventional view, which is more concerned with influencing individuals and groups towards goal achievement. The difference has to do with the democratic and participative formulation of goals versus the unquestioning acceptance and pursuit of prespecified goals.

What is problematic about the latter is that it relies on a socially constructed dichotomy between 'leaders' and 'followers'. We say 'constructed' because such divisions do not have a natural basis to them at all. Because some groups in schools have historically come to exercise power over others, there is now a widespread and largely uncontested view that the basis of the separation is substantive. While it may have substantive effects on the lives of those who are excluded, it is nevertheless founded on an imposed rather than a logical or rational view of reality. As Foster (1986) argues, this is not a legitimate form of leadership, but rather a pernicious form of managerialism masquerading as leadership. Watkins (1985) has rightly pointed out that leadership can come from anywhere within a school, and is not an attachment to status or position. It has more to do with the unique qualities that groups or individuals bring to specific historical contexts. Foster (1986) has arrived at a similar position:

> . . . leadership can spring from anywhere; it is not a quality that comes with an office or a person. Rather, it derives from the context and ideas of individuals who influence each other. Thus, a principal may at times be a leader and at other times, a follower. A teacher may be a leader, and the principal a follower. Leadership is an act bounded in space and time; it is an act that enables others and allows them, in turn to become enablers. (p.187)

If leadership has little to do with hierarchical impositions, then it has a lot to do with enabling the 'best' ideas to emerge wherever they come from, through a process of informed and rational debate. The kind of participative structures that are involved allow all 'voices' to be adequately heard regardless of class, race, gender or position in the formal hierarchy of the school.

If the educative model of leadership is a 'subversive' one as Fay (1977) suggests, and a political *and* 'courageous' one as proposed by Foster (1986), then it is also a 'pedagogic' one. If we take seriously the claim that to operate in an educative fashion is to 'make sense of things' (Pondy, 1978) and to communicate that sense to others, then the substance of any such focus in schools must be primarily upon issues of access, equity and fairness with regard to the pedagogic discourse of schools.

In the remainder of this chapter I argue that the constraining and functionalist view of educational leadership, with its emphasis on administrative notions of efficiency, effectiveness and accountability (Smyth, 1986a), not only makes teachers *invisible* (and hence 'silences' them) in the cultural debate about the nature of schooling and the part they play in it, but it also prevents them from situating their pedagogical practices within the broader social and cultural categories of education (Giroux and Freire, 1987, p.xv). What is required instead is a vision of leadership that begins to embrace how *teachers themselves* might articulate those teaching practices that 'count as valid transmissions of knowledge' (Bernstein, 1975, p.85), how they came about, why they continue and whether they should be altered. This amounts to a dramatic shift from enforcing an unquestioned managerialist ideology with its sanction-ridden practices to what Giroux (1988), Simon (1985), Smyth (1987b) and others label a 'critical pedagogy'. These writers argue for a dialectical approach that examines existing social relationships in teaching so that, according to Simon (1984), in deciding what they might want to do differently, teachers first have to figure out '. . . why things are the way they are, how they got that way, and what set of conditions are supporting the processes that maintain them' (p.380). Treating teachers in this way obviously involves a significant reconstruction of the way knowledge itself is regarded and of the part teachers and schools play in its creation, contestation and distribution. As Simon (1985) put it:

> First, . . . [it] views knowledge as socially produced, legitimated and distributed and seeks to make explicit the ways in which such production, legitimation and distribution takes place. Second, knowledge is apprehended as expressing and embodying particular interests and values, implicating issues of power and ethics in all expressions of knowledge. Third, seeking to negate the 'objective' nature of knowledge and forcing the educator to confront the relation between knowledge, power and control . . . action that would alter the distribution of power and increase the range and scope of possibilities for individually and collectively defined projects. (p.1119)

In slightly different terms Giroux and Freire (1987) claim that the critique involved is one in which there is a relentless pursuit in the '. . .

unmasking of the lies, myths and distortions that construct the basis for the dominant order' (p.xii). They also point out that it is more than merely an unmasking process: '. . . it [is] also a form of practical learning that involve[s] listening to the experiences of others, promoting a capacity for self-criticism, and using such criticism as the basis for developing programmatic discourses for building alternative hopes and realizable visions' (p.xii).

The intent behind such a critique and analysis is to shift the emphasis away from the current preoccupations in schooling which focus on how teachers 'measure up', to assisting *them* instead to look at how particular forms of domination in schools and society have become 'natural' and unquestioned through the social relationships they endorse in their teaching. Pagano (1987) expressed it nicely when she said, 'An education should equip us to recognize the intolerable and to act against it' (p.121). She points out that unless teachers engage in the kind of moral discourse that enables them to reflect critically, while simultaneously exploring the 'emancipatory' as well as the 'enslaving' possibilities of educational practice, then those practices '. . . become fact[s] of nature to be managed scientifically' (p.119). Pagano's (1987) argument is that for teachers *not* to engage in moral discourse about teaching amounts to a form of 'moral abdication' that is a capitulation to those forces which insist on defining the world in their own images and interests. She is not advocating a particular moral content in teaching, so much as she is advocating 'a moral imagination', which is quite different from telling teachers '. . . *what* is intolerable, or what in particular they should value . . .' (p.121). Adopting a moral point of view with respect to one's teaching:

> . . . is to take an attitude towards those who would dictate content, and to combat the claims of those whose power in the world demands that the capacity for moral discourse be atrophied. To take a moral point of view as an educator is to commit oneself to empowering one's students to engage in moral discourse and to make moral judgements. (p.120)

As Giroux (1981) cryptically notes, it is difficult to be prescriptive about precisely what constitutes critical pedagogy: '. . . the goals of emancipation are not like a shopping list that one draws up before going to the supermarket, they are goals to be struggled for in specific contexts, under specific historical conditions' (p.220). To endorse the notion of critical pedagogy is, therefore, to adopt a particular view about the nature of the relationship between knowledge, inquiry, experience and values in teaching; it is the interpenetration of these that constitutes the 'critical' agenda. Claims to a critical pedagogy of teaching rest upon a number of fundamental presumptions, that are considered next.

Linking the Pedagogical with the Political

Much of the debate over forms of leadership in schools is really a struggle over those contending forces arguing for the 'pedagogy of the answer' versus the forces that believe in 'the pedagogy of the question' (Bruss and Macedo, 1985). It is a struggle between those who believe they have definitive knowledge (both substantively and procedurally) about teaching and those who argue that teaching has considerably less to do with procedures and more to do with the pursuit of moral, ethical and political questions. In many respects it is an extension of the broader discussion educators like Freire (1972) are engaged in about mechanistic approaches to literacy, compared with socially and politically informed approaches to literacy that are located in the culture and experiences of learners. It is really a question of whether we can any longer afford to allow discussion of educative issues to remain fixated at the level of 'recycling old assumptions and values concerning the meaning and usefulness of literacy' (Bruss and Macedo, 1985, p.7), or whether other dimensions of schooling that have conveniently been ignored in the past need to be given an airing. What remains largely ignored at the moment is the political nature of education, and of how learning is situated in and reproduced by a particular history and context of power relations. Teachers do not by and large perceive *themselves* as 'active' learners, inquirers and advocates of their own practices — nor are they encouraged to become critical theoreticians of their own teaching, its traditions and the structures within which it is located.

Kohl (1983) claims that unless teachers adopt this kind of informed militant position towards their work, then the door will continue to remain wide open 'to stifling curriculum proposals devised by stodgy academics with no real sense of what goes on in the classroom' (p.28). Allowing others to shape and determine teaching amounts to what Kohl (1983) sees as teachers bargaining away their educational power and giving up their responsibility as intellectuals (p.30). Where teachers and students embrace the 'pedagogy of the question', then they adopt practices that both force and challenge them to think critically about their world:

> The pedagogy of the question requires that learners distance themselves from their bureaucratized daily existence, while they

become more and more aware through reflection of the mythical facts that enslave them. Unlike the pedagogy of the answer, which reduces learners to mere receptacles for pre-packaged knowledge, the pedagogy of the question gives the learners the 'language of possibility' to challenge the very constraints which relegate them to mere objects. [By way of contrast] . . . the pedagogy of the answer . . . lacks any profundity of thought and cannot stimulate and challenge learners to question, to doubt, and to reject. (Bruss and Macedo, 1985, p.8)

What this amounts to is a preparedness to move outside supposed certainties into the less secure, more tentative and problematic arena of complexities, instability and value conflict. In his book, the *Reflective Practitioner: How Professionals Think in Action,* Schön (1983) provides a compelling account of how discipline-based knowledge in a range of professions is proving incapable of delivering solutions to the protracted social, environmental and human problems of our times. What Schön (1983) is saying is consistent with Freire, in that we are confronting a crisis of confidence in which claims to knowledge based on technical rationality are out of step with the changing situations of practice; the rules of the game have changed radically. Accepted and taken-for-granted ways of applying specialized knowledge to resolve particular recurring problems no longer seem to work. The foundations of professional practice, in teaching as well as in a range of other professional areas, seem to have shifted dramatically from 'problem-solving' to 'problem-setting' (or problem-posing); that is, from a rational process of choosing from among possibilities that best suit agreed upon ends to a situation that opens up for contestation and debate the nature of those decisions, the ends to which they are to be directed and the means by which they are achievable. Rather than relying upon tried and tested knowledge to be applied in all circumstances of a similar kind, the scene is increasingly characterized by the application of knowledge acquired from previous particular cases. What this has meant for professionals is a transformation:

* from a position where scientifically derived knowledge is deemed superior, to a circumstance in which artistic and intuitive knowledge may be equally appropriate;
* from an a priori instrumental view of knowledge, to one that reflects knowledge as being tentative and problematic;
* from a view which pre-supposes answers to complex social questions, to one that endorses the importance of problem posing and negotiated resolution. (Smyth, 1986b, p.7)

Reflection-in-Action

In this view of leadership as sense-making, greater attention is therefore given to the 'playfulness' of knowledge and to job-embedded ways of learning that acknowledge the fundamental importance of questioning, criticizing and reformulating taken-for-granted assumptions about the nature of work. It means engaging in what Schön (1983) describes as reflection-in-action, or '. . . reflective conversation with the situation' (p.42). By reflecting upon action, Schön (1983) claims that individuals and communities acquire knowledge, skills and concepts that empower them to remake, and if necessary reorder, the world in which they live. It takes the form of '. . . on-the-spot surfacing, criticising, restructuring and testing of intuitive understandings of experienced phenomena' (Schön, 1984, p.42).

There is, therefore, a growing realization that specialist claims to knowledge, including those by people outside classrooms purporting to know what is best for teaching and learning (see US Department of Education, 1986), are really claims to power. It is to acknowledge Foucault's (1980) point that knowledge and power are inextricably connected and that the knowledge/power relationship is the very basis of most of our social relationships. As he says, 'Truth isn't outside of power, or lacking in power. . . . Truth is a thing of this world: it is produced only by virtue of multiple forms of constraint' (p.131). It could be argued that as long as knowledge about teaching is seen to be definitive, and to lie in the hands of people distant from classrooms (administrators, researchers, policy-makers, etc.), then the actions of teachers will be constrained and directed in ways decided by others.

While professional groups other than teachers are increasingly coming to regard their practice problematically (see Schön, 1983, 1984, 1987), among those who see themselves as self-proclaimed educational leaders there seems to be evidence of a move in the opposite direction. Emphasis in education upon economic 'rationalization' and economic accountability, with their attendant requirements that teachers fit in with notions of 'standardization', 'efficiency' and 'effectiveness', are clear indicators of an intensification of ideological control over schools in the form of scientific management. Like mainstream educational theory, such a scientific management view concentrates on the relationship between knowledge and control, and how what teachers do in conveying that knowledge can best be managed and evaluated. As Fitzclarence and Giroux (1984) put it:

> The underlying concern in this case has generally focused around the best ways to transmit and systematically evaluate what is

construed as 'legitimate' knowledge. . . . [T]he value of school knowledge has become largely linked to the promotion of academic achievement and the implementation of acceptable models of socialization. . . . [M]ainstream educational theory [like traditional views of educational leadership] has generally ignored the relationship between knowledge and power. And in doing so, it has both shifted and avoided a concern with the politics of school knowledge to a concern with the administration and management of knowledge. (p.462)

What is worrying about such technologized approaches is that they detach students and teachers from their language, customs, rituals, experiences and histories; what is posited in their place are managerial forms of discourse about the nature of schooling that are alien to the cultural lives of people in schools. Because of the power of language, what occurs is a pedagogic dislocation as teachers and students become confused about the relative legitimacy and potency of their own lived practical experiences in the light of hegemonic 'management pedagogies' (Giroux, 1985). The imperatives in management pedagogies become the reduction and standardization of knowledge; the measurement of attainment against predetermined objectives and standards; and the allocation of teaching resources so as to maximize output. Because the discourse of management pedagogy is located in the lexicon of the technocrats, and not that of the idiosyncratic and value-laden experiences of classrooms, teachers and students have to struggle continually against the goals and objectives set by others outside classrooms. As Ryan (1982) put it, the technocratic view has an air of pseudo-respectability about it, '. . . its scientistic language, reflecting an instrumentalist orientation to carefully-defined and measurable goals, gives the perennial politics of control a gloss of sophisticated modernity' (p.30).

Even where these externally contrived agenda appear to be rational, sensible and humane, the inability of management pedagogies adequately to understand, let alone grapple with, the complexities in classrooms, creates a situation of opposition for teachers. What must not be overlooked is that unequal power relations in schools (between individuals and groups) are established and constructed through the lived experiences of people in schools. As such, they can be 'disestablished' and 'deconstructed' in the way people choose to live, work and ultimately penetrate the object of their struggles (Smyth, 1986c). What is needed is a faith '. . . in the power of [teachers, pupils and parents] to reflect on and change the oppressive circumstances in which they find themselves' (Giroux, 1981, p.216).

The management pedagogies alluded to by Giroux do not exist in a vacuum: it is not possible meaningfully to discuss classroom processes without at the same time considering their relationship to wider social and economic structures and processes. Carnoy and Levin (1985) have provided an insightful analysis of the direct relationship between changes in the workplace and school reforms. They argue that in the same way that workers are frustrated and alienated from their jobs because of a lack of *real* involvement in their work, so too students in schools are equally alienated from schooling because of a lack of control over their learning. Just as there is a long history of worker resistance, there is also a tangible legacy of resistance in schools in the form of open defiance of: '. . . school norms and standards; others consider success in school a betrayal of their peers; and still others drop out in the classroom, resisting passively by not listening, withholding their enthusiasm, and not completing their assignments' (Kantor and Lowe, 1987, p.71).

According to Carnoy and Levin (1985), conflict of this kind in both school and workplace must ultimately lead to major transformations in both, as distinct from the cosmetic changes of the kind we have witnessed recently. Kantor and Lowe (1987) summarize Carnoy and Levin's thesis:

> . . . these conflicts will eventually generate efforts to reform both the workplace and the school. At the workplace . . . managers will attempt to reduce worker dissatisfaction and raise productivity be redesigning work and increasing worker participation. Initially, these efforts will consist of reforms such as job rotation, flexible scheduling, and incentive pay plans that seek to increase worker satisfaction without relinquishing managerial control of the labor process [which is pretty much the scene as it has happened to date]. . . . Whatever happens at the workplace, however, work reform by itself will not be enough to assimilate dissatisfied workers. As in the past . . . school reforms will also be necessary. . . . Given the current emphasis on the socially reproductive dimensions of schooling, successful reforms will likely be those that correspond to workplace reforms. . . . [R]eforms that inadequately address the sources of worker discontent and alienation . . . are likely to fail. . . . Those reforms oriented to cooperative, participative work relationships will rise in importance. These include programs such as group decision making and peer training which . . . will impart the skills and habits required by the team approach to production that will become necessary to satisfy disgruntled workers. (p.71)

The central argument in this chapter has been that the hierarchically organized and sanction-ridden business management notions of leadership that have to do with efficiency, effectiveness, standardization and quality control have no place in schools. The alternative proposal has been that if there is any meaning attaching at all to the notion of educational leadership, then it lies in teachers making sense of what they do through problematizing their teaching in the social and political contexts in which it occurs. What is being suggested is that teachers begin by unmasking (or unveiling) the historically embedded nature of technicist forms of teaching, as a first step towards teachers regaining faith in themselves. The second step lies in what Shor and Freire (1987) call the 'dialogical method of teaching', based as it is in self-criticism and critique of the taken-for-grantedness of actual contexts of teaching. It is clear that the ideas behind such a critical pedagogy are sufficiently complex as to defy codification. Indeed, there is a host of reasons why such proceduralization should be strenuously resisted; it is more like a 'form of life' than a process.

Strategic Pointers

If teachers are to experience the educative forms of leadership spoken about in this chapter, then they need to be invested with ways of developing a deep sense of the importance of *history as a formative process* in their personal and collective teaching. What needs to be challenged is the cultural conditioning of both students and teacher that causes them to accept forms of schooling that buttress and cement existing social relationships between students and teacher, and between students themselves. In part this process of developing a sense of history of their own pedagogy can come about when groups, working collectively and collaboratively, consider questions like the following:

* where did the ideas I embody in my teaching come from historically?
* how did I come to appropriate them?
* why do I continue to endorse them now in my work?
* whose interests do they serve?
* what power relationships are involved?
* how do these ideas influence my relationships with my students?
* in the light of what I have discovered, how might I work differently? (Smyth, 1987b, p.20)

Working at creating a 'historical memory' of this kind acts as a way of countering oppressive authoritarian teacher-student relationships that are beyond the teacher's own making. At the same time it involves a commitment to *participatory forms of learning* as the way to unfreeze existing power relationships between teacher and students. Allowing learning to connect in a *real* way with lived experiences of students' daily lives amounts to a departure from prescribed (or 'suggestive') curriculum. A passive pedagogy in which the teacher's monologue of words is all that counts actually enshrines 'official' knowledge in a way that promotes a dominant viewpoint, thereby disempowering students. This commitment to a *dialogical method of teaching*, in which there is an engagement in a joint search for knowledge, is the antithesis of didactic teaching, in which the definitive and prescriptive communiqués of teachers are unavailable for examination or contestation by students. Learning that involves political and moral values means that the very '. . . structure of learning itself challenges structures of control' (Shor and Freire, 1987, p.96). Communication is not, therefore, '. . . a mere ping pong of words and gestures. It affirms or challenges the relationships between the people communicating' (Shor and Freire, 1987, p.99). Developing a dialogue enables learners to penetrate the opacity of what passes as knowledge, by challenging them to encounter the 'limit situations' that represent the status quo. As Greene (1978) noted, our predominant concern should be to maintain the 'normative', the 'critical', but above all the 'political' in our teaching, thus empowering teachers '. . . to reflect on their own life situations, to speak out in their own ways about the lacks that must be repaired [and] the possibilities to be acted upon in the name of what they deem decent, humane and just (p.71).

Within such a scheme *learning becomes a social process*, where understandings are arrived at through shared and negotiated means. Individual empowerment is, thus, an empty vessel. Unless learning helps others to attain greater freedom in terms of seeing their own potential, limitations and consequences, then, as Shor (1980) points out, this amounts to no more than a form of 'self-absorption'. Construed in this way, both knowledge and learning are 'transformative' in that they work towards achieving non-exploitative social relationships between people. Refusing to be driven by imposed curricula (with their official version of knowledge) amounts to a way of countering this form of amputation that separates students and teachers from the realities they are supposed to be studying. Adopting *a situated pedagogy,* in which the starting point is concrete descriptions of reality, is clearly going to be opposed by those who favour the imposed curriculum, but only because they have '. . . become ideologized into rejecting freedom and accepting authoritarian and elitist ways of organizing studies' (Shor and Freire, 1987, p.107).

If this is to amount to anything, then teachers need to be able to describe the surface realities of their teaching empirically; that is, there needs to be some evidence rooted in practice, as the basis of assertions about teaching. Minimally this requires describing the 'elements' of the situation; the who, what, when, where of teaching occurrences. This rendering of descriptive accounts of teaching generally amounts to a way of selectively reconstructing personalized records of teaching events. Questions that might guide teachers in this analysis include:

* what counts as knowledge?
* how is such knowledge produced and distributed?
* what concerns do different forms of knowledge production address?
* whose interests are in opposition to the dominant ideology?
* what knowledge would not be consistent with the dominant ideology?
* do certain forms of engaging knowledge help to legitimate one set of interests over and above others?
* how might knowledge be engaged so that alternate forms of knowledge and knowledge production might be considered?
* where ultimately will the teacher and the student stand regarding the interests which underlie the pursuit of knowledge?
* given this pursuit of knowledge, what is to be done?

(Simon, 1985, p.1119)

These *grounded descriptions* provide the basis upon which teachers can begin to share teaching experiences and elaborate with one another on the signification of their cultural and social meaning with students and with colleagues. Narratives of this kind enable an uncovering of the opaque nature of much of what passes as knowledge in classroom teaching, and provide a basis upon which teachers and others can develop genuinely empowering forms of understanding.

References

Berlak, A. and Berlak, H. (1981) *Dilemmas of Schooling: Teaching and Social Change,* London, Methuen.

Bernstein, B. (1975) *Class, Codes and Control: Towards a Theory of Educational Transmissions,* London, Routledge and Kegan Paul.

Bernstein, B. (1986) 'On pedagogic discourse,' in J. Richardson (Ed.), *Handbook of Theory and Research for the Sociology of Education,* New York, Greenwood.

Bruss, N. and Macedo, P. (1985) 'Towards a pedagogy of the question: Conversations with Paulo Freire,' *Journal of Education,* 167,2, pp.7-21.

Carnoy, M. and Levin, H. (1985) *Schooling and Work in the Democratic State,* Stanford, Calif., Stanford University Press.

Carr, W. (1984) 'Adopting an educational philosophy,' *Cambridge Journal of Education,* 14,2, pp.1-4.

Elbaz, F. (1981), 'The teacher's "practical knowledge": Report of a case study,' *Curriculum Inquiry,* 11,1, pp.43-71.

Fay, B. (1975) *Social Theory and Political Practice,* London, Allen and Unwin.

Fay, B. (1977) 'How people change themselves: The relationship between critical theory and its audience,' in T. Ball (Ed.), *Political Theory and Praxis: New Perspectives,* Minneapolis, Minn., University of Minnesota Press, pp.200-33.

Fay, B. (1987) *Critical Social Science: Liberation and Its Limits,* Oxford, Polity Press.

Fitzclarence, L. and Giroux, H. (1984) 'The paradox of power in educational theory and practice,' *Language Arts,* 61,5, pp.462-77.

Floden, R. and Feiman, S. (1981) 'Should teachers be taught to be rational?' *Journal of Education for Teaching,* 7,3, pp.274-83.

Foster, W. (1986) *Paradigms and Promises: New Approaches to Educational Administration,* Buffalo, N.Y., Promethers.

Foucault, M. (1980) *Power/Knowledge: Selected Interviews and Other Writings,* Ed. and trans C. Gordon, New York, Pantheon.

Fried, R. (1980) *Empowerment vs. Delivery of Services,* Concord, N.H., New Hampshire Department of Education.

Freire, P. (1972) *Pedagogy of the Oppressed,* Harmondsworth, Penguin.

Grioux, H. (1981) 'Pedagogy, pessimism and the politics of conformity: A reply to Linda McNeil,' *Curriculum Inquiry,* 11,3, pp.211-22.

Giroux, H. (1983) *Theory and Resistance in Education: A Pedagogy for the Opposition,* South Hadley, Mass., Bergin and Garvey.

Giroux, H. (1985) 'Teachers as transformative intellectuals,' *Social Education,* 49, May, pp.376-9.

Giroux, H. (1988) *Teachers-as-Intellectuals: Towards a Critical Pedagogy of Learning,* South Hadley, Mass., Bergin and Garvey.

Giroux, H. and Freire, P. (1987) 'Series introduction,' in D. Livingstone *et al.* (Eds), *Critical Pedagogy and Cultural Power,* South Hadley, Mass., Bergin and Garvey.

Greene, M. (1978) *Landscapes of Learning,* New York, Teachers College Press.

Greenfield, T.B. (1981) 'Understanding educational organizations as cultural entities: Some ideas, methods and metaphors,' Paper to conference on Administrative Leadership: New Perspectives on Theory and Practice, 13-15 June 1981, University of Illinois, Urbana.

Grob, L. (1984) 'Leadership: The socratic model,' in B. Kellerman (Ed.), *Leadership: Multi-Disciplinary Perspectives,* Englewood Cliffs, N.J., Prentice Hall.

Hextall, I. (1984) 'Rendering accounts: A critical analysis of the APU,' in P. Broadfood (Ed.), *Selection Certification and Control: Social Issues in Education Assessment,* Lewes, Falmer Press.

Jackson, P. (1968) *Life in Classrooms,* New York, Holt, Rinehart and Winston.

Kantor, H. and Lowe, R. (1987) 'Empty promises: Review of schooling and work in the democratic state by Carnoy and Levin,' *Harvard Educational Review*, 57,1, pp.68-76.

Kohl, H. (1983) 'Examining closely what we do,' *Learning*, 12,1, pp.28-30.

Lampert, M. (1984) 'Teaching about thinking and thinking about teaching,' *Journal of Curriculum Studies*, 16,1, pp.1-18.

Lortie, D. (1975) *School Teacher: A Sociological Study*, Chicago, Ill., University of Chicago Press.

Pagano, J. (1987) 'The schools we deserve: Review of Goodlads', "A Place Called School",' *Curriculum Inquiry*, 17,1, pp.107-22.

Pondy, L. (1978) 'Leadership is a language game,' in M. McCall and M. Lombardo (Eds), *Leadership: Where Else Can We Go?* Durham, N.C., University Press.

Reed, D. (1974) 'An experience in Peru,' *New Internationalist*, 16, June, pp.8-11.

Reid, W. (1979) 'Practical reasoning and curriculum theory: In search of a new paradigm,' *Curriculum Inquiry*, 9,3, pp.187-207.

Ryan, B. (1982) 'Accountability in Australian education,' *Discourse*, 2,2, pp.21-40.

Schön, D. (1983) *The Reflective Practitioner: How Professionals Think in Action*, New York, Basic Books.

Schön, D. (1984) 'Leadership as reflection-in-action,' in T. Sergiovanni and J. Corbally (Eds), *Leadership and Organizational Culture: New Perspectives on Administrative Theory and Practice*, Urbana, Ill., University of Illinois Press, pp.36-63.

Schön, D. (1987) *Educating the Reflective Practitioner*, San Francisco, Calif., Jossey Bass.

Schwab, J. (1983) 'The practical 4: Something for curriculum professors to do,' *Curriculum Inquiry*, 13,3, pp.239-65.

Shor, I. (1980) *Critical Teaching and Everyday Life*, Boston, Mass., South End Press.

Shor, I. and Freire, P. (1987) *A Pedagogy for Liberation: Dialogues on Transforming Education*, South Hadley, Mass., Bergin and Garvey.

Simon, R. (1984) 'Signposts for a critical pedagogy: A review of Henry Giroux's "Theory and Resistance in Education",' *Educational Theory*, 34,4, pp.379-88.

Simon, R. (1985) 'Critical pedagogy,' in T. Husen and Postlethwaite (Eds), *International Encyclopedia of Education Research and Studies*, Vol.2, London, Pergamon Press, pp.1118-20.

Smyth, J. (1986a) *Leadership and Pedagogy*, Geelong, Deakin University Press.

Smyth, J. (1986b) *Reflection-in-Action*, Geelong, Deakin University Press.

Smyth, J. (1986c) 'Changing what we do in our teaching: Let's stop talking about it!' *Journal of Teaching Practice*, 6,2, pp.16-31.

Smyth, J. (1987a) *Educating Teachers: Changing the Nature of Pedagogical Knowledge*, Lewes, Falmer Press.

Smyth, J. (1987b) *Rationale for Teachers' Critical Pedagogy: A Handbook*, Geelong, Deakin University Press.

US Department of Education (1986) *What Works: Research about Teaching and Learning*, Washington.

Watkins, P. (1985) 'Alternatives to traditional views of organisational leadership: Human agency and practice in the restructuring of education,' *The Australian Administrator,* 6,3, pp.1-4.

Chapter 8

In Defence of Organizational Democracy

Fazal Rizvi

The papers in this volume are highly critical of the traditional notions of leadership in education. Central among their criticisms is the contention that these traditional, mostly functionalist, accounts of leadership assume erroneously that organizational hierarchies are inevitable. The functionalist view, implicit in much of the recent educational management literature, deems administrative hierarchy to be a technical necessity, essential for the efficient and rational realization of organizational goals. The functionalist sees leadership in terms of a process which involves the exercise of organizational authority, an authority which is believed to derive its legitimacy from the overriding concerns of efficiency and effectiveness. Such instrumentalism assumes leadership to be neutral with respect to particular organizational goals, concerned solely with the most efficient means for the realization of the given organizational ends. Leadership is regarded as a function of the most rational arrangement of social activities and relations. The authors of the papers in this volume deny that in education such organizational neutrality, and an absolute means-ends distinction, is either empirically feasible or morally defensible. Thus the functionalist accounts of educational leadership are criticized both for portraying an inaccurate picture of educational organizations and for presenting a normative view of leadership which is inappropriate for the educational enterprise.

Rejecting the assumption of the technical necessity of hierarchy, the authors believe that it is indeed possible to conceive of and pursue various democratic alternatives to the kind of organizations the functionalist views of educational leadership imply. In exploring these alternatives, the authors call for greater and more broadly-based participation in educational decision-making. Watkins is supportive of the thrust of the Victorian Ministerial Papers in their commitment to the principles of 'genuine devolution of authority and responsibility to school community' and 'collaborative decision-making processes'. Angus is critical of the recent corporatist views of leadership which, while acknowledging the importance of values and culture, nevertheless assume unequal power relationships to be perfectly natural. Arguing from a feminist perspective, Blackmore suggests that the democratization of social relationships is a fundamental requirement of human emancipation. Foster contends that in education leadership should be concerned with transformation of values and that this purpose is best achieved in organizations which are themselves committed to such social ends as democracy, justice and liberty. Codd views leadership in terms of reflective action which is guided by democratic values. Following critical theorists like Habermas and Fay, Bates and Smyth argue for an emancipatory view of the educational enterprise in which the hierarchical notion of leadership does not assume an overriding significance. They believe that the critical perspective on educational leadership implies a reformulation of the way social relationships in schools are currently defined, towards, among other things, democratic decision-making and broadly-based educational participation.

Of course, the emphasis on the value of broadly-based participation in educational decision-making is not confined to the writers generally sympathetic to critical theory. A wide variety of recent educational thinkers have reasserted the importance of participatory democracy to education, in much the same way as Dewey did more than fifty years ago. Writing from within the liberal-democratic tradition, Patricia White (1983) has argued that the case for democratic organization of educational decision-making is a strong one. From a socialist perspective Wood (1984) has attempted to demonstrate how a transformation of social order through education is impossible unless radical changes are made to the current hierarchical structure of schools and its bureaucratic decision-making procedures. More recently Maxcy (1985) has used the rich reservoir of Dewey's educational writings to illustrate how notions of 'participation' and 'education' are philosophically linked.

The view of organizational democracy in education advocated by these writers suggests an obliteration of the distinction between leaders and followers that is structurally defined. The phenomenon of leadership is not denied, but its institutionalization is. It is assumed that in organizations committed to democracy, leadership would emerge organically, and, since it would not be fixed to institutional positions, it could be contained democratically. In accepting this assumption, the authors of the papers in this volume present organizational democracy as not only morally desirable but also practically feasible. But can complex organizations like schools and school systems function effectively without hierarchical designation of positions and roles? How realistic is it to expect *all* individuals to participate in organizational decision-making? Can the mass of people really bear the strain of playing public and political roles? In short, how plausible is organizational democracy?

This century a large number of theorists have suggested that the basic premises upon which the idea of organizational democracy is based are fundamentally mistaken. Many political scientists, sociologists and management theorists have argued that hierarchical leadership is inevitable in complex organizations. In this chapter I shall examine this conclusion by referring in particular to two key arguments of the Italian sociologist, Robert Michels (1958; written originally in 1915), as they apply to decision-making in educational organizations. Both of these arguments relate to Michels' 'iron law of oligarchy' which, as I will show, continues to be highly influential. Indeed, it could be argued very plausibly that more recent attempts to demonstrate the impossibility of organizational democracy amount essentially to a restatement of Michels' original position. Michels' arguments therefore need to be examined and countered by all those who subscribe to the values of direct democracy, including those advocates of the critical perspectives on educational leadership whose papers are included in this volume.

The Iron Law of Oligarchy

The most widely known and influential of all arguments against the possibility of organizational democracy this century go back to the writings of a number of early Italian sociologists. Prominent among these are Pareto (1935), Mosca (1939) and Michels (1958). Writing at the beginning of this century, each of these writers argued that hierarchical leadership was an inevitable and necessary phenomenon in modern society. They contended that as societies become more complex, organizational democracy increasingly represents an unrealizable and unrealistic dream. Elite governance is inevitable, regardless of any human efforts to counteract it. In this chapter, I shall examine Michels' arguments, ahead of those of Pareto and Mosca, not only because his writings are the most recent and influential but also because Michels intended his arguments to apply specifically to those organizations which had aspired to, and yet had failed to, achieve democracy. Michels was a writer generally sympathetic to democratic ideals, who sought to explain what he saw as its failure in practice.

Michels attempted to theorize on the nature and scope of elite power in a most systematic, empirical fashion; indeed, the current empirical character of political science is at least partly due to his methodological innovations. While nineteenth century political theory had been largely normative and speculative, Michels' contribution was to make it rigorously empirical. He argued that writers in the past had largely been concerned to make recommendations about politics rather than to discover the principles according to which political and administrative systems operated. He therefore presented his explanations of the nature of control in organizations and the role of leadership in society as scientific claims — neutral and objective, free from any ethical contamination. He claimed that his analysis of elite leadership was only one part of a much wider scientific analysis of society and the role of politics within it.

Thus Michels' views are offered as laws and facts, which do not themselves reveal any ethical comment on the phenomena described. Hierarchical leadership is not presented as either good or bad, just or unjust, desirable or undesirable — in Michels' view it simply exists and must therefore be incorporated within a scientific understanding of the politics of organizations.

For Michels, to investigate a phenomenon scientifically involves the testing of a hypothesis against the accrued facts. The hypothesis which Michels wants to test is his 'iron law of oligarchy'. It states that leadership is a necessary phenomenon in every form of social life and that it is necessary for organizational survival. In his book, *Political Parties,* Michels seeks to test the hypothetical 'iron law of oligarchy' by examining a number of organizations which prima facie seemed to him to represent outstanding counter-examples to the law. The organizations he selected to study were all committed to preserving equality and democracy in their internal decision-making structure. In them power was claimed to be equally distributed, and their leaders were elected to act as mere agents of the mass membership. Even in such organizations, Michels claims, he found tendencies towards elite control since only a small minority took the major decisions. In these organizations the dominant minority could not be controlled by the majority, despite the use of various democratic mechanisms. The minority was always in a position to manipulate the electoral processes to fulfil its own interests, by means of a range of measures from sheer coercion to the skilled use of propaganda. Not only did the minority control the decision-making processes but, Michels suggests, the majority was happy enough to be governed, led and manipulated. Therefore no strategy of ensuring the accountability of the leaders to the majority was sufficient to prevent the supremacy of the minority. Because of their power, their organization, their political skills or their personal qualities, the leadership was always potentially capable of preserving its domination. To Michels, these observations confirmed the iron law of oligarchy.

The nature of organizations, Michels concluded, is such that it gives power and advantage to a group of leaders who cannot then be checked or held accountable by their followers. Michels (1958, pp.365-6) insists that 'the formation of oligarchies within the various forms of democracy is an outcome of organic necessity, and consequently affects every organisation, be it socialist or even anarchist.' But how is this necessity to be explained? Michels argues that there are two factors which cause this organic necessity — an organizational factor and a psychological factor.

For Michels, oligarchy is an inevitable product of the very principle of organization. Whenever we encounter organization, we find oligarchy there as well. According to Michels:

> Organisation implies the tendency to oligarchy. In every organisation, whether it be a political party, a professional union, or any other association of the kind, the aristocratic tendency manifests itself very clearly. . . . As a result of organisation, every party or professional organisation becomes a minority of directors and a majority of directed. (Michels, 1958, p.37)

Michels' much-quoted phrase, 'Who says organisation, says oligarchy' (Michels, 1958, p.418), implies that organizations could not continue to exist unless they were rationally and hierarchically structured. He argues that the size and complexity of modern organizations are such that technical expertise is required if the organizational goals are to be attained. He insists that attempts to involve all members in organizational decision-making must, by necessity, involve amateurishness and confusion that is totally self-defeating. Organizations, to be effective, need to establish a coordinated policy, a plan for action and an administrative structure, including clearly defined lines of accountability, to ensure consistency and efficiency. The logic of organizations is such that they require expertise which the majority of members of a group typically do not have the aptitude to develop and for which they certainly lack interest and time. The idea of mass participation in an organization therefore conflicts with the principles of professional and technical administration.

For Michels, a second set of explanations of the oligarchical phenomenon is psychological. That is, oligarchy derives from the psychological characteristics of human personality, of both the leaders and the followers. Leaders, according to Michels, are psychologically predisposed to consolidate their political power. Power once acquired by individuals naturally leads them to ensure that it is preserved. In the course of organizational behaviour leaders are psychologically so transformed that they view others in unspontaneous and calculated ways. The exercise of leadership transforms human personality.

Oligarchy is also reinforced, in Michels' view, by the psychic transformation of the followers. He maintains that while democratic theorists often assume a high degree of political interest and spontaneity on the part of all individuals, in fact most people are apathetic towards public matters. Most people are concerned with organizational decision-making only insofar as it affects their personal interests. They have no interest in how decision-making takes place, and it is therefore only a small group which constitutes the active membership of any organization from which the leadership is derived.

Michels believes moreover that most people lack technical compe-tence associated with public decision-making. With this feeling of incompetence, they are only too happy to let others make decisions. He insists that the majority in fact fears participation and has a psychological need for guidance. Majority apathy, submissiveness, lack of expertise and deference all combine to provide ideal conditions for the few, the elite, with the interest, knowledge and the organizational ability to lead. Michels concludes, 'The majority of human beings, in condition of eternal tutelage, are predestined by tragic necessity to submit to the dominion of a small minority, and must be content to constitute the pedestal of an oligarchy' (Michels, 1958, pp.33-4).

The themes central to Michels' iron law of oligarchy have recurred in a range of recent political writings. Schumpeter (1950), Dahl and Lindblom (1963), Verba (1961) and Lasswell (1958) have all argued against the empirical possibility of implementing a radical programme designed to democratize communities and organizations. They have in effect suggested that the idea of direct democracy is incompatible with the organizational imperatives identified by Michels. Many recent management theorists too have followed Michels in arguing against developments in industrial democracy and participatory decision-making. Organizational democracy is thought to be unrealistic because it is thought that to operate efficiently modern organizations require expertise in decision-making skills which only a few possess, or could develop. Organizational effectiveness is assumed to require well defined specialisms and professionalism.

Leaders are believed to be needed because they possess many personal qualities and resources which make them indispensable for organizational survival. These resources include superior technical knowledge, control over the formal means of communication and greater skills in organizational politics. Leaders can ensure the realization of organizational goals more quickly and efficiently, without the unnecessary time-consuming debates that typify amateurish decision-making processes of many community organizations. But such an appeal has a self-perpetuating effect. The professionals come to have a personal interest in maintaining the status quo because it is only then that it is possible for them to benefit from the claims to professional expertise. It is a claim which can be used to exclude people from any but the most minimal input into decision-making.

Citing his debt to Michels' insights, an Australian writer, Higley (1980), has strongly reiterated the oligarchic thesis. He has suggested that our society and social organizations must inevitably be governed by an elite; and even that a certain type of elite is necessary to safeguard our current form of weak democracy. He has maintained that any attempt to create a more equal and participatory democratic society will not only inevitably fail but also, in the process, lead to social discord and political chaos which could threaten existing forms of limited democracy. In examining Higley's claims, Pateman (1982, p.97) suggests that the case presented by Higley stands on two related assertions: first, that in complex societies like ours social organizations must necessarily be hierarchical and largely undemocratic, and second, that individuals are always, because of their inherent human nature, self-interested and apathetic with respect to public issues.

It is clear that much of the use that has been made of Michels' basic position in recent studies of organizations has centred on his two main arguments. First, the 'efficiency argument', derived from Michels' reference to organizational factors, has been used to suggest that organizational democracy is inefficient. Second, the 'mass apathy' argument, derived from Michels' reference to psychological factors, has *assumption* been used to contend that democracy is impossible because generally people are socially and politically apathetic and mostly do not wish to be involved in decision-making. In what follows I want to examine these two arguments in some detail.

The Idea of Efficiency and Its Ideological Uses

Among its many advocates Michels' 'efficiency argument' has been supported by a number of recent philosophers of education who have found the notions of 'democracy' and 'participation' largely rhetorical and therefore particularly unhelpful. Wilson and Cowell (1983), for example, argue that democracy is a 'myth', 'a matter of style, doctrine or ideology'. As a theoretical notion it lacks conceptual determinacy and should not therefore be accorded a place in that form of educational thinking which aspires to philosophical clarity. Similarly Barrow (1981) finds the whole issue of democracy in educational decision-making irrelevant. He insists that: '. . . I would see no reason to complain at variations between schools, some autocratically led by wise and inspired heads, others given over to democracy. All that does matter, both in theory and practice, is that decision-making should be carried out by those with requisite qualities, which must include philosophic competence.'

Both Barrow and Wilson and Cowell suggest that democracy may be a less efficient way of developing educational policies than those modes of decision-making which rely on specific expertise or '. . . the requisite qualities'. In their view efficiency demands that educational decisions be made by those who are capable of making rational decisions; that is, those who possess a particular range of skills and knowledge. Competence in the sphere of policy-making, however, should not be defined exclusively in terms of information. Our rational decision-makers should also be 'philosophically competent', so argues Barrow.

The efficiency argument is no less common in modern administrative theory. It is derived partly from the writings of Michels, but perhaps more directly from a particular (functionalist) interpretation of the writings of Max Weber (1970). This interpretation of Weber is familiar enough (see Weiss, 1983). It is argued that effective and efficient decision-making requires a clear hierarchy of command and responsibility. It is obvious that many decisions, particularly those of a technical or detailed character, or those involving great speed of response, cannot be taken by all the members of a community in some democratic manner. Decision-making of this kind must be left in the hands of an elite body of people, qualified by experience, technical skills, connoisseurship or any other host of criteria, including 'philosophical competence'. The technical indispensability of leadership for the efficient conduct of organizations is believed to render participatory modes of decision-making undesirable. Participation is thus thought to be inimical to 'efficiency'.

In confronting the claim that participation is inimical to 'efficiency' we need to be clear about how the notion of 'efficiency' is understood. To understand the use of the notion of efficiency both Michels and Weber employed, something must be said about the form of rationality within which it is located. This view of rationality centred on the positivist claim that statements of fact and judgments of value are logically distinct, and that only facts can be rationally assessed. Values are outside the province of rationality and the only practical rationality that is possible is the rationality of matching means to ends efficiently and effectively.

Modern administration theory is fundamentally embedded within this 'bureaucratic' view of rationality. It systematically eschews making judgments on the morality of organizational ends, for it rests on the assumption that ends cannot be subjected to the scrutiny of reason. The task of the administrator is seen as one that is concerned with formulating rationally designed *means* for the explicit realization of given *ends*. Bureaucracy itself is viewed as an instrument of efficiency, neutral with respect to the goals it has been created to serve. Efficiency, then, is viewed as a morally neutral value, concerned with the realization of whatever goals which have been set. Administrative decisions are thought to be rational only if they are considered to be the most efficient means of achieving predetermined goals. This account of efficiency raises a number of conceptual problems.

The first point which should be noted is that the administrative notion of efficiency is an extremely general one: it lacks any specific reference. As Fay (1975) has pointed out, 'efficiency' cannot be judged without reference to some further, more specific criteria. We need to ask the question, efficiency in terms of what — monetary costs? human labour? suffering? the consumption of natural fuels? time? or what? Fay argues that 'until this question is answered there is literally no way of choosing between alternative courses in terms of efficiency' (Fay, 1975, p.50).

MacIntyre (1981) has shown how there is a crucial gap between the generalized conception of efficiency used in administrative discourse and any criteria which are precise enough to be usable in particular situations. Questions of when and how efficiency should be judged are of crucial importance, yet, the positivist tradition of Michels and Weber provides no clear-cut standards of judgment. Quoting Bittner, MacIntyre claims that 'the inventory of features of bureaucracy contains not one single item that is not arguable relative to its efficiency function'. He argues further that:

> Long-range goals cannot be used definitely for calculating it because the impact of contingent factors multiplies with time and makes it increasingly difficult to assign a determinate value to the efficiency of a stably controlled segment of action. On the other hand, the use of short-term goals in judging efficiency may be in conflict with the ideal of economy itself. Not only do short-term goals change with time and compete with one another in indeterminate ways, but short-term results are of notoriously deceptive value because they can be easily manipulated to show whatever one wishes them to show. (1981, p.72)

What these arguments clearly illustrate is that it is impossible to conceive of purely technical and neutral criteria of efficiency, and that substantial value judgments are made in determining the 'most efficient means' to achieve a given goal. The notion of 'efficiency' is a value-laden concept and cannot therefore be used to make a sharp and enduring distinction between what is an end and what is a means. With educational issues in particular, as Peters (1966) has observed, the means-end distinction cannot be strictly applicable, for education is an enterprise shot through with moral, political and cultural concerns. In education any attempt to calculate efficiency must involve reference to notions of significance, appropriateness, worth and the like, and it is not at all clear how choices of this kind can be made in a value-free manner.

The idea of administrative efficiency is a goal, the preference for which over other goals, such as mass participation, has to be argued for in specifically moral and political terms. Efficiency is, moreover, not an ideal which is self-evidently worth pursuing — especially when it conflicts with other human interests. Indeed, as Callahan (1962) has demonstrated, in American educational thought the pursuit of efficiency for its own sake has served to subvert other more important educational goals. It has played a specifically ideological role.

The argument that participation is inimical to efficient decision-making is ambiguous between the claim that the processes of democratic decision-making *are* inefficient and the suggestion that these processes *produce* decisions which are necessarily less efficient, and less rational, than those which are made centrally by independent 'experts'. This ambiguity highlights yet another problem with the argument that the tradition of Michels' oligarchic thesis represents. It concerns the account of decision-making implied in such an argument.

The 'efficiency argument' assumes that decision-making is a single, once and for all, act of the decision-maker. A decision is often seen as an 'expression of an attitude', as a choice made by 'the acting willing person' on 'the basis of his or her conscience and his or her *personal* view of the world'. Apart from the problem of value relativism implied in this formulation, there are other problems with this account. In the *process* of decision-making, at what point is a decision reached, what is meant by a decision-maker and how is he or she to be recognized? These are notoriously difficult questions to answer.

Decision-making is seldom, if ever, carried out by the individual acting in the privacy of his or her own thoughts; nor are decisions made in a social and historical vacuum. A 'decision' can always be broken down into a number of stages. There is the stage in which a project is initiated, it is then discussed, deliberated over and perhaps put into a more coherent form and a consistent shape. There is also the stage at which support for the project is mobilized whether by public actions or by private bargaining or, in some cases, even threats. These are all overlapping stages in the process of policy deliberation and the organization of political support. A decision should be seen as the outcome of an accumulation of lesser 'decisions' in which many people might have taken part, in which compromises might well have been made and in the course of which the original objectives themselves might have changed. To say that X 'took part' in 'the decision' to introduce local selection of principals in a Victorian school, for example, does not tell us a great deal about the part X took in the process of decision-making. The form and the extent of participation must be made more specific if an individual's responsibility is to be discussed or if it is to be claimed that more of those affected should have had the opportunity to participate.

This account of decision-making, as a process rather than a single act, is more accurate, but still not complex enough. We are still not clear as to how one can recognize a 'decisional outcome'. A decision can perhaps be understood as the formal act which ends the deliberation of the issue. A decision defined in this way is thus procedural. The decision is what Austin (1961, p.220) has referred to as a 'performative utterance', meaning a verbal formula such as 'I promise' or 'I decide', which does not describe the act of promising or deciding but is itself the act of promising or deciding, providing that certain necessary social preconditions are fulfilled. These contextual preconditions range from the trivial, such as that all parties understand that the sounds 'I decide' constitute deciding, to the important and complex, such as that the person uttering the words has the authority to say 'I decide' in the circumstances in question.

The important point to arise from this discussion is that while the formal performative utterance may only be made by a relatively few people, whom we might recognize as the 'experts' in the field or the 'philosophically competent' or indeed as 'administrative leaders', the decisional outcome reflects an accumulation of steps often involving a host of modifications to the original policy — concessions, additions, syntheses with rival policies and so on. Indeed, some steps often appear crucial to the final outcome only in retrospect, whereas at the time they may not have seemed to amount to much. Many decisions are only stumbled upon, made inadvertently.

This account of decision-making, as dynamic and historically informed, highlights the fact that there exists a logical space, something which is denied by the epistemological assumptions of the traditional account of Michels and his followers, for a whole host of people being involved in deliberations over policies, and not simply the 'experts'. Insofar as educational decision-making is concerned, there would seem to be an important participative role for the wider school community, which includes students, parents and teachers. This does not mean that there is no place for 'experts' in the participative decision-making process. In democratic contexts the claim to 'expertise' would have to be publicly defended and established. The 'experts' would clearly be required to provide the kind of information which laypersons could not possibly have access to. But it is important to point out that, given our account of the decision-making process as an undifferentiated activity, there are always stages which require, and which could benefit from, widespread participation of all those who are affected, however remotely, by the decisions in question.

Nor is the claim that organizational democracy always produces inefficient decisions entirely accurate. In a recent paper Evers (1988) has employed arguments from the Popperian theory of knowledge and the recent economic decision-making literature to suggest that the claim that hierarchical modes of organization are most likely to produce efficient decision-making is, in general, untrue. Given that knowledge of directives in an organization is always fallible, Evers argues, a democratic decision-making structure enables decisions to be made adaptively, on the basis of successive instances of learning and feedback loops. In democratic systems errors can be more effectively and comprehensively corrected, which would clearly ensure more efficient decision-making. It has been argued by a number of recent social scientists that instead of organizational democracy being inefficient, as a follower of Michels might claim, it can in fact, if carried out within genuine participatory structures, be expected to increase organizational 'efficiency'. Thus the empirical assertion regarding the inefficiency of democratic organizations, made by Michels, can be challenged by this research.

Contrary to Michels' view, many recent organizational thinkers, such as Fischer and Siriaani (1984) and Crouch and Heller (1983), have gathered a great deal of empirical evidence to suggest that participation is a necessary condition for bringing about greater 'efficiency', if the term is to mean satisfying long-term interests rather than short-term technical goals which have been broken down into smaller 'manageable' objectives. Fischer and Siriaani's argument is based on the belief that participation encourages and arouses commitment to the common goals which the participants have had a say in formulating. Participation induces, they claim, enterprise, intitiative, imagination and the confidence to experiment in a variety of directions, and must rebound to the greater utility of the whole organization. They argue, moreover, that the people who actually belong to local communities know their interests best. Efficient decision-making requires that people be encouraged to come forward, actively say what they need and help administrators identify the social and moral context in which policies have to be developed. Participation could then be expected to promote efficiency — raise productivity and assist material progress or, more neutrally, better achieve whatever ends might have been chosen — on the grounds that it will arouse a commitment to the community and to the organizational ethos.

The 'efficiency argument' may be confronted in another way. Parry (1970) has argued that the generalized notion of 'efficiency' that followers of Michels might assume nevertheless presupposes some allegedly objective conception of a 'public interest' which is divorced from the interests of the individual participants. It can be shown, however, that an objective computation of 'public interest' is impossible, for public interest is necessarily constituted by the ends which the individual participants themselves choose by means of some accepted procedure. Given this understanding, it is logically odd to contrast some 'objective' criterion of 'efficiency' supposedly met by organizations with low degrees of participation with the allegedly inferior achievements of organizations which aim at maximizing participation. If people 'choose to maximize participation in all possible areas of political life then this is not to be contrasted with "objectively better" policies which have been rejected' (Parry, 1970, p.35).

In opposition to this line of thinking it might be argued that each participant will still have to choose between the realization of certain, say, material benefits and the maximization of participation. If an individual prefers maximizing participation, then he or she may well find that he or she has incurred a loss to set against his or her gain. The costs, when measured in terms of the time and effort involved in gathering information, debating, making and possibly implementing decisions, may well be very high, and most people can be expected in such circumstances to settle for less participation. If such is the case, then Parry argues that:

> it remains possible to describe certain forms of action as less efficient than others if they leave certain individuals worse off where 'worse' is measured by their actual choice. It might then be the case that high levels of political participation, because of the amateurishness or the slow procedures involved, left individuals worse off in respect of other values previously acknowledged. (Parry, 1970, p.35)

It would appear, therefore, that if material losses are the consequence of greater participation, then some individuals may find that the costs of participation are very high indeed. Of course, we cannot afford to dismiss judgments about material losses in any cavalier fashion. It has to be admitted that participation would not amount to much if it leads to material disaster. But all that this argument implies is that in concrete circumstances we need to be extremely careful in weighing up the costs and gains of instituting and extending particular forms of participation. The issue of costs and gains is an empirical one which needs to be explored in each particular context. However, this argument does not establish in any a priori way the implausibility of organizational democracy.

Apathy and Its Social Origins

The issues raised here are linked to Michels' 'mass apathy argument', which states that since most people are politically apathetic, they are happy enough for a minority, which thrives on leadership, to make decisions on their behalf. Michels argues that widespread democracy is not possible because of this existence of certain permanent psychological dispositions among both the mass membership of an organization and its leadership. He maintains that the mass has an immense need for direction and guidance which only a few have the requisite qualities and desire to provide.

The 'mass apathy argument' was most influential among the political scientists of the late 1950s and early 1960s. While writers such as Dahl (1961) did not entirely accept the logic of the iron law of oligarchy, and presented instead pluralist analyses of power structure, they nevertheless accepted Michels' assumption that widespread public apathy was inevitable in all organizations and that political scientists simply had to accept this fact. Finding considerable apathy in his studies of voting behaviour, Dahl argued that a degree of 'realism' was required in thinking about the nature and scope of democracy in modern Western societies. According to Dahl, the making of state policies was not so much a matter of articulating the wishes of the great masses, but a steady appeasement of a relatively small number of interest groups whose preferences are negotiated by their elite leaders. In much the same way as Michels had done, the new 'realists', as Dahl and his followers have come to be known, saw themselves as empirical social scientists interested in understanding the existing forms of political behaviour and interests. They wanted to find out those features of political behaviour which could be empirically established or could be shown to be feasible. Finding masses to be disorganized, ignorant and apathetic, they concluded that organizational democracy was impossible, and denied the meaningfulness of phrases such as 'the public interest', 'the common good' or 'the democratic voice'. Recommending a fundamental departure from classical normative democratic theory, they sought to redefine democracy in procedural terms. Democracy became a matter of electing 'leaders' who could be relied upon to act on behalf of the voting public. The acceptance of the apathy premise was translated into the belief that no more could be expected from the masses than the casting of a vote every so often.

More recently the mass apathy argument has reappeared as elite theory. It has been argued by Dye (1981) and Zey-Ferrell and Aitken (1981), for example, that, given mass apathy, political and organizational decision-making is best seen as elite competition. Similarly Higley (1980) has argued that the 'real basis' of the inevitable existence of elite is the presence of widespread apathy and an absence of any common interest in complex societies. Furthermore, Higley maintains that since decisions that supersede individual preferences have to be made and enforced, hierarchies of power commanded by individuals would seem to be necessary.

The 'realist' social scientists and elite theorists argue that the notion of organizational democracy mistakenly assumes that people actually want to participate in decision-making processes. They argue that there is a great deal of evidence to suggest that the mass of the people are socially and politically apathetic and do not wish to be involved or participate. Very few people would, given the choice, elect to spend their free time on what are essentially political activities. The masses wish to be left, in Voltaire's phrase, to cultivate their own garden. It is suggested further that to expect people to develop a sense of responsibility to participate in decision-making is to deprive them of their freedom to remain disinterested.

It is difficult to deny the empirical proposition that there is widespread apathy in contemporary society. But we need to be cautious about how we interpret the supposedly 'objective' evidence showing apathy, and ask what causes this condition. Apathy and general disinterest need not be seen as intrinsic to human nature, as Michels and his followers seem to imply. Apathy has historical sources and is engendered as a result of human organization and bureaucratization. Walker has argued that:

> political apathy obviously has many sources. It may stem from
> personal inadequacy, from the fear of endangering important

personal relationships, or from a lack of interest in the issues; but it may also have its roots in the society's institutional structure, in the weakness or absence of group stimulation or support, in the positive opposition of elements within the political system to a wider participation; in the absence, in other words, of appropriate spurs to action, or the presence of tangible deterrents. (Walker, 1966, p.290)

Apathy is not an intrinsic feature of human life; it is something conditioned by an overorganized and paternalistic society. Human beings can be politically engaged only in an organization in which they are encouraged to participate. Evidence of apathy is clearly an index of the extent to which contemporary institutions have fallen short of the democratic ideal, not a proof of its impracticality. As Plant (1974, p.71) has pointed out, it is *because* social and political structures in contemporary society have become so unresponsive to the wishes of ordinary people and have become so large, remote and bureaucratized that widespread apathy prevails.

The 'mass apathy argument' involves the assumption that facts about individual characteristics and forms of social organization are somehow 'natural', fixed and unchanging. This crude assumption needs to be challenged. As Pateman (1982, p.95) suggests, human conduct, far from being fixed, is dynamically linked to the wider social and cultural processes. '"Modernisation" does not occur independently of fixed or "natural" facts about individuals and social life, but is part of the same specific historical developments that give rise to complex bureaucratic organisation and a certain pattern and form of political consciousness and political participation.' The 'mass apathy argument' assumes that, because of some alleged 'natural' facts, democratic citizenship which aims to initiate organizational reform cannot be created — a claim that ultimately denies the very possibility of education. It accepts the prevailing social formation as given, and yet through education social divisions and attitudes can and often do change. Appropriate social structures can help to reinforce divisions between the politically active and inactive. If children are encouraged to accept participation as inherent in our social relations, then it is likely that as adults they would want to participate. In such circumstances apathy would be considered just as odd as it might now be accepted as perfectly understandable, or as an instance of the individual's right to exercise his or her freedom not to participate.

Nor is self-interest inevitably the outcome of an individual's exercise of freedom. It is true that in liberal democratic societies, where individualism is encouraged above all other virtues, self-interest prevails. Indeed, as Pateman has correctly observed, in a society 'where commercialisation and commodification has reached the point that today almost everything can be offered for sale in the hope of profit, it is not surprising that it is so widely believed that self-interest is the key to social order' (Pateman, 1982, pp.98-9). It is a mistake to assume that all individuals operate from the motivation of self-interest. Indeed, it could plausibly be argued that women as a group have always been held 'naturally' to act from love, altruism and self-sacrifice, despite social structures that might encourage the opposite. So, since neither self-interest nor apathy is intrinsic to the human condition, our goal ought to be to create structures that facilitate altruism and a concern for democratic activism.

Given the alleged tension between participation and freedom, those who stress the value of a participatory institution can only respond to the allegations of its impracticality by pointing out that in cultures orientated to maximizing participation more people will *want* to participate. Participant cultures will cultivate further participation. The response to this evidence of apathy should not be, argues Bachrach (1967, p.33), to be 'realistic' and accept the alleged facts about human nature and its poorly formed social motivation, but to develop human potential by attempting to make its institutions more participative and democratic. This should be seen as an *educational* objective.

Democracy and Educative Values

Michels' arguments against the possibility of organizational democracy are based on the supposedly objective empirical evidence about the nature of modern social organizations and human motivation. It is argued that the participatory democratic ideal simply does not square with existing political realities, since it can be shown that all previous attempts at bringing the less visible and audible parts of organizations into the decision-making arenas have failed. But such a charge can surely be met by pointing out that even if this empirical generalization is true, it does not follow that the achievement of democratic community is in principle impossible. It is simply fallacious to suppose that empirical evidence concerning contemporary democratic practices can be taken as a refutation of the ideals of participatory democracy. As Duncan and Lukes (1963) argue, to suggest that reference to empirical realities refutes the normative case for greater participation in decision-making is to commit a 'category mistake'. They point out that classical advocates of participatory democracy were perfectly well aware of the difficulties of translating their normative goals into reality. Rousseau, for example, was not concerned with 'men as they are' but 'laws as they might be'; that is, with human potentialities for political action. Duncan and Lukes maintain that it is still viable to argue for a framework for a freer and more moral society than has existed hitherto. The fact that contemporary organizations have failed to advance democratic goals does not in itself demonstrate that they are inherently incapable of achievement.

Hierarchical and elitist practices are, moreover, inevitable only under certain empirical conditions, conditions which no doubt currently exist in a society which is so dominated by social conditions defined in terms of bureaucratic relationships. But these conditions themselves are far from inevitable. The 'iron law' of oligarchy or indeed the 'inner logic' of bureaucratic organizations need not be regarded as inescapable. It is only under certain structural conditions that bureaucracy, or oligarchy, presents itself as natural and necessary — there is no reason to suppose that under different conditions human relationships might not be ordered differently. Human beings have options, and it is the norms to which they subscribe more than some given external social reality that determine which options they exercise. Social reality itself is a historical condition. Gouldner (1970) challenges the so-called 'realist' political scientists in the following terms:

> Instead of telling men how bureaucracy might be mitigated, they insist that it is inevitable. Instead of explaining how democratic patterns may, to some extent, be fortified and extended, they warn us that democracy cannot be perfect. Instead of controlling disease, they suggest that we are deluded, or more politely, incurably romantic, for hoping to control it. Instead of assuming responsibilities as realistic clinicians, striving to further democratic potentialities whenever they can, many social scientists have become morticians, all too eager to bury men's hopes. (Gouldner, 1970, p.126)

Viewed in this way, the a priorism of the apathy and efficiency arguments becomes evident. For even if it could be shown that some inefficiency would result from allowing more broadly-based participation in decision-making, it has not been demonstrated that Michels' argument is correct. There are strong moral arguments in favour of the view that we should still aim at maximizing participation in decision-making.

Kariel (1966, pp.63-5) has argued that it may be necessary to choose between efficiency and other human goals such as 'self-development' through participation. In comparing the relative costs of pursuing either the value of participation or the value of organizational efficiency, the notion of costs must, Kariel suggests, be broadened to include costs for the good life for the individual and the community as well as the monetary costs. We must estimate not only the monetary costs of participation but also the human costs — in terms of repression of character of non-participation; of lost opportunities to allow self-education of people. This practical deliberation may lead one to conclude that efficiency and material progress, which are the virtues of organizations and bureaucracies, are less important than the education of character — of self-reliance and political imagination. As Norman (1987, p. 174) argues:

> even if radical democracy turned out to be less efficient in promoting the material prosperity of the least well-off, we should have to set against the loss the distinctive gains of equality of power — the goods of co-operative relations between people and the opportunities for people to control their own lives and employ to the full their distinctive human capacities for discriminative choice and judgement.

The gains of democracy are not always immediately evident. Long-term and short-term gains have to be weighed against each other, and the idea of 'gains' itself needs to be viewed in its broadest sense. In exploring one of the dimensions of the term 'gains', Maxcy has recently demonstrated that there is a close conceptual link between the idea of democratic participation and education. Maxcy (1985, p. 34) has argued that 'democracy is a normative conception, in the sense that it represents a set of criterial conditions toward which persons ought to strive if they are to enlarge and increase their capacities in life.' Through participation, growth in the habits of critical sense and judgment becomes possible.

The idea that participation is part of a process of political and moral education is, of course, not new. Rousseau's entire political theory revolves around the idea of, as Pateman puts it:

> the individual participation of each citizen in political decision-making and in his theory participation is very much more than a protective adjunct to a set of institutional arrangements; it also has a psychological effect on the participants, ensuring that there is continuing inter-relationship between the working of institutions and the psychological qualities and attitudes of individuals inter-active in them. (Pateman, 1970, p. 22)

For Rousseau, participation is indeed a way of protecting individual interests and ensuring good governance, and perhaps even promoting efficiency. But more importantly Rousseau asks us to consider how social order affects the structure of human personality. What effects do institutional arrangements have on the development of human personality? A centralized authoritarian social structure, such as the modern school, can be expected to teach people to be timid, suspicious and self-interested. Participatory structures are surely necessary if we value the reversal of these trends. For Rousseau, then, the central function of participation is an educative one, with the term 'educative' understood in its widest possible sense. Rousseau envisages a dialectic between the development of participatory structures and the psychological development of the participating individual. Participatory structures provide the incentive and the appropriate motivation for individuals to become socially and politically involved, and this involvement, in turn, means that participatory structures are strengthened, acquiring legitimacy and credibility which they currently do not have. Once participatory systems are strengthened, they become self-sustaining because 'the very qualities that are required of individual citizens if the system is to work successfully are those that the process of participation itself fosters and develops' (Pateman, 1970, p.25).

The charge of utopianism is often levelled against Rousseau. It is argued that since people generally misuse the limited opportunities for participation they have now, what would happen if more extensive opportunities were provided? Children especially lack the sense of responsibility, the decision-making skills and requisite knowledge to be informed participants. As we saw earlier, this argument is explicitly put forward by Barrow.

However, if we were to accept Rousseau's contentions, then this would appear to be a highly dubious argument. According to Rousseau, participation is part of a process of political and moral education: it is an education in responsibility. A sense of responsibility and the decision-making skills, which Barrow would like to see inculcated in children, can only be developed by their actual engagement in participation, not by waiting for the day when some external authority decides that the requisite skills and attitudes have been obtained. Indeed, we cannot even assume that it is possible for that authority to know what requisite skills and attitudes are required to qualify as an informed participant. The point of participation is to 'stretch' the individual's mind, forcing him or her to develop his or her intellectual qualities. As de Tocqueville saw it: 'when I am told that the laws are weak and the population is wild, that passions are excited and that virtue is paralyzed, and that in this situation it would be madness to think of increasing the rights of the people, I reply that it is for these very reasons that they should be increased' (quoted in Parry, 1970, p.26).

Like Rousseau and de Tocqueville, Dewey (1975, pp.57-69) emphasized the development of the social and intellectual capacity of the individual through participatory processes. For Dewey, educational institutions had an important role to play in helping the development of the individual's character. He believed that the quality of institutions is shaped by the quality of its subjects, but equally importantly the converse is also true; that is, a test of the quality of social institutions is the quality of the citizens it produces. Dewey recognized that his view of democracy rested on a certain 'faith in the capacities of human nature; faith in human intelligence and in the power of pooled and cooperative experience'. He went on to maintain, however, that this 'faith' was grounded as much in reality as the assumptions of those who hold a more pessimistic view of human nature. For Dewey, it was the 'inability' of our 'intellectual habits' critically to examine currently held assumptions which restricted the development of truly democratic communities. He believed that such intellectual habits are not native to human life, intrinsically and independently possessed; they are learnt in social situations such as those found in schools. Schools must therefore bear a large responsibility for the development of appropriate attitudes and skills required for people to take part in, and develop further, participant cultures. It is only by providing students with practical experience in decision-making, by transforming schools into participant cultural sites, that we can hope to realize the good of widespread and direct democracy.

Possibilities of Organizational Democracy

Implicit in Dewey's view of democracy is a complex view of what it means to be human, simultaneously both a creature and creator of history. Humans are a species that creates itself through accretion of its values, customs and culture, which are both reproduced and transformed through education. Education can be simultaneously conservative and creative. In Dewey's view, for it to be creative, teachers need to devise experiences which involve making available to each student the opportunity to make a contribution to the enrichment of cooperative life. It is only through considerable political learning that students recognize their potentialities, becoming citizens capable of deliberating about what they are doing, setting goals and priorities for themselves; in effect, taking charge of their history-making. Importantly, for Dewey, however, this learning is not an individualized practice; it requires constant negotiation and collective judgment. Only *public* deliberation allows citizens to become aware of their powers as responsible agents and judges. Dewey maintains that it is through participation that the needs of all and the unique judgment of each can be taken into account.

Participation, according to Pitkin and Shumer (1982, p.47):

> is an encounter among people with differing interests, perspectives and opinions — an encounter in which they reconsider and mutually revise opinions and interests, both individual and common. It happens always in a context of conflict, imperfect knowledge, and uncertainty, but where community action is necessary. The resolutions achieved are always more or less temporary, subject to reconsideration, and rarely unanimous. What matters is not unanimity but discourse. The substantive interest is only discovered or created in democratic political struggle, and it remains contested as much as shared.

All this is not to deny that in modern nation states genuine and serious difficulties are encountered in pursuing democratic ideals. Direct participatory democracy often seems impossible in societies confronted by the spectre of enormous technical complexity and large-scale organizations serving diverse needs, but, as Pitkin and Shumer (1982) point out, *we cannot afford to concede that it is impossible.* This is so because conceding it makes it self-fulfilling. In schools in particular we should be in the business of exploring possibilities for emancipation, for creating new futures, rather than shutting off options.

Dewey (1975, p.66) argues that in modern nation states democratic forms have become

> limited to Parliament, elections and combat between parties. What is happening proves conclusively, I think, that unless democratic habits of thought and action are part of the fibre of people, politial democracy is insecure. It cannot stand in isolation. It must be buttressed by the presence of democratic methods in all social relationships. The relations that exist in educational institutions are second only in importance in this respect to those which exist in industry and business, perhaps not even to them.

The issue of how it might be possible to generate and sustain democratic relationships in schools is a difficult one. Indeed, while it is possible to mount a strong philosophical case for organizational democracy and defend it from possible objections, it is more difficult to envisage how democratization might work in schools, and how one might proceed towards greater democracy and away from hierarchical organizational arrangements.

To begin with, we must question the universal applicability of that notion of democratic practice which might be suggestive of the abstract idea of everyone participating in all decisions all at once. The idea of a single assembly is neither necessary nor sufficient for democracy. What is essential is the possibility of some face-to-face interaction through which specific interests can be communicated, discussed and taken into account when final decisions are made. As Pitkin and Shumer (1980, p.50) argue, 'representation, delegation, co-operation, federation, and other forms of devolution are entirely compatible with democracy, though they do not and cannot guarantee it.' Nor does democracy imply an absence of organizational structure and leadership. 'The point is not to eschew all organisation and all differentiated leadership, confining democracy to the local and spontaneous, but to develop those forms and those styles of authority that sustain rather than suppress member initiative and autonomy' (Pitkin and Shumer, 1980, p.51).

In developing democratic institutions, what is necessary is that collective power is always 'kept responsible to its participatory foundations' (Pitkin and Shumer, 1980, p.51). Beyond this generalized condition there are no formulas, general rules or neatly packaged models for bringing about democracy in schools because democratic action is always localized. Indeed, it would be logically odd to believe that it could somehow be imposed from above. Each organization and each school is unique in some aspect, and it is for this reason that the rationalist linear model of educational change is totally inappropriate. Each situation has to be examined in the context of its own unique historical and social features. Changes can only come about when the individuals who belong to a particular organization can see the point in changing. While it is not possible to provide general, comprehensive, alternative models to hierarchy and bureaucracy, to the dictates of the 'iron law of oligarchy', it is nevertheless possible to provide historical examples that show that degrees of democratic forms are possible. Indeed, it may be useful to examine and learn from the attempts which have been made in a variety of settings around the world to democratize schools. Such an examination might not only provide useful practical pointers but could also indicate the range of concrete problems and issues which must be addressed.

Among the widely discussed examples of school democracy are the progressive schools of the 1930s in the USA, inspired by Dewey, the kibbutz schools in Israel and the self-governing schools in Yugoslavia. While it is not possible to discuss these experiments in any depth in this chapter, they are nevertheless illustrative of democratic possibilities. The kibbutz movement in Israel has been in existence for more than half a century. It has always been profoundly committed to egalitarian and democratic values. A kibbutz school is basically organized within the framework of a community of families governed by a general assembly based on the democratic principle of one member – one vote, exercised through a weekly community meeting. A kibbutz is owned by its members and cannot be sold; its assets cannot be divided by its members. This means that since a kibbutz operates as an amalgam of industries, agricultural branches, cultural networks and educational institutions, there is a greater possibility of social cohesion, and a sense of mutual obligation within the group. The education of children within the kibbutz is a shared communal responsibility. Whyte and Blasi (1984, p.397) point out that their research in a variety of kibbutzim reveals that 'people who work together meet together to discuss community affairs, serve on educational committees that oversee their children's schools, participate in community cultural events, and together elect community economic and social officials and decide community policy.' While kibbutzim attempt to maximize participation, they do not reject reliance upon expertise and authority; though the issues of the degrees of authority and the areas of expertise most appropriate for different participatory institutions are clearly delineated and regularly reviewed. Those assigned tasks requiring expertise are held directly accountable to the community as a whole.

Of course, the Israeli experience is not directly translatable to Western situations. For one thing, kibbutzim are homogeneous communities in which all individuals are committed to the religious ideology of Zionism and, therefore, have a collective interest. Western nations are mostly pluralistic societies with a tradition of interest groups and conflictual politics. It is worth noting, moreover, that only 3 per cent of Israelis belong to kibbutzim, the rest preferring to live in institutions which are, in essence, little different from their Western counterparts. In recent years the Israeli government has moved in 'to coordinate and rationalize' regional kibbutzim, with the expressed aim of providing them with many services and the opportunities which are not available to small communities (Rayman, 1984). The government has also attempted to link the productive efforts of kibbutzim to the broader context of national economic policies which have sought to expand military bureaucracy and increase world markets. Rayman (1984, p.406) argues that these developments have to a large extent undermined some of the original democratic goals of the kibbutz movement. The egalitarian democratic ideology has, Rayman suggests, come under increasing pressure as Israel as a developing industrial nation attempts to bring 'efficiency' to its organizations.

While there are considerable problems with the further development of the kibbutz movement, the lessons which can be learnt from it are also instructive. It is clear that no sooner than the efforts of democratic organization are captured by state interests and state bureaucracies, democratic goals become subverted. The size of organization is also important. On the basis of Israeli experience the possibility of bringing *direct* participatory democracy to larger organizations appears limited. This point is made convincingly by Halsey (1983) in his examination of the way schools function in Yugoslavia.

The Yugoslavian state does impose certain regulations and constraints regarding taxes and structure and procedures for governance, and the state also establishes certain educational requirements for everyone, but beyond this schools in Yugoslavia work as self-governing institutions. School communities — teachers, parents, students and other members of the community — govern themselves. Halsey points out that schools in Yugoslavia are 'socially owned', and that adversarial relationships between teachers and parents, which characterize British schools, seem to be absent in Yugoslavian schools. Watson (1985, p.21) claims that schools in Yugoslavia are organized as 'self-managed communities of interest'. Self-managed communities of interests are associations formed by working people directly or through self-managed organizations and communities to satisfy common needs. Watson argues that the purpose of self-managed communities of interest is 'to form a bond between workers, the community, and schools in order to facilitate personal development, educational development and economic development' (Watson, 1985, p.21).

All decisions in Yugoslavian schools are made by a workers' council which, in many cases, is comprised of the whole staff. Principals and others in positions of responsibility are elected by the whole community of interest, and jobs are rotated so that not only is the workers' commitment to the egalitarian ideology strengthened but also the workers begin to develop confidence in their own ability to function in a cooperative. An important educational consequence of 'self-management' in schools is that students begin to learn about democracy by seeing it work at first hand and by participating in student councils themselves. As Watson (1985, p.22) points out, 'the expectation is that all students will end up working in self-managed enterprises, and that therefore they should have experienced and learned about the concept of self-management.'

Any impression that Yugoslavian schools organized on democratic lines always work in the way hoped for would be misleading. For there are considerable problems, both of practical logistics and of widespread commitment. Halsey (1983) observes that it is only in the smaller communities that direct democracy appears to be working effectively in Yugoslavia. As institutions expand in size and functions, self-management becomes more difficult because every worker cannot in practice be consulted about all policies. In larger institutions there arises a need to build representative structures that often have the effect of subverting direct participatory democracy. But if hierarchies are unavoidable, then it must not be assumed that it is impossible to devise mechanisms 'to make them the servants rather than the masters of the workers in the enterprise' (Halsey, 1983, p.197). The Yugoslavians, according to Halsey, have long been addressing themselves to the problem of devising appropriate mechanisms, but this has proved to be an extremely difficult task.

There remains, even in Yugoslavian schools, the problem of unequal distribution of organizational power. Even those committed to participatory democracy are often reluctant to give up the power once they manage to achieve it. As Boyd (1984, p.18) asks, why should the administrators with their powerful interests 'shoot themselves in their own foot'? Lindblom (1977, p.337) has observed that in Yugoslavia, as elsewhere, managers and administrators often use their own technical knowledge to 'reduce the workers' councils to rubber stamps'. While there are other researchers (for example, Spinard, 1984) who have shown Lindblom's analysis to be exaggerated, there does appear to be some agreement that in larger organizations in Yugoslavia participatory democracy often becomes 'managed participation'. The creation of a democracy in which there is equality of power relations thus remains one of the most perplexing challenges.

However, to claim that there are problems in achieving greater democracy is not to suggest that it is an ideal not worth pursuing. Indeed, the recognition of the problems inherent in democratizing organizations should enable us to be much better equipped to detect circumstances in which those in power seek to subvert democratic participation by obscuring egalitarian interests. Educators should especially seek to prepare students for democracy in such a way as to provide them with critical skills which enable them to identify and challenge sources of domination and oppression.

Though these vary considerably, opportunities for democratic reform exist everywhere. In the state of Victoria in Australia, for example, a series of Ministerial Papers (Education Department of Victoria, 1986) has committed the Victorian educational system to the principles of democratic and collaborative decision-making. Successive governments in Victoria, for whatever motives, have attempted to devolve more power to local communities. Schools are now encouraged to develop, within certain very broad, state-wide guidelines, their own policies in respect of curriculum, teaching/learning style and school organization. Most secondary schools in Victoria now have representative administrative committees to make decisions which were previously the sole prerogative of the principals. Other initiatives in Australia, such as the Commonwealth Participation and Equity Program (PEP), have provided school communities with an opportunity to examine systematically their practices in an effort to increase democratic participation at all levels of decision-making. While research into these developments (see, for example, Rizvi and Kemmis, 1987) has demonstrated some small measure of success in democratizing schools in Victoria, these achievements have been limited. Moreover, there is emerging evidence that many of these initiatives have been co-opted within the bureaucratic structures of the state. While the rhetoric of democracy remains, its practice has been made increasingly difficult.

Despite this note of pessimism, so long as Victoria and other educational systems retain democratic rhetoric, it provides local communities with the opportunity to take up the government on its rhetoric and demand changes to its bureaucratic structure and initiate unilateral reforms to school organization, even without the support of officialdom. Indeed, some schools have done, or are following precisely this course. Democratic reform does not necessarily require a complete overhaul of the entire system — it can always be gradual and piecemeal.

The structural changes required to facilitate extensive democracy in schools are considerable, and they vary from context to context. Because the capacity of schools to bring about change is limited by broader administrative, social and economic constraints, it might be tempting to suggest that unless broader administrative, social and economic conditions change, schools cannot proceed with democratic reforms. But such a conclusion would be self-defeating, because larger changes will not come about unless we first initiate small-scale and incremental changes on every possible front. As Pitkin and Shumer (1982, p.54) argue, 'We must not postpone the practice of participatory democracy until after such changes are achieved, nor expect it to emerge automatically from them. Democracy is our best means of achieving social change and must remain our conscious goal.'

Since there can be no definitive prescriptions for change, our strategy must involve a thoughtful understanding of our own situation. An historical understanding of our own discourse, practices and institutions would appear to be an important part of any direct political action. But beyond this we must attempt to extend the scope of those democratic practices and institutions which already exist. In Western countries democratic rhetoric abounds. We must use this rhetoric in creative ways to ensure the extension of democratic forms with which we are familiar. Thus we could try extending the current powers of participatory decision-making structures in schools and build upon the more radically conceived community education movement. We could incremently begin to challenge anti-democratic practices and structures by devising alternative modes of organization. The charge of utopianism, often levelled against democrats, can only be met by ensuring that proposals for reform are grounded in experience. We must be prepared to regard reforms as tentative and experimental, and, as Burnheim (1985, p. 186) suggests, subject to 'continual, detailed reflection, speculation, evaluation and struggle. We have no assurance of ultimate success, and indeed no clear idea of what would constitute success.' Democracy implies that 'such criteria are continuously changing, not arbitrarily, but in light of new and unforeseen problems.'

Democracy, as Norman (1987, p. 174) has argued, is not simply an abstract ideal which bears no relation to what human beings want and need. It is a value grounded in experience and it directs experience. We value democracy because it is our only way of achieving fulfilment in a co-operative community in which we run our lives not only individually but also collectively. Democratic practice provides grounds for optimism, and surely such optimism remains the most important of all ingredients in education.

References

Austin, J. (1961) 'Performative utterances,' in *Philosophical Papers*, London, Oxford University Press.

Bachrach, P. (1967) *The Theory of Democratic Elitism: A Critique*, Boston, Mass., Little, Brown.

Barrow, R. (1981) *The Philosophy of Schooling*, New York, John Wiley and Sons.

Boyd, W. (1984) 'Competing values in educational policy and governance: Australian and American development,' *Educational Administration Review*, 2,2, pp.4-24.

Burnheim, J. (1985) *Is Democracy Possible?*, London, Polity Press.

Callahan, R. (1962) *Education and the Cult of Efficiency*, Chicago, Ill., University of Chicago Press.

Crouch, C. and Heller, F. (Eds) (1983) *International Yearbook of Organizational Democracy*, Chichester, John Wiley and Sons.

Dahl, R. (1961) *Who Governs?* New Haven, Conn., Yale University Press.

Dahl, R. and Lindblom, C. (1963) *Politics, Economics and Welfare,* New York, Harper and Row.

Dewey, J. (1975) *Philosophy of Education: Problems of Men,* Totowa, N.J., Littlefield, Adams.

Duncan, G. and Lukes, S. (1963) 'The new democracy,' *Political Studies,* 11,2, pp.156-77.

Dye, T. (1981) *Understanding Public Policy,* 4th ed. Englewood Cliffs, N.J., Prentice-Hall.

Education Department of Victoria (1986) *Ministerial Papers 1-6,* Melbourne, Government Printer.

Evers, C. (1988) 'Schooling, organisational learning and efficiency in the growth of knowledge,' Paper presented at conference on school-based decision-making and management, Woodend, Victoria, April.

Fay, B. (1975) *Social Theory and Political Practice,* London, George Allen and Unwin.

Fischer, F. and Siriaani, C. (Eds) (1984) *Critical Studies in Organization and Bureaucracy,* Philadelphia, Pa., Temple University Press.

Gouldner, A. (1970) 'The denial of options,' in H.S. Kaviel (Ed.), *Frontiers of Democratic Theory,* New York, Random House.

Halsey, A.H. (1983) 'Schools for democracy,' in J. Ahier and M. Flude (Eds), *Contemporary Education Policy,* London, Croom Helm.

Higley, J. (1980) *Elites in Australia,* London, Routledge and Kegan Paul.

Kariel, H. (1966) *The Promise of Politics,* Englewood Cliffs, N.J., Prentice-Hall.

Kariel, H.S. (1967) *The Decline of American Pluralism,* San Francisco, Calif., Stanford University Press.

Lasswell, H. (1958) *The Political Writings of Harold D. Lasswell,* New York, Free Press.

Lindblom, C. (1977) *Politics and Markets,* New York, Basic Books.

MacIntyre, A. (1981) *After Virtue: A Study in Moral Theory,* London, Duckworth.

Maxcy, S.J. (1985) 'The democratic myth and the search for a rational concept of education,' *Educational Philosophy and Theory,* 17,1.

Michels, R. (1958) *Political Parties,* Chicago, Ill., Free Press.

Mosca, G. (1939) *The Ruling Class,* New York, McGraw-Hill.

Norman, R. (1987) *Free and Equal: A Philosophical Examination of Political Values,* Oxford, Oxford University Press.

Pareto, V. (1935) *The Mind and Society,* New York, Harcourt-Brace.

Parry, G. (1969) *Political Elites,* London, George Allen and Unwin.

Parry, G. (1970) *Participation in Politics,* Manchester, Manchester University Press.

Pateman, C. (1970) *Participation and Democratic Theory,* Cambridge, Cambridge University Press.

Pateman, C. (1982) 'Elitism, equality and democracy,' in M. Sawer (Ed.), *Australia and the New Right,* Sydney, George Allen and Unwin.

Peters, R.S. (1966) *Ethics and Education,* London, George Allen and Unwin.

Pitkin, H. and Shumer, S. (1982) 'On participation,' *Democracy,* 2, Fall, pp.43-54.

Plant, R. (1974) *Community and Ideology,* London, Routledge and Kegan Paul.

Rayman, P. (1984) 'Collective organization and the national state,' in F.

Fischer and C. Siriaani (Eds), *Critical Studies in Organization and Bureaucracy,* Philadelphia, Pa., Temple University Press.

Rizvi, F. and Kemmis, S. (1987) *Dilemmas of Reform: An Overview of the Victorian Participation and Equity Program,* Geelong, Deakin Institute for Studies in Education.

Rousseau, J.J. (1953) *Rousseau: Political Writings,* Trans F. Watkins, London, Nelson.

Schumpeter, J. (1950) *Capitalism, Socialism and Democracy,* 3rd ed., New York, Harper and Row.

Spinard, W. (1984) 'Work democracy: An overview,' *International Social Science Journal,* 36,2, pp.195-215.

Verba, S. (1961) *Small Groups and Political Behavior: A Study in Leadership,* New York, Princeton University Press.

Walker, J. (1966) 'A critique of the elitist theory of democracy,' *American Political Science Review,* 60, pp.85-95.

Watson, H. (1985) *The Democratization of Schooling,* Geelong, Deakin University Press.

Weber, M. (1970) *From Max Weber,* Ed. G. Gerth and C. Wright Mills, London, Routledge and Kegan Paul.

Weiss, R. (1983) 'Weber on bureaucracy: Management consultant or political theorist?' *Academy of Management Review,* 8,2, pp.242-8.

White, P. (1983) *Beyond Domination: An Essay in the Political Philosophy of Education,* London, Routledge and Kegan Paul.

Whyte, W. and Blasi, J. (1984) 'Worker ownership, participation and control: Toward a theoretical model,' in F. Fischer and C. Siriaani (Eds), *Critical Studies in Organization and Bureaucracy,* Philadelphia, Pa., Temple University Press.

Wilson, J. and Cowell, B. (1983) 'The democratic myth,' *Journal of Philosophy of Education,* 17.

Wood, G. (1984) 'Schooling in a democracy: Transformation or reproduction?' *Educational Theory,* 34,3, pp.219-39.

Zey-Ferrell, M. and Aitken, M. (Eds) (1981) *Complex Organizations: Critical Perspectives,* Glenview, Ill., Scott.

Notes on Contributors

Lawrence Angus is a Lecturer in the Faculty of Education at Monash University. Prior to that he was on the staff at Deakin University, where he completed his doctorate. Lawrence has just published *Continuity and Change in Catholic Schooling* with Falmer Press. His research interests are in educational reform, school effectiveness, and critical approaches to the study of educational administration.

Richard Bates is Professor of Education and Dean of Education at Deakin University. He has published extensively in educational journals, and is an active member of numerous national and international professional associations. His research interests are in the development of a critical theory of educational administration, studies of schools as negotiated realities, and research into policy formulation in education.

Jill Blackmore is a Lecturer in Social and Administrative Studies at Deakin University, prior to which she was at Monash University. She undertook both her MA and PhD at Stanford University. Jill's current research interests are in the areas of gender relations, teacher unionism, and school-based decision-making.

John Codd is a Reader in Education at Massey University where he teaches in educational theory, policy analysis and curriculum design. As well as co-editing three books he is a frequent contributor to the *Journal of Aesthetic Education*. John's research interests in education are interdisciplinary.

William Foster is an Associate Professor in the Division of Leadership and Administration in the School of Education, University of San Diego. He has had his work on critical practices in educational administration published in a range of journals. His most recent published book is *Paradigms and Promises: New Approaches to Educational Administration*

(Prometheus Books). Bill's research interests are in the relationship of critical theory and sociology to educational administration.

Fazal Rizvi is a Senior Lecturer in Social and Administrative Studies at Deakin University. He completed his doctorate at King's College, University of London. He was a major author of *Dilemmas of Reform: The Participation and Equity Program in Victorian Schools.* Fazal's research interests are in policy studies, ethics, and educational reform.

John Smyth is Associate Professor in Social and Administrative Studies and Chair of the Education Studies Centre at Deakin University. He has held positions at other Australian and overseas universities, and completed his doctorate at the University of Alberta. As well as publishing widely in journals his recent edited books are *Learning about Teaching through Clinical Supervision* (Croom Helm); *Educating Teachers: Changing the Nature of Pedagogical Knowledge* (Falmer); he has also jointly authored with Gitlin *Teacher Evaluation: Educative Alternatives.* John is the editor of *The Australian Administrator* and *Critical Pedagogy Networker.* His research interests are in teachers' professional knowledge and development.

Peter Watkins is Senior Lecturer in Social and Administrative Studies at Deakin University. Prior to completing his PhD at Deakin University, Peter taught extensively in Victorian high schools. He is a regular contributor to journals on educational administration, and has research interests in the areas of the relationship between school and work, workplace democracy, and the critical analysis of organizations.

Index